BURGESS HILL

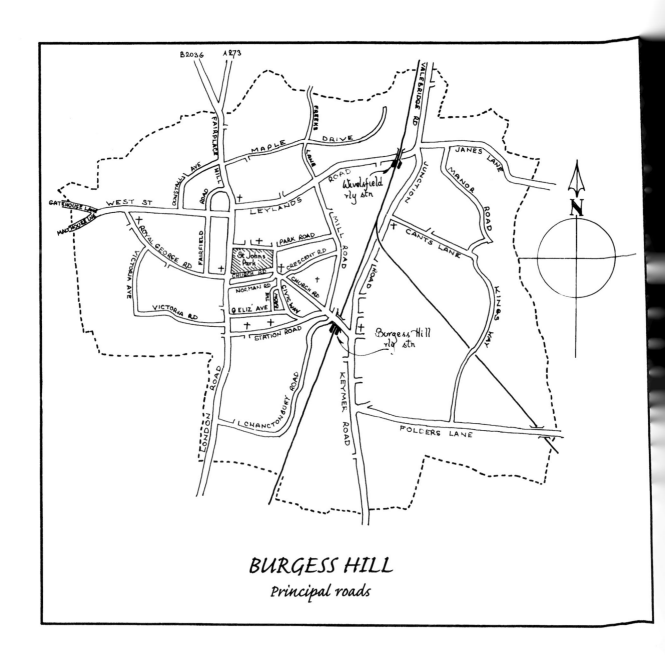

BURGESS HILL
Principal roads

BURGESS HILL

Hugh Matthews

with a final chapter by
Mark Dudeney

Phillimore

First published 1989
This paperback edition 2006

Published by
PHILLIMORE & CO. LTD
Shopwyke Manor Barn, Chichester, West Sussex, England
www.phillimore.co.uk

ISBN 1-86077-437-7
ISBN 13 978-1-86077-437-9

Printed and bound in Great Britain by
CAMBRIDGE UNIVERSITY PRESS

Contents

To Joan,
my wife and devoted companion for more than 40 years

List of Illustrations

List of Maps

Photographs 1, 2, 7, 9, 11, 13-15, 21, 27, 29 and 35 were taken by the author. Nos. 42-46 were taken by Mark Dudeney. The remainder are reproduced by courtesy of Mr. F.M. Avery and the Burgess Hill Local History Society, and were copied by Mr. John D. Sharp. The maps and line drawings were produced by Mr. Tony Archer. The author is grateful to all these people for their assistance in making this book visually attractive.

Preface

To the newcomer to Burgess Hill it must come as a disappointment to discover that there exists no comprehensive history of the town. The works of two earlier writers, Historicus (C.D. Meads) in the late 19th century and A.H. Gregory in the 1930s have long been out of print; such copies as still exist are jealously guarded and can only be borrowed by those intimately known to the owners. Both works covered the growth of the town from the enclosure of the commons and the coming of the railway, concentrating to a large extent on the period between about 1850 and 1890 which witnessed a momentous change from a rural community into a town in its own right.

In recent years much research has been done part of which has resulted in the publication of a new book covering the period from 1840-1914.[1] This excellent work, based on a detailed study of the census returns 1841-81 and supplemented by study of some hitherto untapped sources, has broken new ground and adds much to what has already been written by the two previous authors. But we are still left with an enormous gap between pre-history and the early part of the 19th century. This book is an attempt to bridge part of that gap.

On making enquiries about the history of the town, the newcomer can expect to be told either that it has no history worthy of mention since 'it all began in the 19th century', or he may be told of the existence of a Roman road that runs through the town centre, which vaguely suggests that Burgess Hill can lay claims to origins of great antiquity. Neither would be entirely true. So far as can be said with any degree of certainty at the present time, the Roman road, which did of course exist, almost certainly cut a dead-straight swathe through unpopulated waste land on its way towards London; the existence of an early brickworks cannot be ruled out. On the other hand, as we shall see, Burgess Hill was not entirely a tract of uncultivated and unpopulated waste before the early part of the 19th century.

It is with the period prior to the enclosures and the advent of the railway that this work is chiefly concerned. Inevitably there will be some overlap with the work of the previous writers, but it is hoped that what is said in the following pages will supplement rather than duplicate what has already been published.

The research on which this book is based has been carried out jointly by the writer and Mrs. Heather Warne both of whom, having started to work independently, met and decided to pool their knowledge. Research, involving travel to one or other of the County Record Offices, the supply of paper and writing materials, photocopies of some of the particularly interesting documents – all are expensive in terms of time and money. It was agreed therefore that for both to pursue the same areas of research would be a waste of effort. Since the writer has had no specialist training in historical research and because his knowledge of Latin and palaeography was minimal when he embarked upon this major project, the work contributed by Mrs. Warne has been invaluable. She it was who frequently travelled to London to spend long hours poring over, and extracting information from, such ancient documents as still exist for our immediate area; she it was who spent many months transcribing the early Keymer manorial court rolls and court books in the County Record Office at Lewes; and she it was who kindly helped me with some of my attempts to translate the Latin entries in the records I studied myself. Much of the material that was recorded in Latin between c.1600 and 1733 which she so competently translated and summarised has been generously passed over to me. I am deeply grateful for this vital material.

Over a period of some eight years the staff of the County Record Offices have been most helpful, in several instances giving assistance far in excess of their normal duties as later did the staff of the *Mid Sussex Times*. Mr. Wyn Ford and Mrs. Warne kindly commented on the early chapters. Mrs. Ann Phillips, our local Librarian, obtained copies of the 19th-century tithe awards and the enclosure maps for Clayton and Keymer, and she, too, offered helpful and constructive criticism on the whole of the first draft of this book. The maps, diagrams, and illustrations are the work of Mr. Tony Archer. To all I express my sincere thanks.

The book is intended primarily for local residents anxious to learn more about the origins and early history of their town. Nevertheless it is hoped that parts of it may be of interest to the serious student of local history. The main sources are given in the Bibliography on pages 179-80 and references are shown for some of the more interesting quotations for the benefit of those wishing to check the authenticity of any specific statement.

It will quickly become evident to the reader that the general theme of the book is what may loosely be termed 'Land and Folk'. 'Land' because under our houses and gardens, places of work, shops and banks, roads and open spaces lies virtually unknown territory. Little is known of its early history and little has been written about it. 'Folk', because our present environment and many of the older things we see around us were created by people, just like ourselves, who until recent times lacked the benefits of the technological age in which we now live, and produced what they did with a minimum of mechanical aids, relying largely on muscle-power – always at low wages and frequently whilst being undernourished. Anyone who has moved into the town to a new house built on virgin soil, and who has started from scratch to create a new garden using only spade and fork, will readily appreciate the immense physical effort involved. They are only the last in a long line who have cursed at, and struggled to tame, the intractable clay on which we live. Those who have moved into more mature accommodation have, of course, reaped the benefit of the vast efforts of someone before them.

We shall attempt to show how people acquired and held their property, and how the land was used, and to say something about those people and their life-style over the past three centuries or more. If, as a result, the lives of only a minority of the present population of the town are enriched, then the years of research and the labour of trying to write this book will have been well worth while.

In a work of this nature there are bound to be errors although every effort has been made to avoid them. It is hoped that these will be so few as not to detract from the accuracy of the book as a whole, responsibility for which is mine alone.

1986   H.G.M.

Introduction

The roots of the town lie buried deep in the ancient parishes of Clayton and Keymer both of which once extended from the top of our beautiful South Downs some six or seven miles north into the Weald. Keymer, in fact, until comparatively modern times terminated at Ashenground Road and Wivelsfield Road, Haywards Heath where two old houses, once part of both the manor and the parish, can still be seen. The 40-acre farm near Butlers Green, Cuckfield, lying to the north of the Heaselands estate and called Burnt House, formed a detached part of the parish until the boundaries were adjusted in the 1930s. Clayton, similarly, was another of those long, narrow, downs-foot parishes. It once extended to the north to include Bridge Farm and Bridge Hall Farm along the Ansty Road, and Woodfield Lodge in Isaacs Lane together with a large 160-acre detached part now forming the Heaselands and Heasewood Farm estate. Map 1 gives a general indication of the extent of both parishes and shows how the Burgess Hill area was related to them.

Both are mentioned in the Domesday survey and it is clear from the entries that each (even then with its own church) was well established in 1086 and had been in existence for some centuries. Some of the villagers and cottagers listed may well have lived within the town boundaries in the area near the present railway station and perhaps to the north, south, and west of the old commons where the Clayton boundary abutted that of Hurstpierpoint. All the indications are that most of the remaining land once adjoining the former commons was enclosed after the Conquest and before 1350.

So to a large extent the early history of the town is the history of these old parishes. As so frequently happens, the child outgrew the parents which today are left to the south of the town boundaries, basically much as they were several hundred years ago. An old Claytonian of the time of the first Queen Elizabeth would feel entirely at home if he could return and walk along Underhill Lane at the foot of the Downs from the church towards Westmeston. He might ask himself why there are virtually no more houses than there were four hundred years ago. He would be astonished at the huge areas of arable land that today are worked by so small a labour force. He would be equally astonished at the enormous yields produced from those same acres on which he and his forebears laboured so long and mightily for so small a return.

The two-cell parish church nestling at the very foot of the northern escarpment of the Downs has changed little since a permanent building was erected about a thousand years ago. The massive Saxon chancel arch and the early medieval wall paintings, discovered in the 19th century and beautifully restored, would have been as familiar to our Tudor forebears as they are to the present generation. The existing patchwork of fields and hedges, too, has changed little during the past 400 years. People of c.1600 walked the same hedgerows, cleaned out the same ditches, tilled the same fields and grew crops very similar to those grown today. Only the method of cultivation and the huge difference in yields have shown any marked change.

If the newcomer to Burgess Hill wants to find a true starting point in the long search for his roots then he should go to Clayton, beginning at the church which is by far the oldest extant building in the parish. He should park his car and walk, for only on foot can one assimilate and recapture the true atmosphere of this ancient settlement. Go into the church, sit for a few minutes and let your imagination take you back through the centuries. What momentous changes it has seen: the Norman conquest and occupation, the horrors of the

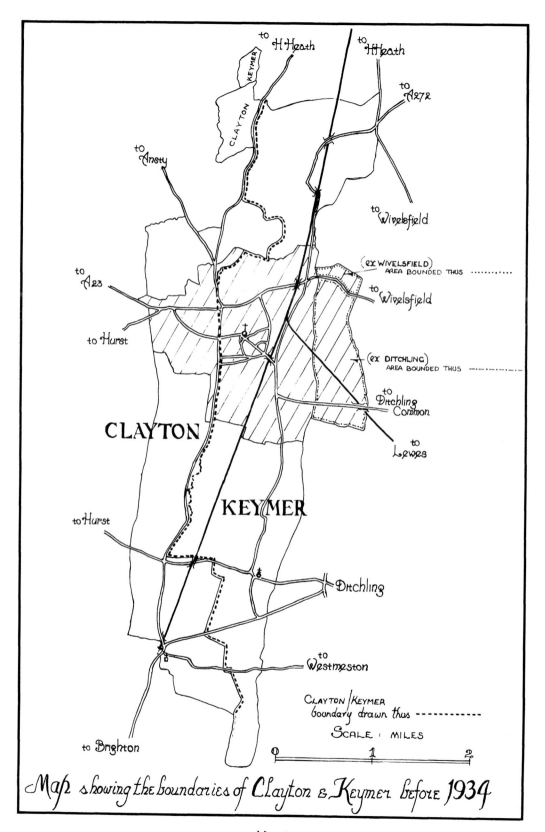

to H Heath

to H Heath

CLAYTON KEYMER

to A272

to Ansty

to Wivelsfield

(ex WIVELSFIELD)
AREA BOUNDED THUS ....

to A23

to Wivelsfield

to Hurst

(ex DITCHLING)
AREA BOUNDED THUS ─·─·─·─·─

to Ditchling
Common

CLAYTON

to Lewes

KEYMER

to Hurst

Ditchling

to Westmeston

CLAYTON / KEYMER
boundary drawn thus ------------
SCALE : MILES

0   1   2

to Brighton

Map showing the boundaries of Clayton & Keymer before 1934

Map 1

Black Death and the slow haul back to normality during the 15th and 16th centuries, the Civil War and the two more recent World Wars, to mention but a few. The small commemorative brass to Richard Iden a former rector, now on the south wall of the chancel, originally lay to the left of the altar; it was moved to its present position during the 19th-century restoration. Outside, the churchyard stands much higher than the surrounding levels, mute testimony to earlier nameless generations of parishioners whose mortal remains lie mouldering beneath it. But remember that it is still an active church that continues to minister to the spiritual needs of its people today as it has done for so many centuries.

Adjoining the churchyard to the west and abutting the parish boundary of Pyecombe is a 19th-century house built on land once forming a small holding called Birdshole which now stands a few yards to the rear. The site is very old and could perhaps once have been occupied by the parish priest.

From here walk in an easterly direction: adjoining the churchyard on your right is Clayton Court Farm, the focal point of the former demesne lands of the manor of Clayton where once were held the manor courts. A little further along on the left is a large house built on a north-south alignment, formerly the rectory, but now for some reason that is not apparent called Clayton Manor. In its grounds in the 19th century were unearthed (and subsequently again covered up) the remains of a Roman bath house which suggests that a Roman villa, yet to be discovered, existed in the vicinity.[1] Fragments of Roman tiles can still be picked up in the grounds, lying on or very near the surface. The village street with its scatter of 17th-, 18th- and 19th-century cottages swings abruptly to the north and becomes a rough bridle track much as it did at the beginning of our period.

You may now return to your car, for you have seen the original heart of the parish. Today the centre of population is concentrated at Hassocks (originally a field by the railway containing rough tussocks of grass) but now embracing the area extending from Spittleford Bridge in the east to the Hurstpierpoint boundary in the west. Just off the road that leads from Stone Pound crossroads to Hurstpierpoint is The Ham, once part of the demesne lands of the manor of Wickham (mentioned from time to time later) and now the home of the Campion family formerly of Danny Park in Hurst. The present Mr. W.D.S. Campion is still lord of the manors of Clayton and Wickham, and still enjoys such residual privileges as appertain to that age-old title. So far as we can tell he is possibly the first lord of the manor of Wickham to live within the bounds of the manor since Saxon times.

Near the crossroads is the site of a Roman cemetery, a sure indication of a substantial Roman presence in the area during the occupation. Here are the remains of two Roman roads, one going from east to west to join Stane Street a little to the south of Pulborough, the other leading to the north passing through the centre of Burgess Hill.

North and north-east of Stone Pound crossroads on the way to Burgess Hill the area today is heavily built up and, although away from the busy main road to the west one can still see old field patterns, intensively farmed today, the atmosphere of the church and the village street has gone. It is as if one has moved through four centuries in a matter of two or three miles, and in almost as few minutes. Still further north where Clayton abuts the town boundary is the town's industrial estate, part of which until recently stood in Clayton having burst its Burgess Hill seams. It is all a far cry from the tranquil scene a mile or two to the south.

Much of Keymer on the other hand has changed substantially, particularly in the past 135 years, mainly as a result of the coming of the railway. Our time traveller would still recognise the church, for although it was rebuilt in the 19th century, it largely retained its 14th-century plan and elevation. But Lodge Lane and the main east-west thoroughfare, now called Keymer Road, would be to him an alien world, as would most of Ockley Lane and the modern development to the west. Further south, by Lodge Farm and near the foot of the Downs, little has changed. The old water mill disappeared about the middle of the 18th century when it was replaced by a windmill on the top of the Downs, but the mill pond can still be seen much as it was at the Conquest.

The northern escarpment of the Downs has changed little, if at all, over the centuries; it still presents a truly rural pastural scene. Only when one has climbed to the top and witnessed the almost total destruction of downland grass, which for generations supported large flocks of sheep, and seen the result of large scale conversion to arable necessitated by two World Wars in the space of a single generation, is the full impact of the modern agricultural revolution felt.

To the north of the village centre the areas around Oldlands and Ockley Manor have changed little in four centuries though, as our time traveller neared the town boundary, the modern water tower and the (to him) palatial suburban residences would no doubt create a sense of wonder.

The former boundary between the two parishes within the modern town followed very approximately the line of the present London Road. It snaked from one side of the road to the other making it difficult to trace today. Yet if one studies carefully the 19th-century O.S. map, with time and patience remnants *can* be seen though not always in unbroken sequence. Much easier to follow are parts of the former boundary between Keymer and Ditchling and, north of Janes Lane, between Keymer and Wivelsfield. Here clearly visible are remnants of a typically early hedge – in places a double hedge – planted alongside a sort of three-feet wide no-mans-land. The best example can be found on the eastern boundary of Janes Lane Recreation Ground where it runs alongside Manor Road, and where at the southern end a double line of trees marks a boundary now over a thousand years old. There are easily recognisable remnants, too, in the vicinity of Charlwood Gardens that continue towards Theobalds Road.

We do not propose to devote more time and space to a discussion of our parent parishes than is necessary to set the scene for what follows. It is important for the reader to associate our modern town with these ancient settlements rather than to think of it as having developed from a stretch of waste land belonging to nobody in particular and having no association or roots with anything. Meanwhile we will attempt to show that our immediate area has for long been a centre of some importance, and to trace its development from about 1600 to modern times.

Chapter One

The Manorial Background

As stated earlier, the history of Burgess Hill prior to the first half of the 19th century is closely linked with the parishes of Keymer and Clayton and it is the records of these parishes and their manors that provide most of the information on which this and the following chapter are based. The town did not acquire full independence as a civil parish in its own right until 1934 when parts of Wivelsfield and Ditchling were added to the former Urban District to establish its boundaries as they are today. It has therefore been necessary to examine the records which relate to those areas of Ditchling and Wivelsfield that now form part of Burgess Hill (in addition to those of Clayton and Keymer) – a task simplified by the fact that all the land in question was held of the manor of Ditchling.

The later years of the reign of Queen Elizabeth and the period from 1600 throw a flood of light on the activities of the people of this area for the first time.

Wills proved in the Lewes Archdeaconry Court dating back to 1541 continue without a break until the middle of the 19th century. Parish registers of baptisms, marriages and deaths for Clayton and Keymer have been transcribed from 1601 to the early 19th century. There exists a useful collection of Inventories covering mainly the first half of the 18th century as well as a large number of property deeds dating from Tudor times and even earlier. In addition to these valuable primary sources there are the records of the local manor courts.

The court books of the manor of Ditchling cover the period 1597 to 1842,[1] but later information about land and property ownership is available in two surviving rentals. The earliest rolls (apart from those of the mid-14th century held at Arundel Castle mentioned in Heather Warne's article on Burgess Hill (S.A.C.123, pp. 127-43)) cover one half of the manor of Keymer for the years 1587 and 1589.[2] The Keymer court records then continue, mainly in book form, from 1598 to 1924 with gaps from 1618-22 and 1629-30.

About this time John Rowe, steward of the Abergavenny manors, compiled a record of the rents and customs of all the manors in his care, later published by the Sussex Record Society under the title *The Book of John Rowe* (S.R.S. vol 34). In this are detailed rentals of both Keymer and Ditchling manors and he quotes from the court rolls then in his possession, mostly of the reign of Queen Elizabeth but in one or two instances as early as the time of Henry VII. These early rolls have unfortunately now disappeared. The Clayton court books date from 1588 to 1922,[3] but here again there are gaps, and there is no manorial information for the years 1589-95 and 1597-1600. A valuable set of court records dating from 1665 to 1901 also exists for the ancient manor of Wickham,[4] part of the land of which extended into Burgess Hill, later to be incorporated into the western part of the present West End Farm.

The court records serve as deeds of all copyhold tenements. They show changes of ownership over the centuries, sometimes in considerable detail, and in some cases provide a useful pointer to the age of a house or barn that may still be seen today.

Another primary source not previously studied in depth for our immediate area is the Quarter Sessions records. The Order Books, dating from 1642 to 1967, provide valuable information about crime and punishment and the plight of the poor, and give an insight into how local public services – roads, bridges, etc. – were administered before the great reforms of the 19th century which led to the formation of County, Borough, Urban and Rural Councils. In addition there is a fine set of Quarter Sessions Rolls, some now cut up and preserved in book form, covering the period 1594-1950. These supplement the details shown in the order books and contain original depositions, accounts and other claims for expenses and fees incurred by those engaged on public business, removal orders for vagrants, names and signatures of men summoned for jury service, and so on.

Other sources consulted include Sussex Archaeological Collections (hereafter S.A.C.), Sussex Records Society (hereafter S.R.S.), the tithe surveys of c.1840, the enclosure awards of the 19th century, the Sussex Archaeological Society (hereafter S.A.S.) calendars of deeds and other legal documents, and Land Tax Returns of the late 18th and early 19th centuries.

Other sources are quoted in the notes and references.

The Land

For a relatively new town Burgess Hill has much to commend it. Substantially developed from the mid-19th century and followed by a second, even more massive, development since the early 1950s, it is old enough to have established an identity yet young enough not to be one of those closed communities where it takes a couple of generations before one ceases to be a 'foreigner' and is only then reluctantly accepted as a full member of local society equal in social status with those whose forebears have been there for generations. Fortunately this sort of community, in Sussex at least, is fast disappearing if it has not already gone, for the half century and more that has elapsed since the ending of the First World War has seen changes that would have seemed impossible to the fathers and grandfathers of many of the older inhabitants today. No longer are people bound to the land as they were at the beginning of our period; no longer do they live, work and die within the narrow confines of a village from which there was almost no opportunity for escape. Man's horizons have been broadened beyond measure by the introduction of radio, television and cheap travel; increasingly so since the Second World War and in particular since the 1960s and 1970s. With improved transport, relatively cheap fares, good roads and a car, or other motorised vehicles within the reach of almost everyone today, it is perhaps not surprising that populations now are so mobile. But how did it start?

In simplest terms it all began in Burgess Hill with the enclosure of the commons in 1828 and 1857, and the coming of the railway in 1841. Before then much of what is now the very heart of the town was a wild, barren waste called St John's Common which must have appeared to the passing visitor much as parts of the still unenclosed Ditchling and Chailey commons look today. Yet it would be quite wrong to assume that Burgess Hill was entirely an area of unpopulated waste land and rough commons before the 19th century. It is true that much of what is now the town centre – the area bounded roughly by Mill Road, part of Leylands Road, Fairfield Road leading into West Street to West End Farm, Royal George Road, part of London Road, and Station Road – was once common land but there were numerous farms, small holdings and cottages, some with an acre or two of land, on the periphery. By the early 17th century St John's Common to some extent had become a focal point for the parishes of Clayton and Keymer, superseding the loosely scattered settlements in Clayton village and the slightly more densely populated centre of Keymer near the church, with its small farms and cottages strung out along the highway, then known as Keymer Street, leading from Hurstpierpoint to Ditchling.

The annual fair attracted dealers and visitors from a wide area of mid-Sussex when it was held each summer on the feast of St John the Baptist (24 June) and there are sound reasons to believe that trading from stalls or temporary shacks on the common took place throughout the entire summer and possibly through the winter, too. This was certainly done in the 18th century as the Marchant diary shows,[5] and there is no indication that trading of this nature was in any way new. The common itself, though strictly regulated by the manor courts, increasingly attracted men and their families who, through no fault of their own when they found themselves homeless, erected temporary shelters and continued to occupy them either until they were thrown out or until they could prove to the locals that they were honest, capable of earning a living given the opportunity, and were not likely to become a burden on the parish. As will be seen later, a number of ancient sites on the fringes of the common began in this way. By the middle of the 17th century St John's Common had become a magnet, attracting those who had nowhere else to live and, although many were driven out on orders from the manor courts, some did manage to survive. The sites of several of these early settlements are still identifiable to the present day.

Before discussing in detail some of the many problems that faced both landowners and tenant farmers at the turn of the 16th century, it is necessary to consider briefly how land was held. Manorial land can be said to fall into one of two categories:

1. Customary freeholds were held at a nominal rent, usually a few shillings a year but often only a few pence. They were subject to a heriot of the best beast on death or alienation, and to a 'relief' equivalent to one year's rent for any admission either by inheritance or purchase. A typical example is the 30-acre holding called Collins and Westup Mead (now part of West End Farm) which paid only 12 pence a year rent and of course the same amount for a relief. Thus when Richard Parson died in 1620 his best ox worth £3 10s. 0d. was seized for a heriot and his son George paid another 1s. 0d. upon entry as the relief.

2. Copyholdings were the direct descendants of the medieval villein farms and cottages which owners held 'by copy of court roll at the will of the lord'. These in turn may be sub-divided into:

(a) the virgate or yardland (or part thereof) subject to a fixed annual rent (again of a few shillings or a few pence), a heriot of the best animal on the premises and a 'fine at the will of the lord'. 'Fine at the will of the lord' meant that the sum payable when a property changed hands could vary depending upon the state of the local economy at the time. The fines paid for example by the incoming owners of the land once called Peppers alias Tibballs (held at a rent of 6s. 8d. and later the site of Victoria Pleasure Gardens) show a steady increase from £6 3s. 4d. in 1601 to £160 in 1867 – a 26-fold increase in about two and a half centuries.

(b) cottages with a little land varying between a few square rods and a few acres. These paid only a few pence annually by way of rent – usually 6d. but occasionally as much as 1s. 0d. – sometimes only 2d. or 3d. In these cases heriots and entry fines were both fixed and were almost always 6d. in each case.

Normally on our local manors the best beast of neither freeholders nor copyholders was seized if the previous owner had leased his premises and was not living there at the time of his death.

Non-manorial land was truly freehold and paid no rent, heriot or relief to the lords of the manor. We have examples of two such estates lying partly within the town boundaries: Franklands and Hammonds Place.

The Courts

In this section a few examples are quoted of the type of business transacted at both the Hundred and the Manor Courts; and an attempt is made to show how locals were affected thereby.

In the heyday of the manorial system in the Middle Ages, some courts performed a dual function. The Court Leet dealt with minor offences, e.g. infringements of local by-laws, weights and measures, nuisances caused by failure to clear waterways and to trim hedges overhanging the highways, selling beer at less than the statutory strength, selling bread that was under weight, and so on. In this part of Sussex these offences seem to have been heard at the Hundred courts. For example at a View of Frankpledge held for the Hundred of Buttinghill we find:[6]

2nd May 1587 (Clayton)

Thomas Parson, headborough came with his tithing and paid the common fine, 2s. 6d. And presented that Thomas [blank] had not cleansed his ditch towards the highway between Clayton and Seynt John's Common by the date given him at the last View, therefore he forefeits 6s. 8d.

8th October 1587 (Keymer)

John Beche is a common beer tippler and broke the assize and therefore he is in mercy 2d.

15th April 1589 (Clayton)

The occupiers of the land called North Wickham [a little to the south of the Burgess Hill boundary] late in the tenure of John Streter, have not cleansed their ditch nor cut back the hedge overhanging the highway and the penalty imposed in the former View is now therefore forfeited (3s. 4d.).

A few years later:

29th September 1613.[7]

Francis Reps, gent, has not repaired the bridges called Eylesforde bridge and the bridge by Hammons near St. John's Common by the date given to him at the last View so he forfeits (blank).

Thomas A Lye is to cleanse his diches beside the King's Highway from St. John's Common gate to Gorwood Common and to receive the water from such highway in the lands called Fowles Mead by the feast of All Saints next under penalty 5s. 0d.

The jurors lastly say that Henry Smith about the feast of St. Bartholomew last by force and arms broke the pound at St. John's Common in Keymer and took away divers animals viz: one gelding and five wenyers impounded there by John Anstye alias Holcombe and was fined 3s. 4d.

10th October 1614

The farmers of the lands and tenements called Hamonds in Clayton are to repair a bridge near Hamons gate before the feast of St. Andrew under penalty of 10s. 0d.

2nd October 1615

Edward Michelborne esq, is to repair two bridges in Clayton one of which is near Hamonds house and the other is called Eylesford bridge together with the road next adjacent which is often inundated by penninge of the water by John Haselgrove the miller at Hamonds mill.

30th September 1618

Nicholas Jenner has not cleansed his ditches next the highway at the fayre place in Keymer and Edward Michelborne Esq. has not received the water from the highway leading from Hammonds gate to the church of Clayton and led the water there into his meadow whither it ought to flow.

The above extracts demonstrate how difficult it was to force local land owners and occupiers to devote time and money to repairs and maintenance of public rights of way. Eylesford bridge, which crosses the main road near New Close Farm a little to the south of the town boundary, had remained unrepaired over a period of two years or more and the entries suggest that nobody really knew who was responsible. The fact that it is not mentioned after October 1615, however, suggests that some effort had been made to alleviate the nuisance. Gorwood Common was another name for the southern part of St John's Common that lay in Clayton, west of the London Road: Fowles Mead was part of what was later to become Shelly's to the west of Royal George Road. Nicholas Jenner was living at Sheddingdean in 1618 having acquired the farm from his father, Stephen, the previous year. The fact that Henry Smith was presented in 1613 for breaking the pound at Keymer shows that this category of offence, once tried by the manor courts, was now a matter for the Hundred court.[8] Nevertheless, as we shall see later, tenants of the manor were in no doubt that responsibility for *providing and maintaining* the pound rested firmly with the lord (see below page 67). The entry of October 1589 when John Beche was fined 2d. is the only example found to date of a person selling sub-standard beer in the Burgess Hill area.

Petty criminal offences were, of course, dealt with by the Justices of the Peace, usually at Petty or Quarter Sessions but not infrequently summarily in their own homes. Other former functions of the Court Leet were probably taken over by the parish vestry, early records of which, sadly, no longer exist.

The Courts Baron, of which such a splendid series of records exists, were basically concerned with the transfer of title to property and the means of collecting manorial rents, heriots – payable when an owner died or sold his property – and entry fines payable by the incoming tenant. In addition, however, they protected the lord's other interests whenever those interests were threatened. A tenant was bound to keep his house and buildings in good repair and was liable to a fine if he failed to do so. Fishing and hunting rights on copyhold land were vested in the lords and taking fish or game without authority was also punishable by fine. Standing trees on copyhold land were the property of the lords and could not be felled and used, even for essential repairs, without first obtaining permission. Hay and corn grown on manorial holdings could not be sold and transported out of the manor without a licence, the granting of which attracted a small fine. An owner could, and frequently did, lease his premises to a sub-tenant; for this privilege he paid a standard fine of 4d. per annum regardless of the area involved in the transaction. The tenants' rights were also protected by the umbrella afforded by the Courts Baron particularly in regard to the use of the commons. Illegal encroachments; overgrazing by animals; the taking of bracken and furze; illegal digging of clay – all came before the courts at one time or another during the period under review. A grant of common land to create a new tenancy could not be made by the lord alone, but by the lord (or the steward acting on his behalf) *with the assent of the homage* (representing all the tenants). A few examples of the business transacted at these courts are discussed in more detail below.

For the local property owner conditions in the early 17th century seem at first sight to have changed very little since the violent social changes that occurred after the Black Death and subsequent outbreaks of plague in the 14th and 15th centuries. Whether a freeholder or a copyholder, he was still required to attend the manor court, usually held twice a year, whether he had business to transact or not. The manor of Keymer had 11 freeholders and 65 copyholders in 1600 when three freeholders and seven copyholders were fined for non-attendance (one was pardoned). As the century wore on, however, the lists of defaulters became longer and longer until by 1679 eight freeholders and 44 copyholders were recorded as having made default and were fined the standard 3d. The levying of fines on those not attending the courts unless they had business to transact seems generally to have been abandoned in the early 18th century.

Yet although freeholders were expected to attend the courts in accordance with long established custom, the early 17th-century records show them becoming increasingly independent of the manor. They were no longer obliged by law to use the Court Baron when they wished to sell their land, though normally they could expect to be summoned for the purpose of agreeing what should be handed over to the lord for a heriot, and to make fealty.[9] Even so, many failed to put in an appearance and information about changes in ownership is sparse, indeed in some instances virtually non-existent. To quote just one or two examples of freehold properties lying in the eastern part of town:

(1) Little Otehall farm, part of which lay between Manor Road and Janes Lane, comprised six small freehold parcels of land subject to rents varying between 4d. and 5s. 9d. Each was subject to a heriot of the best beast and a relief in cash of one year's rent; yet nowhere are any of these premises mentioned in the court records until 1842 by which time they had long been engrossed to form a single composite working farm.

(2) Moore's Inholmes (later called Folders farm) gets only a brief mention in 1723 and again in 1780. This 36-acre holding, too, was subject to an annual rent and relief (in this instance of 18d.) and a heriot of the best beast.

(3) Similarly the important 200-acre farm lying to the east of Junction Road called Cants, which in the early 17th century included 80 acres called Anchor farm (later Doubledays) and a smaller property to the north called Frankbarrow, although quoted in the Book of John Rowe as paying a yearly rent of 10s. 0d. is not mentioned once in the court books.

So what record was kept and how were the lords' interests protected? There seems no doubt that they were; a conscientious steward would have seen to that. The duty of collecting manorial rents fell to the Reeve in his year of office, and these and other of the lords' dues were paid to the steward at regular intervals. The Reeve rendered an annual account, though unfortunately only one has survived.[10] The increasing use of formal legal documents ensured that changes in ownership were properly recorded. Many of these deeds, some dating back to the 16th and 17th centuries and even earlier, have been preserved and may be seen at both the County Record Offices. Anyone who is seriously studying the history of a specific property should not fail to consult these documents. Nevertheless, notwithstanding what has been said about the paucity of written records concerning freehold property, the court books do in some instances give details, albeit frequently with long gaps, until well into the 19th century.

If the manorial grip on freeholders had to some extent weakened by the year 1600, the same cannot be said of the copyholders who remained firmly tied to the manor until the latter half of the 19th century; indeed in a few cases until well into the present century. They held their premises 'by copy of court roll at the will of the lord according to the custom of the manor by the rents, customs and services due and of right accustomed . . .', a formula virtually unchanged since medieval times which continued to be written into all copyhold deeds either until a property was enfranchised,[11] or on 1 January 1926 when copyholds were abolished.

Owners of copyhold land were no longer subject to 'services', which in the Middle Ages meant working a given number of days each year on the lords' demesne. In the early years of the period under review they, and incidentally the freeholders, were required to 'make fealty'; that is, when taking over a tenancy for the first time to swear to be good and faithful tenants of the lord. But in practice this had become a mere formality; they simply acknowledged that in theory their land and premises were the property of the lord of the manor. Like the freeholders they were required to attend the courts when summoned, or send a valid excuse if unable to attend through illness: like the freeholders increasing numbers failed to turn up as the 17th century wore on until by the 18th century only those having business to transact were prepared to give up part of a day, or a whole day depending upon how far away they lived, for the doubtful privilege of seeing the now obsolescent procedure in action. They probably paid their 2d. or 3d. fine willingly if the alternative meant neglecting a cow due to calve or losing a favourable day to do essential work on the land.

Yet although this suggests a breakdown of manorial control, copyhold tenants almost always appeared promptly when taking up a new holding either by inheritance or purchase. In accordance with long established custom three proclamations were made in court when a tenant died; if no-one came the premises were seized into the hands of the lord who was then at liberty to re-grant them to another tenant.

As previously noted, the courts, in addition to dealing with property transactions, also maintained strict control of the disposal of the crops and minerals on manorial land:

> 1589. A licence was granted to Stephen Jynner to carry away from his customary land called Sheryndene [later Sheddingdean] soil called marl dug by Henry Boyer esq. with the excavations of earth there called myne paying a fine 4d.

This refers to shafts dug by Henry Bowyer the Cuckfield ironmaster (who built Cuckfield Park) in an attempt to find iron ore, traces of which were again revealed in recent years when the western half of Maple Drive was developed. Small quantities of iron ore were in fact found and mined for a time in the late 16th century in the course of which the presence of marl (a mixture of clay and carbonite of lime then highly valued as a fertiliser) was also revealed. Stephen Jenner was quick to seize the opportunity to exploit the unexpected find.

1. Pollards Farm on the eastern boundary of the town was probably built in the late 15th century.

     1598. A licence was granted to Roger Adderton, gent, to carry away from his native lands in Keymer called Burges Hilland [later Burgess Hill farm] three cartloads of hay paying a fine 12d.
     1598. A licence was granted to Henry Jenner to carry away from his customary lands called Pollards Inholmes [adjoining Ditchling Common on our eastern boundary] one cartload of wheat paying a fine 4d.
     1602. A licence was granted to Elizabeth Atree to carry away from her customary land called Brokeland [Brooklands farm a little to the north of the town boundary] one cartload of wheat and one cartload of pease paying a fine 8d.

There is little point in quoting more. Technically, the produce of a copyholding was still the property of the lord and could not be removed or sold outside the manor without his authority. By about 1600 the custom had become simply a means of adding to manorial profit; the lord probably cared little about the disposal of a few cartloads of hay or grain, it was the money that mattered. The small amount, 4d. per load, was little enough but like so many ancient customs the sum had probably been fixed in medieval times and, as with rents and fixed fines and heriots, no attempt was made to allow for inflation. Had this been suggested the homage, on behalf of all the tenants, would doubtless have fiercely resisted it, for gone, too, were the days when a lord could impose his will arbitrarily upon the tenants. In any event the custom declined rapidly during the first half of the 17th century and by 1650 had died out entirely in this area.

The provision of adequate fencing was a major concern at the time and indeed has continued through to the present day, for straying animals could, and still can, create untold damage in a field of growing corn or roots. The following are one or two early examples:

> 1599. The homage present that Edward A Wood who holds in the right of his wife Anne for the life of the said Anne certain customary lands called (blank) by right ought, and all those who are in future seised of the premises ought, to make the usual enclosure and fence between the said lands and the lands of Thomas A Wood called Curles [later Broadhill farm]. He is given until Easter to do so upon pain of 5s. 0d. And further they say that the fencing (or enclosure) between the free lands called Ockley lands and the customary land there from time to time and from time immemorial has been and ought to be made by the farmers and possessors of the said free lands and not by the customary tenants.[12]

This was settlement of a dispute between the owners of Ockley Manor and the adjoining Broadhill farm which lies near our southern boundary. Both were tenants of the manor of Keymer.

> 1600. James Godman [who held Dartfords north of Janes Lane formerly in Wivelsfield] was ordered to repair his fences at the cottage of Joan Godlye before the feast of Penticost on pain of 4s. 0d.
>
> Oliver Mockett was ordered to repair the fences next to the house of Edward Johnson on pain of 2s. 4d.

Such cases were comparatively rare. It was in the interests of the whole community to ensure that fences were kept in good repair. If animals did stray they were quickly rounded up and confined to the manor pound and normally only released on payment of a fine. As previously noted occasionally a man would take it upon himself to regain possession of his stock without proper authority. A little earlier we find:

> 1608. It was presented that Richard Parkes had broken the common pound within the manor [Clayton] and was in mercy 12d.

In this instance the offence was tried in the manor court for the last time.

From time to time disputes arose over rights of way. A typical example comes in 1633 when:

> John Johnson who farms certain lands called Hamonds lands within this manor [Clayton] is ordered to lay open a tenants way,[13] leading from Scotches as far as Sinjun's common within the manor and across land called Hamonds land on pain of 10s.

John Johnson was then not only farming Hammonds but was also the copyhold tenant of the adjoining land to the north called Tibballs alias Peppers, later to become the site of the Victoria Pleasure Gardens and now partly the site of the trading estate. The right of way had been stopped up some years earlier by Sir Edward Michelborne (of Hammonds Place) who 'had placed a wayne gate and a pair of bars across the road leading from the land of Richard Amore called Shotters [Scotches] to St. Joane's common to the inconvenience of Richard Amore and other tenants of the lord'. In July 1635 nothing had been done and Johnson was ordered to remove the obstructions before Michaelmas next on pain of 20s. Another year elapsed and, because of his failure to comply with the previous orders, the penalty of 20s. was executed. The case dragged on for three years before John Johnson finally succumbed to manorial pressure. As a yeoman farmer he would have had neither the status nor the ready cash to wage a prolonged struggle over a problem which he had inherited from his landlord. He probably took the view that the dispute was really between

2. Hammonds Place. The east front was rebuilt in 1566 by Edward Michelborne.

3. Hammonds Place from the north. This timber framing dates from c.1500.

Sir Edward Michelborne and the lord of the manor, and saw no reason to become involved in a court case which he could reasonably claim was not his direct concern. The fact that he had to pay the 20s fine and comply with the order demonstrates that in allowing the blockage of the road to continue he was in breach of the law and that the manor was still a force to be reckoned with.

Although a copyholder 'owned' his land insofar as he could sell it, bequeath it, lease it, and mortgage it, the lord, as we have seen, retained many rights. In addition to those examples already mentioned was the perennial problem of repair and maintenance of the tenants' houses and buildings. By the year 1600 a number of copyhold premises were owned by absentee landlords who leased them to local farmers. These owners were not vitally concerned if the farm houses or barns were in a state of decay; they did not live there and so long as their rents were paid promptly they were probably content to leave the management of both land and buildings to their sub-tenants on the basis that, if the roof leaked, the farmer would in his own interests take steps to have it repaired. Legally, however, owners were responsible to the lord as the following examples show:

> 1600. It was presented that the barn of Roger Adderton, gent, at Burgeshillande was in a dreadfully ruinous state for lack of timber. He was given until the feast of Penticost next to repair it on pain of 20s. Meanwhile timber was allocated by administration of the court.
> 1601. The homage presented that the residence of Edward A Wood called Batchelors [in Keymer Road] was extremely ruinous and in decay. He was given until the Assumption of the Blessed Virgin Mary,[14] to repair it on pain of 20s.

Edward A Wood did not comply with the court order. He was presented again a year later when the beadle was ordered to levy the fine and he was ordered to make repairs to both the house and the barn by the feast of St James the Apostle on pain of 40s. Yet it was not until 1605 that repairs were finally made; even then six oak trees had been cut down and used without authority. So he was in trouble again.

> 1607. Thomasine Aderton was given until 25th July to repair her tenement and barn at Burgeshill on pain of 40s.

Roger Aderton had died, apparently having failed adequately to repair his buildings as ordered in 1600. He probably spent a minimum whilst he was alive; his unfortunate widow inherited not only the premises but also the liabilities that went with them. She was, for example, elected Reeve in 1609 though she almost certainly paid a deputy to perform this thankless duty for her one year's term of office.

> 1633. Edward Pierce was ordered to repair the barn on his native lands called ye Inholmes by the feast of St. James the Apostle on pain of 10s.
> 1637. It was presented that the house and barn of Edward Pierce were in decay and needed repair.

Edward Pierce held 25 acres of land called Hothers Inholmes on our eastern boundary in the right of his daughter Margery who had inherited the premises on the death of her mother in 1627. Since he was also occupying the house it seems strange that he neglected it and the barn; but then, like so many small landowners at the time, he was probably living from hand to mouth and suffering from what in modern parlance is called a 'cash-flow' problem.

Before we leave this subject we will mention just one more example:

> 1635. Thomas Winchester's customary barn was in need of repair. He was in court and acknowledged the decay and asked for timber to be allowed him. Whereupon the lord's Supervisor of Woods was ordered to look over the said barn and allow a suitable amount of wood to be taken from his customary lands and not elsewhere.

He was presented again in 1640 and nine years later:

1649. It was presented that the barn of Thomas Winchester was in a ruinous condition. Timber for repairs was to be allocated after inspection by Thomas Canfield, Supervisor of the Woods.

Thomas Winchester held 16 acres of land called Warelands part of which adjoined London Road and was later incorporated into the Hammonds estate. It had taken nearly 15 years to reinstate the dilapidated barn into a reasonably watertight building. It may well be that he had no particular use for a barn on this isolated part of the small estate, but in accordance with ancient custom he was obliged to maintain it and the court was still sufficiently powerful to make an order for its repair and to ensure that the order was carried out.

4. Groveland Cottage, to the south of Hammonds Place, once called Warelands.

It must not, however, be thought that neglect of houses and farm or cottage buildings was widespread in the area throughout the period under discussion; the majority of copyholders rarely, sometimes never, made a court appearance to face charges such as those quoted above. When they did there may well have been special reasons for their negligence; illness, financial difficulties, or, where a man was struggling to bring up a large family with little help from anyone except perhaps his wife, sheer lack of time. Man's basic instinct for warm and reasonably comfortable shelter for himself and his family, and proper protection for his livestock and stores of grain and fodder must have been as strong in the 17th century as it was to be seen later. It is highly likely that the root of the trouble was lack of working capital.

When a tenant applied to the court for an allocation of timber to repair his buildings, permission was invariably given:

> 1601. Two doles of timber were allocated to John Dumbrell for rebuilding the barn on his native lands [later called Leylands farm] to be taken from the common of St. John by assignation of John Dansey and John Cooke.
>
> 1606. Thomas Nutley was granted three doles of timber for the repair of his house and barn to be taken from his native lands (Holmebush farm, a little to the north of the town boundary) by assignation of the lords' verderers.

In both these cases the tenants had acted strictly in accordance with the law and had sought an allocation of timber before they were presented at the court for neglecting their buildings. In neither case was a fine levied, the timber having been allocated as 'botes'. This age-old custom is admirably explained by John Rowe,[15] who records that:

> All the great wooddes and timber trees of oake, beech, ashe, and elme growinge on the copiholds ar the Lords; savinge that the Lord must leaue growinge on the copihold unto and for the tenants use not onely all trees of luith for the defence of the buildinges from the violence of stormy windes, but also sufficient timber trees for reparations of all buildinges there from time to time, and likewise for all maner of bootes for the use of the tenant and benefitt of the tenement viz: howseboote, fireboote, ploweboote, carteboote, paleboote, stakeboote, postes, rayles, barrs, hedgboote, and all other necessary bootes . . .

The custom persisted until well into the 19th century when two cases were recorded – one in 1838 and one in 1840. The one in our area, paraphrased, reads:

> 1838. Henry Marten was granted a licence to fell 12 trees for repairing buildings and fences belonging to his farm called Little Burgess Hill [to the north of the present Burgess Hill railway station]. No fine was levied the trees having been assigned for Botes.

The other case referring to land in Worth held of the manor of Keymer need not concern us here.

Growing timber and underwood, although the property of the lord, could be sold to a copyholder sometimes as part of a deal involving partial enfranchisement. Burgess Hill farm, for example, had been acquired in 1612 by John Rowe the well-known steward of the Abergavenny manors. From 1644 the premises were no longer subject to a heriot of the best animal and a fine at the will of the lord on death or alienation – these manorial dues had been converted to a nominal 6d in each case and in addition the lord relinquished his rights to 'all trees, woods and underwoods' on the estate in accordance with a charter dated 20th June of that year. There are, unfortunately, no details of the cost of this transaction. It would not have been cheap by the standards of the day; lords, and stewards acting on their behalf, jealously safeguarded their rights and manorial dues were not abandoned lightly, for once sold it was highly unlikely they could ever be re-purchased. As a point of interest it is worth mentioning that one or two pockets of woodland formerly part of Burgess Hill farm have survived the ravages of modern development and can still be seen today (1986).

As mentioned earlier (page 5) the right to take fish from manorial water was vested in the lord(s). This age-old custom had been established centuries before local records begin, probably in pre-conquest times, but even as late as the 17th century was still being observed.

When, for example, six acres of Valebridge common was granted to Edmund Attree in 1606 for the purposes of forming a new mill pond, one of the conditions was that fishing and gaming rights were to be reserved to the lord(s). He (Attree) was to repair the bridge over the water-course at the highway from time to time. Similarly, when the 60-acre holding called Fielders (later known as Ashenground and now Catts Wood) was enfranchised in 1676, the deed specifically mentioned the exclusion of 'hunting and fishing rights over the said lands', which remained reserved to the lord.

Cases of poaching for fish rarely came before the manor court though to what extent this was due to strict observance of the local bye-laws by the villagers or how much to the fact that offenders were seldom detected is anybody's guess. All the cases recorded appear in a 20-year period between 1688 and 1706 which suggests that the homage or the steward, or both, had suddenly become aware that fishing, other than by permission of the lord, was illegal. The five cases to come before the courts can be summarised as follows:

1688. Richard Goddard and James Hasleden had illegally fished in a certain pond on Varlebridge common within the waste of the manor and were each fined 10s.

1690. Henry Scrase and Thomas Gearing were each in mercy 2s.6d for fishing with nets in certain ponds on the manorial waste where they had caught and taken away many fishes.

1695. John Hill, George Parker and John Whiteman were presented that on 2nd May they had fished with a net in a stream called Spittleford Brook and had caught many fishes. Each was in mercy 12d.

1705. Walter Welfare had caught several quantities of fish in Varlebridge pond without a licence and was in mercy 10s.

1706. Walter Welfare had fished with nets in Varlebridge pond and had destroyed many fish. If he ever fished again in the said pond he would be in mercy 20s.

Walter Welfare, about whom more will be said later, was owner and occupier of Valebridge mill from 1695 until his death in 1725. If food was in short supply and there were fish outside his door for the taking it is, perhaps, not surprising that he helped himself and hoped to get away with it; but then Walter Welfare was no ordinary mortal; his illegal fishing was probably done in the same spirit as the other offences with which he was charged around this time.[16] These were the only examples found involving poaching of fish. It seems strange that all occurred within such a short period – 18 years out of a time-span of three and a quarter centuries. No cases of illegal hunting were recorded at the manor courts.

It is hoped that these examples will throw some light on the difficulties experienced by, and restrictions placed on, copyhold tenants at the beginning of the period under review. There was to be little significant change until about 1840 when increases in population and the great leap forward in the fields of manufacturing and transport made the need to simplify the system of land transactions a matter of urgency. As previously stated the only major change in the manorial system over the next two and a half centuries came about the middle of the 17th century, when the need for a licence to carry away farm produce from the manor was dropped.

One cannot escape the impression that as early as 1733 tenants were prepared to try to bend the rules. In October of that year Francis Warden of Butlers Green House, Cuckfield, had just taken up duty as steward of the manor of Keymer. After the homage of six had dealt with the list of property transactions they presented:

It is the custom of this manor that if a tenant die seized of several copyholds he shall pay but one heriot.

Also that freeholders pay no heriot only Reliefs on death or alienation.

Also that the freeholders and cottagers of this manor have no right to commonage on the lord's waste.

And that copyholders ought not to turn out any more cattell on the commons in the summer than they can keep on their land in winter.

A footnote by the steward indicates that he 'did not find the customs well warrented particularly as for freeholders not paying heriots there being many instances in the court rolls where heriots have been seized on the death of freehold tenants'. He could have added that a tenant holding several copyholds paid a heriot for *each* property. And when, a century later, the Keymer commons were enclosed he would have found that several cottagers and one or two freeholders had proved they had rights of common and were therefore given an allocation in the Enclosure Award.

What conclusions, then, can be drawn from this brief entry? The members of the homage were all men of substance. They included three holding premises in Balcombe; the others were Richard Turner of Oldland, Keymer, Richard Allcock of Woodwards in Burgess Hill and Stephen Laugham of the Rookery, Haywards Heath. Did they really believe that their joint statement was accurate and that it would be accepted without question by the new steward? Or was it an attempt to change the rules whilst the game was in progress? Had Mr. Warden given his blessing he would have created a precedent which would have been quoted by the tenants *ad nauseam* thereafter. In the circumstances he was not being over-cautious in deciding to check previous entries in the court records before giving or withholding his agreement.

But here for the time being we must leave our local farmers and landowners and turn our attention to the commons which were later to form the town centre. There was to be little real change until well into the 19th century.

Chapter Two

The Infant Community: The Burgess Hill area in the 17th century

In this chapter an attempt will be made to show how settlement on the commons was begun during the 17th century, and reference will be made to an activity that was to have far reaching effects upon the future of the town. This was, of course, the brick, tile and pottery manufacturing industries which began here a century or more before the date of 1714 recorded by A.H. Gregory in his *Story of Burgess Hill*.

The actions of men during the 17th century resulted in the earliest serious beginnings of colonisation of the commons that was to continue on and off for the next two hundred years. Minor looting of the commons had already begun during the Tudor period but the great wave of 'common-grabbing' from about the time of the Civil War had a much more dramatic effect. It was during this period that the area we now call Burgess Hill began to develop into a small community becoming more and more removed from the ancient centres near Clayton and Keymer churches.

The Commons

Records show that tenants were still grazing their cattle in 1733, a custom that probably persisted until the early 19th century. There is ample evidence that *unauthorised* persons sometimes turned out their animals on the commons:

> 1692. Thomas Burtenshaw had grazed a horse on the waste of the manor [Clayton] where he had no right and was in mercy 20s.
>
> 1693. Thomas Burtenshaw had continued to graze a horse on the waste where he had no right and was in mercy 20s.
>
> 1716. The homage present that divers persons not having right of common do daily make encroachments, surcharges and trespasses upon the commons and waste grounds . . .[1]
>
> 1731. John Hebberden had put out a horse on the manorial commons where he had no right.
>
> 1732. Richard Sanders had put out his horses and animals on the waste at Broad Street Green [now part of Keymer Road] where he had no right of common pasture and was in mercy 2d.

Although there are more examples of this type of offence it should be said that it did not occur very frequently; indeed, most of the recorded offences were committed between the dates shown above. Equally rare were offences involving cutting down and carting away fern and furze:

> 1691. John Attree of Frick [now Lowlands farm on the northern boundary of the town] and James Nye of Clayton were presented for cutting down quantities of fern and carrying it away from Valebridge common. Each was in mercy 5s.
>
> 1812. John Ashfold of Hurst, farmer, and Nathaniel Holford of Clayton were presented for committing trespass on the wastes of this manor [Keymer] by cutting and carrying away furze and brake [bracken] therefrom having no right of commonage or licence to do so.

The fern was almost certainly used as bedding for animals when straw was in short supply. The furze was probably used as fuel, or it could have been crushed and used to supplement animal feed though the process would have been a laborious one at a time when no crushing machinery was available.

If unauthorised grazing and taking of litter was a relatively unusual offence the same cannot be said of encroachments. Such was the pressure from the growing population for land during the 17th century that men were constantly in trouble at the manor courts. Those whose holdings abutted the commons frequently took in additional land without authority; others with no land of their own simply 'squatted' after hastily throwing a few materials together to provide some sort of house. Offences of this kind were recorded from the early years of the period under review and continued on and off until the early 19th century:

> 1607. John Baker had encroached on the lord's waste called St. John's Common with a certain building and was in mercy 4d. He was ordered to take it down before the feast of St. James the Apostle [25th July] on pain of 3s. 4d.
> Henry Eston had encroached upon the said common with a certain shop called 'a smythes shopp' and was in mercy 4d. He was ordered to remove it by the above stated date [i.e. 25th July] on pain of 2s.[2]
> 1623. John Savage had encroached on the waste to the west of his cottage which was seized by the lord.
> William Nutley was presented for encroaching on the waste.
> John English was presented for a similar offence.

Of these five examples those of 1623 probably involved little more than three men moving the stakes forming the boundaries of their holdings. John Savage apparently temporarily lost his house until he had thrown open the common – a drastic measure but one that was probably considered necessary at the time if the tenants were not to lose their common altogether. Henry Eston must have demolished his smithy since there is no record of its having been formally granted by the manor court. Thirty years later, in 1637, Robert Easton (probably his son) was to try again, this time on Valebridge common, again without success. Indeed there is no evidence to suggest that any of the five men were able to retain land they had, in effect, stolen from their neighbours. One can understand the concern of the other tenants: if one person was allowed to take even a square yard without authority what was to stop others taking two, five, ten square yards ending up with a free-for-all and no common left.

Something of a free-for-all did occur during the Commonwealth when the locals seem to have made a concerted attack on the commons as the following examples show. In 1655, for instance, instead of the usual one or possibly two presentments[3] for encroachments we find:

> 1655. Samuel Marten and James Saunders had dug earth, sand and turffe on St. John's Common and each was amerced 5s.
> Stephen Jenner, Samuel Marten, Stephen Hockham, John Marten, William Jenner, Thomas Marchant, Thomas Wiggens, Robert Leggat and John Standen had encroached and made enclosures on St. John's Common. They were given until Christmas to lay it out on pain of 20s.
> Samuel Snashall and Widow Budd for the like encroachment on St. John's Common. They were given until Christmas to lay it out on pain of 3s. 4d.

Thomas Peckham had erected a cottage on St John's Common but 'because he was a poore man and laborious in his calling the homage desired that the said cottage might be continued and that a little parcel of ground might be assigned to him for a garden'. Three tenants were appointed to set out the land and provision was made to provide land for a 'work-house' for Henry Peckham [who must be the same man], wheeler.[4]

The story of Henry (or Thomas) Peckham is interesting since it records one of the very few grants to a man who began his business by setting up illegally on the common. Normally, as shown above, the court simply recorded that such and such had encroached and was ordered to throw down the enclosure or be fined. To this extent Henry (as we shall call him) was something of an exception. In pleading his case he clearly impressed members of the homage, which at this court comprised only two, and they in turn must have convinced the steward that he was what today would be called 'a deserving case'. Be that as it may, poor Henry did not survive in business very long. In September 1659 his 'Tenement, work-house and garden plott' were surrendered to his father and brother John who were to sell them and pay his debts, and if any money was to remain it was to be divided among his children. The site later became the Fair-field in Fairfield Road and the lane which once led to the house and workshop can still be seen today.[5]

Avis Budd occupied a cottage and half an acre of land on the east side of the present Mill Road. She had been admitted to the premises *as the first tenant* in June 1655 and here she was, less than three months later, in court for attempting to increase her holding by stealing part of the common. She may very well have felt that if others were apparently getting away with their encroachments she might just as well try for a share for herself; there was much to be gained and nothing to lose if she complied with the court order and restored the common before the following Christmas. In the event it seems that she did get away with it and that her successors to the property were equally successful in extending the boundaries at the expense of the other tenants. When, nearly two centuries later following the Tithe Commutation Act, the parish was accurately surveyed, it was found that Avis's site comprised no less than four and a half acres. Three acres of this had been acquired by purchase and a quarter of an acre more allocated to the then owner when the common was enclosed in 1828, but even so about three quarters of an acre had been encroached piecemeal some time between 1655 and 1828.

Samuel Snashall acquired Smeeds (the smithy near the present *King's Head*) in 1655 and was granted an additional quarter of an acre of land the same year. This was almost certainly the encroachment he had made on the common which probably adjoined his premises.

When Thomas Marchant appeared in court in 1656 for 'enclosing part of a pond on St. John's Common' he was probably taking advantage of an old pit (originally dug for clay and never filled in) for watering his cattle. His house and land (later called Grove farm) were very close to some of the finest sources of clay on the common. With Thomas in court in 1656 were Thomas Wickens, Stephen Jenner, Nicholas Jenner and Samuel Marten – all presented for making unauthorised enclosures.

Some of the illegal encroachments made about the middle of the 17th century became formal tenancies, the sites of which can still be seen today. Take for example the case of Henry Marten. He was hauled before the manor court in 1649 when it was presented that he 'had erected a cottage on St. John's Common between the messuage of John Johnson and the messuage and land called Barbers'. He was ordered to remove it before Michaelmas on pain of 40s. Twelve months later nothing had been done; indeed, Henry had also enclosed two more acres. He had died in the meantime but this made little difference so far as the court was concerned. His widow, Anne, was ordered to demolish the cottage and throw open the waste before the next court on pain of 40s. A year later:

> 1651. Anne Marten had not pulled down the cottage built by her late husband on the lord's waste at St. John's Common near the lands of John Johnson, nor had she laid out the two acres with it.

More than 20 years were to elapse before anything more is heard. In 1673 'a cottage and two crofts on St. John's Common near the land of James Wallnut (or Warnett) called Barbers' was granted to Thomas Parker 'on condition that Anne Marten, widow, remains in possession of the little room in which she is living for the rest of her life'. The rent was fixed at 4d. p.a. Anne Marten was still occupying the cottage in 1678 when it was sold to Edward Michelborne of Hammonds Place, but she seems to have died shortly after having outlived her husband by about 30 years. Part of the site later became the property of Norman and Burt, the former well-known local builders in London Road.

On the Clayton side of the common several cottage properties dating from the second half of the 17th century can be associated with enclosures almost certainly made during the upheavals of the Civil War and the Commonwealth. This is the complete list so far as can be established from the official records:

1. Dunstalls – granted in 1659 to James Sanders (or Saunders) but already containing what was described as an 'Auncient tenement or cottage'. There is no way of determining how old was 'Auncient'. When the Keymer commons were enclosed in 1828 the term 'ancient enclosure' was given to anything that had been enclosed for 20 years or more. We suspect, however, that it was not all that ancient since in July 1653,[6] James Saunders, then described as 'of Clayton, lyme-burner' appeared before the Quarter Sessions at Lewes charged with 'erecting and continuing a cottage [there]'. He pleaded not guilty and, six months later when his case was heard, he was acquitted. On the basis that not more than a year or two elapsed between his building the cottage and his appearance before the magistrates, it would appear that in this instance the house was less than 10 years old.

2. 'Cottage and half an acre enclosed from St. John's Common' now the site of the *Weald Inn*, was first mentioned in 1654 when it was mortgaged for £5 6s. 0d. by the then owner Edmund Turner. There is no indication of when it had been built but it could well have dated from the early years of the Civil War.

3. 'Cottage and half an acre at St. John's Common' (now the site of The Mount, 73 London Road) first mentioned in 1669 but built some years earlier.

4. 'Cottage and half an acre at St. John's Common next the land called Brewers farm' (now part of West End farm) granted in 1672.

5. 'Cottage, shopp, stable, orchard and garden and several closes of land on St. John's Common otherwise Starford Heath' (later called The Gattons) first mentioned in 1684 but enclosed earlier.

6. In 1692 Richard Bennett was presented for erecting a cottage on the waste of St John's Common and was ordered to demolish it on pain of 5s. In 1694 the cottage together with eight rods of land was granted to Richard Bennett for the term of his life. All was well until 1701 when he died and the premises reverted into the hands of the lord leaving Elizabeth his wife high and dry. However she continued to occupy the house since in 1705 she was ordered to demolish it before the next court on pain of 10s. She did not do so, of course, and the following year she, too, was granted a formal tenancy for the term of *her* life. The site of the cottage in Fairfield Road can no longer be identified, having been entirely obliterated by modern houses. The cottage, or its re-built successor, however, stood until well into the present century.

7. The cottage in Fairfield Road erected by Henry Peckham in 1655 (see p. 16).

On the Keymer part of St John's Common the sites of no fewer than seven cottages erected during this period can be identified:

1. 1689. John King, deceased, had erected a cottage on St John's Common near le Faire Place and had enclosed a small parcel of land which he had held for many years. It was now granted to his widow, Mary King, for her life with remainder to Elizabeth King only daughter of William King [? John's brother]. The house, opposite the *King's Head* and adjoining the Post Office and Stores, is today called Fayre Place.

2. It was presented at a court held on 21 October 1651 that 'a cottage and two acres lately enclosed on St. John's Common',[7] was held by Stephen Ansty. This was the first time the premises were mentioned in the official records which suggests that the cottage and the enclosure were relatively new. The court ruled that Stephen could continue to occupy them until further notice.

3. A similar situation arose a little further to the south in what is now Mill Road when Avis Budd, a widow, was admitted in 1655 to 'a cottage and half an acre at Starford

Common'.[8] This was a formal admission and put a former illegal enclosure on a proper footing.

4. In 1663 Samuel Marten was granted 'ten acres of land lately assarted and enclosed on the waste at Starford Heath with barn and lyme kill thereon' (later to become part of the site of Norman's brickworks). A house was built on the site about 1683 by Thomas Butcher and for many years thereafter it was known as 'Butchers'.

5. South of the present Station Road (adjoining part of the grounds of Oakmeeds school) in 1671 was 'a cottage and two acres lately built and enclosed at Starford Heath or St. John's Common'. It was granted to John Marten who was to establish the brickworks later known as 'Meeds' now remembered in a residential road of that name.

6. By 1685 another cottage had been built on land adjoining 5 above and was owned by John Marten's widow, Jane Marten.

7. Adjoining the lane that led to Freeks farm was a two acre site granted in 1660 to Stephen Jenner who by 1663 had erected a cottage for himself.

From the middle of the 17th century, therefore, there were substantial new settlements in Burgess Hill, some on the very heart of St John's Common. The earlier encroachments were almost entirely made by land owners whose holdings abutted the commons. It was a relatively simple matter for them to move the stakes a yard or two into the common when they needed replacement. But in the examples quoted above we see a quite different approach. Here men boldly marked out a parcel of land on the common, fenced it and often put up cottages or other buildings before they were reported to the manor court. It says much for the flexible attitude of both lords and stewards that some, at least, of the offenders were given grants of these previously illegal plots. To provide access to the new sites, tracks were made across the common and would have been metalled to prevent wagons sinking up to the axles in wet weather. Pottery Lane, now called Station Road, must have started life about this time as would part of the present Mill Road, since Stephen Ansty and Avis Budd would have had to create a track or path to their cottages. It is highly likely that anyone who could demonstrate that he was hard working and enterprising and was not likely to become a charge on the parish could expect to have a sympathetic hearing when he appeared before the court to explain his actions. The majority of offenders were probably local people; sons who had no hope of inheriting property of their own, who wanted desperately to marry and to have children and whose only hope of achieving this was to gravitate to the only open land left in the area. If the alternative was that these unfortunate people all became a charge on the Poor Rate, local land owners and/or tenants would have been only too glad to recommend continuance of an illegal encroachment, for an increase in the Poor Rate was always something to be fiercely resisted.

It seems natural that the surplus population in our parent parishes of Clayton and Keymer should tend to drift towards St John's Common. There was no surplus land anywhere else. If they tried to obtain work outside the parish they were promptly returned to their places of birth when that temporary work had come to an end and they needed parish relief. We shall be discussing this in more detail later. Meantime we may look upon the 17th century as the beginning of the development of Burgess Hill – still a scattered community but one that was now becoming more and more concentrated on what was later to become the town centre.

The Brickmaking Industry

It is difficult to say precisely when the clay-based industries were established in Burgess Hill. One cannot escape the impression that local entrepreneurs would have been very conscious of the great rebuilding that commenced during the reign of Queen Elizabeth and continued for 40 years or so after her death, and that these men would have been anxious

5. Station Road c.1920, looking east. A corner of Meeds Potteries can be seen in the background to the right of the picture. Brickworks were first established on this site in about 1670.

6. Mr. William Meeds' house in Station Road was built c.1884 and is now used as offices, although it looks much as it did in the late 19th century.

to cash in on the building boom. It may well be that the rebuilding programme came late to this part of the country. On the other hand the difficulty of transporting the finished product, other than to the immediate vicinity, must have been enormous given the state of the roads at the beginning of our period. It may perhaps be proved one day that bricks and tiles were made here in Roman times. The Roman settlement near the sandy ridge at Stone Pound, Hassocks, was little more than a couple of miles away from the southern part of St John's Common where later some of the finest deposits of clay were to be found and exploited, and only about three and a half miles from the foot of the Downs where, you may recall, the remains of a Roman bath were discovered in the 19th century.

So far, however, there is no documentary evidence of any activity in this field until the late 16th century. One reference comes in 1578 when Richard Parsons left to his son Richard: 'one moitie or half of a parcel of land lying in Clayton called Cowpers Croft and the *brickplace thereunto nigh adjoining*'.[9] Coopers Croft adjoined West Street and is now part of West End Farm. Just outside the north-west corner of the field is a large pit which could possibly have resulted from digging for clay. But that is all. It would be wrong to claim that the 'brickplace' was in fact a kiln and that the extant pond was a former clay pit; but it remains a possibility.

References in the manorial records bring us on to much firmer ground:

> 1589. It was presented that John Pomfret had dug 'terram' called Erthe upon the common called Seynt John's and had similarly dug sand upon the lords' common called Burgeshill.[10]

It seems reasonably certain that the 'Erthe' was being dug to use in the manufacture of bricks, tiles or pottery and it must be assumed that John Pomfret was digging for clay. The above entry is also interesting in its reference to the digging for sand. The 'common called Burgeshill' was of course St John's Common where it abutted the land of Burgess Hill farm. It is not generally known that a stratum of sand exists on this part of the former common. It may well have been discovered originally when men were searching for clay suitable for manufacturing. Its existence was again revealed when part of Station Road was opened up in connection with drainage work a year or two ago.

No more is heard of John Pomfret's enterprise and it must be assumed that his efforts either proved abortive and he did not find clay of the quality for which he was searching, or that the weight of public opinion was against him and that he abandoned his project for lack of support.

A quarter of a century later there was no doubt about the purpose of a similar offender:

> 1615. Samuel Marten had dug out clay *for making tiles* without licence and was in mercy 2d. He was given until the next court to fill in the pit he had made on penalty of 5s.
> 1616. Samuel Marten had not filled in the pit he had made by this court's date and forfeited 5s.

There is, unfortunately, a gap in the records between 1618 and 1622 so it is not known whether Samuel Marten complied with the order. Certainly he was still active in 1623 when he was again presented for 'digging earth on the common of St. John's without a licence'. He was fined 3s. 4d. and ordered to fill in the whole area before the next feast of St John the Baptist [in 11 months' time] on pain of 3s. 4d. A year later:

> 1624. Samuel Marten had not mended the place excavated by him on St. John's Common and was in mercy 3s. 4d.

With another gap in the records for 1629 and 1630 no more is heard of Samuel Marten until 1633 when he acquired a cottage called Slutswell (north of the present Queen Elizabeth Avenue in the vicinity of Sussex House) from Thomas Booker who was to have 'part of the cottage whilst he remained celebate and unmarried viz. the chamber in the outlet on the south and west side'.

There seems little doubt that Samuel had continued to manufacture clay products without

7. Sussex House, offices of Van den Burghs and Jurgens, was built on the site where Samuel Marten started making tiles in 1615.

a break from 1615 and, indeed, had founded the first permanent brick and tile works in Burgess Hill. He may therefore be properly termed the 'father' of the industry that continues to the present day. He died in 1636 leaving his son, a minor, to carry on.

By the 1640s Samuel junior, continuing where his father left off, had managed to enlist the help of two other local men:

> 1644. Samuel Marten, John Marten and James Saunders had dug 'lutum' (clay) on the waste of Keymer common. The case was to be advised upon after consultation with the lord.
>
> 1647. John Marten, Samuel Marten and James Saunders had dug up clay on St. John's Common. The matter was to be advised upon after consultation with the lord.

It will be noted that no longer were these men summarily ordered to stop their work on threats of severe penalties; the steward and the homage, comprising half a dozen and more substantial local landowners, were clearly in sympathy with the aims of these offenders. They must have recommended to the lord that the enterprise should continue, for a year later Samuel Marten was 'granted a licence to dig clay upon the common called Keymer rendering [to the lord] 3s. 4d. p.a. for so long as he continues to dig clay'.[11] Whether there was a temporary cessation of clay digging causing the licence to lapse, or whether the court refused to continue to renew it is not known, but in 1655 Samuel, and James Saunders, were each fined 5s. for digging clay, sand and turf on the common. In the same year (1655) Samuel and John Marten had crossed the parish boundary and moved into Clayton where they were presented for 'digging clay upon the common called St. John's Common *to make bricks* to the greate damage of the lord and tennants of this manner. Therefore each of them is amerced 5s.'.

James Saunders was apparently still engaged in the infant brick-making industry, since three years later (1659) it was presented that: 'James Saunders hath made a breach upon the common by digging earth *to make bricks* without a licence'. He was not threatened with a fine, nor was he ordered to cease production and fill in the pit he had made. The reason quite simply is that James, as we have seen, was granted 'an auncient cottage and one acre of land near the ffayre place at St. John's Common, paying an annual rent of 6d., a heriot of 12d. on death or alienation and an initial entry fine of 10s.'.[12] Within a few years the Dunstalls were to appear on the scene, take over the business and bequeath their name to the town now perpetuated in Dunstall Avenue and Dunstall Farm Road.

With the two brickworks now established, Samuel Marten's at Slutswell and James Saunders' at the present Dunstall Farm Road, no more is heard of illegal digging of clay for some years. In 1663 Samuel Marten had extended his original half acre holding by acquiring 10 acres of newly enclosed land that, 150 years later, was to be acquired by the Normans of Chailey.

Samuel died about 1675 and left the business to John his son who at once mortgaged the 10-acre site for £31 to Thomas Butcher a local farmer. By 1682 Thomas Butcher had become the sole owner and clearly carried on making bricks.

In the meantime, as previously noted, in 1671 John had been admitted to a 'cottage and two acres lately built and enclosed at Starford Heath or St. John's Common' and was busy establishing a similar works there on the south side of the track, later to be called Station Road, on what was until recent times known locally as the 'Meeds Site'.

In 1685 Thomas Butcher and Thomas Croucher were presented (separately) for having 'dug clay from the waste of this manor [Keymer] to *make bricks and tiles*. Each was in mercy 2s. 6d'.

Little is known about Thomas Croucher. He had sold his cottage alongside the main road leading to Clayton village in 1670 and was probably a tenant farmer with land in the south of the parish. So far as is known he did not establish a brick or tile works in our area. What can be said with certainty is that he was again in trouble with the court the following year when he was fined 20s. for a similar offence. Thomas Butcher had apparently found a richer vein of clay on the common just outside his own land and was probably willing to risk a small fine for the benefits gained by exploiting it before someone else discovered it.

In 1690 Thomas Pockney, then the farmer of Burgess Hill farm, was fined 10s. for 'having dug and carried away large quantities of clay from the manorial waste'. At the next court a few months later both he and William Pockney [? his son] were fined 1s. each for a similar offence. They, too, may well have discovered a particularly suitable vein of clay on the common and had merely dug it out to sell to one of the three manufacturers. On the other hand they may even have been operating their own brick and lime kilns. In June 1705 the Rector recorded in his tithe book that he had 'reckoned with Thomas Pockney and paid him for two cord of wood, £1 12s. 0d. and there remains due to me £1 0s. 6d. [Added later] 'Since, a cord of wood 16s, a load of lime and *500 bricks*'. It is thought unlikely that Thomas would have offered lime and bricks in part payment of his tithes if he was not then manufacturing them on his own (leased) land.

On the Clayton portion of the common:

> 1692. It was presented that Thomas Giles had dug clay on the waste called St. John's Common. He was ordered not to dig clay on the common in future under penalty of 40s.

Nothing whatever is known of Thomas Giles. He is one of those shadowy figures who appear from time to time on an occasion such as this. He was probably a small farmer leasing a few acres of land barely sufficient to provide a basic living, and could have been trying to 'make a little extra on the side'. No more is heard and it must be assumed that with a fine of £2 hanging over his head he decided it was not worth taking any more chances.

In 1692 John Marten, still carrying on business on the south side of the present Station Road, was also fined 10s. for digging clay and making pits on the manorial waste. Two years later Thomas Pockney, whose land adjoined John's works, was again in trouble and was fined 5s. for 'having dug up quantities of clay as well as having cut and dug turf on the common'.

There was probably no need for all this. Had they waited for a few months and taken the matter to the next manor court they would doubtless have received a sympathetic hearing. For example, in 1694, a Richard Jordan was granted a licence to dig out 12 cart loads of earth on St John's Common, a privilege that cost him only 12d. 'Earth' in this context almost certainly meant clay which was no doubt sold to one of the manufacturers. This example shows what could be done if a man tackled his application in the correct manner.

It is difficult to say with certainty how the agricultural land on the present town boundaries was used in the 17th century, mainly because of the paucity of written evidence. There exist no inventories of the 17th century, but late 16th and early 17th century wills make occasional references to animals: cows, sheep and lambs, bullocks and 'all the geese and the poultrie about the house'.[13] Also mentioned are wheat, barley and malt – in one or two instances 'ote malt' which together with the live stock suggests that here in the weald mixed farming was practised: rearing of live stock, cows for milk, cheese and hides; bullocks for beef; sheep for wool and mutton; poultry for eggs and for the table, with the land itself devoted to grazing and the growing of grain and hay. Hops were also grown, for a survey of Burgess Hill farm in 1631,[14] shows a plot of about one and a half acres called 'The Hop Garden', now the site of part of Queen's Crescent and the nearby open space.

One can imagine the scene from the latter half of the 17th century: smoking kilns from the three now well established sites; horse or ox-drawn carts lumbering ponderously over the deeply rutted tracks taking clay to the works and bringing out a finished product; children in charge of a few head of sheep or cattle grazing on the common during the hours of daylight; an occasional cart or wagon trundling along one or other of the main roads; perhaps a stall or two on or near the Fair Place. Around the recently erected cottages owners or their wives would be busy tending poultry and perhaps a pig and trying to create a garden on which to grow a few vegetables and herbs – a scene far removed from the bustle of modern Burgess Hill.

The Fair

During the two days at midsummer (23 and 24 June) the common near the top of Fairplace Hill was a hive of activity. The annual fair held on 24 June attracted large numbers of people from the surrounding area as it had since the 14th century. Yet little is known of its early history. In view of this we are fortunate that an evocative description of a fair day incident of 1648 has survived in the Sussex Quarter Sessions records.[15]

In July 1648 one Edward Good late of Cowden, Kent, appeared before Robert Spence J.P. accused by Anthony Penny of Keymer, bricklayer,[16] of 'stealing one cupple of salt fish and a paire of shooes'. Anthony and Mercy his wife said that 'being at St. John's Common on mid-sommer day selling beere upon the faire day and having a basket with a copple of salt fish in it and a paire of shooes in the booth where they sold drink . . . Edward Good came unto them and called for some drinke and whilst they were busy about filling of beere for others Edward took the basket with the goods in it and went his way'. Mercy, 'hearing that such things weare at the house of John Geere went thither and found the goods which John Geere said he had bought from Edward Good'. John Geere had apparently put up Edward Good in his barn for the night and in the morning had struck a bargain, Geere selling Good a shoulder of mutton for 18d., Good selling the two salt fish for 14d. whilst Joan Geere, wife of John, paid Edward Good 2s. for the shoes. Good emphatically denied the charge and claimed that he had never seen Penny or his wife. He denied that he had taken any basket or goods whatsoever but 'he doth acknowledge that he sold a copple of fish unto John Geere'. Despite his pleas he was found guilty and sentenced to a flogging.

Posterity must remain indebted to Anthony Penny, Edward Good and John Geere for the picture their actions have painted. One can see the stalls; the hub-bub within the booth where beer was sold, hot, stuffy and smelly; and see human nature spanning the centuries as weak then as it is today. There will always be some ready to take advantage of another's lapse of vigilance, steal another's goods and hope to get away with it.

It is not known whether the fair was predominantly a sheep fair as indeed it was in the 19th century, but it seems reasonable to assume that it was. Nevertheless the goods stolen, salted fish and shoes, indicate that the mid-summer fair provided an opportunity to exchange all manner of things, a useful and welcome event in the lives of the local agricultural community. It is interesting to note that the thief was not a local man and that he had been offered a night's rest in a local barn. Two and a half centuries later little had changed, for when Bob Copper's uncle John drove his sheep from Rottingdean to St John's Fair – a leisurely journey taking three days to ensure that the sheep arrived in prime condition – he recounts how 'on the road the same as when we got there we used to doss down where we could'.[17]

There is an interesting entry in the Journal of Giles Moore,[18] the 17th-century rector of Horsted Keynes, in which he recorded that, at 'St. Jones's Fair' on 24 June 1670, 4s. was spent by his maid, Bess Falconer on a new hood for his young niece Mat (Martha). Both Bess and Martha must have made the journey to Burgess Hill for the general attractions that the fair offered rather than simply to buy a hood which would have been available much nearer home. After the hum-drum existence of a country rectory the outing must have been one filled with excitement. It needs little imagination to picture the scene as the two girls prepared for, and actually made, their journey cross country over atrocious roads before finally arriving at St John's Common. To them the journey would have been almost as exciting as that of the late 19th-century traveller when he embarked at Southampton or Liverpool for the New World or Australia. It was probably Bess's only outing in 1670. But all this apart, it does confirm that the fair in the 17th century existed as a centre for trading in goods as well as livestock.

Five years earlier in the middle of July 1665 when the Great Plague was raging in London and elsewhere, an order was issued,[19] drawing the attention of local parish officers to a lack of diligence on the part of citizens of the country in failing to report 'diverse disorderly persons [who] doe travell up and down the country and persons selling goods and wares as [for example] Chapmen, and Pedlers contrary to the law. It is ordered that all Constables and Headboroughs and other His Majesty's Officers and Ministers within this county of Sussex doe from henceforth keepe watch and ward in all Townes and parishes . . . And that they shall take all travellers, Chapmen and Pedlers and other Idle persons which shall travill contrary to the law and all other persons coming from London. And all other places infected with the plague And convey them by passe to the place of their legal settlement. And if that cannot be found or known then to the place of their birth. And it is further ordered that the Bailiffs, Criers and other officers of all Townes and places . . . where any fairs have been kept doe immediately uppon sight hereof make all usual proclamation at all usual places for the publique notice and for prevention of such conventions and fairs . . . And every Constable of each Hundred where any such fairs have been usually kept shall cause the day before and the dayes when such fairs should be kept a sufficient Guard to keepe out all Chapmen whatever . . . except all Drovers, Graziers and buyers and sellers of Cattle . . .'

This was a standard order that had been issued in times of plague since the days of Queen Elizabeth,[20] but it is worth quoting here to demonstrate the concern of the County authorities lest unauthorised strangers should introduce the dreaded disease to a hitherto uninfected area. In the event St John's Fair was not affected in 1665 since the order was issued about three weeks too late.

A further discussion about the fair is given in more detail in Chapter Nine. In the next chapter we shall be examining the social conditions of local people in the 17th century and will attempt to show how standards of living improved and how the poor fared throughout the period to about 1700.

Chapter Three

Yeomen and Poor of the 17th Century

From the local evidence available there is little to suggest that the medium sized farmer of c.1600 with between 70 and 80 acres of land was able to provide for much more than the bare essentials of day-to-day living. What then must domestic life for the farm worker, the smallholder and the small tradesman have been? So far as the small landowners and tenant farmers were concerned, living standards, though much improved through the 16th century when people were hauling themselves out of the middle ages, were far below what they were to be towards the end of the 17th century. Where, for example, a yeoman farmer of c.1600 was mentioning in his will such things as beds, pots and pans and one or two animals, a century later his successors in similar circumstances were sometimes leaving to their wives and children pounds instead of shillings, silver spoons and gold rings and coins, things almost unheard of at the beginning of our period.

The landless working man seldom, if ever, left a will, for the simple reason that he had next to nothing to leave. Such ready cash that he may have had would have quickly been appropriated by his widow or, if she was already dead, by the children; as would the few sticks of furniture and a bundle of old clothes. In the event of a dispute among the children letters of administration would be taken out and dealt with by the Probate Court at Lewes. It is, therefore, with the very poor and the more well-to-do that this chapter, which is based chiefly upon 16th- and 17th-century wills and the Quarter Sessions Records, is concerned.

W.E. Tate, in his classic book *The Parish Chest*,[1] gives a valuable summary of the former Poor Laws dating from the 14th century to modern times. As early as 1388 it became the practice for parishes to return vagrants to the place of their birth immediately they became a charge on the local poor rate – a procedure that was to continue almost unchanged for centuries.

With the suppression of the monasteries between 1536 and 1539 a new law imposed upon individual parishes the duty of caring for the impotent poor. An important Act of 1601 was to be the foundation of the local poor law administration for over two centuries (until 1834). Among other things it ordered that the Churchwardens and between two and four substantial householders be nominated each year as Overseers of the Poor imposing on them the duty of maintaining and setting to work the poor, the funds being provided by local taxation.

Later Acts were designed to set up the building of Houses of Correction to which 'rogues and vagabonds' were to be committed by local magistrates. 'Lewd women who have bastards' and parents leaving children chargable to the parish were also committed to the same establishments.

Whipping of women was officially abolished by an Act of 1792 though the Quarter Sessions Order Book entries of 1798 and 1800 both record such sentences.[2]

The great Act of 1834 saw the end of the old parochial system. Parishes were amalgamated into 'Unions', the governing bodies of which were Boards of Guardians centralised under the overall control of the Poor Law Commissioners.

It is hoped that these brief notes will help the reader better understand the full significance of some of the examples that follow in this and following chapters.

Wills of the 16th century normally followed a standard format. They usually began: 'I

[name] being sycke in bodye but by goddes goodness whole of mynd and havinge good remembrance make my last Wyll and testament as here followeth'. Then followed the testator's concern for his soul: 'I bequeth my sowle to almightie god trusting it to be associate with the blessed companye in heaven thorowe [through] the meryts of our Savyor Chryst and the intercession of the blessed virgin marye and all the holie company of heaven.' He then goes on to give instructions as to the disposal of his body which was usually to be buried in the local parish churchyard. Then followed legacies to the poor, the parish church and sometimes to 'the mother church of Chichester'. The testator then gives instructions as to the disposal of his estate which is often given in considerable detail.

The practice was followed with little substantial alteration throughout the 17th century and beyond, though after the Reformation the reference to the Virgin Mary and the Saints was dropped. Pre-Reformation wills sometimes made provision for the saying of masses and dirges 'for my sowle' not only on the day of the funeral, but 'at my monthes mynd' and 'at my year's mynd', a custom that continued for a short time after the break with Rome. For example:

> 1542, March 17 William Virgo, yoman of the parysh of Keymer,[3]
> . . . also I will have at my buryeng day v masses. Item at my monyth day v masses and at my yeres day v masses and also at all iij tymes brede, mete and drynke to refreshe the poore people to pray for my soule.

William Virgo owned (or was related to the owner of) Bedelands farm on our northern boundary.

> 1543, May 3 John Virgo of Kymer [probably a brother of William].
> I will have at my burieng five masses, at my monthes mynd v masses and at my yeres mynd v masses. Also at my monthes mynd I will have calffes [sic] and brede and drynke accordingly to be distributed to the poore and to such other people as then shalbe ther.

There is no way of establishing what was meant by 'calffes'. He may have given instructions to kill a calf to be roasted and served with the bread and drink but we cannot be sure. The interesting point is that after the masses the poor were to be treated to a good square meal; sufficient incentive, one would think, to ensure heartfelt good wishes for the soul of the departed.

The saying of 'masses for the soule' of the deceased was revived during the short and tragic reign of Mary Tudor who tried, not very successfully, to reinstate the Catholic faith. After her death the practice seems to have died out. One of the very last comes in the will of Joane Dobbyn of Clayton 'given by word of mouth to Edward Fawkener, Richard Dobbyn [her father] and Margaret his wife and others of Seynt John's in the parish of Clayton on 16th February Mclviij [1558-59]'.[4] She directed that her body was to be buried in the churchyard of Clayton . . . 'one masse to be said at my monthes mynd and one other at my years mynd . . . and I Wyll that breade and drink shalbe distributed unto them that shalbe at my buryall at the discretion of my Executors'. Other items in this Will are of interest. She left:

> To the mother church of Chichester iiijd for to be prayed for there.
> To my father Richard Dobbyn xiijs which my sister dyd bequeathe me upon her deathbed which xiijs is in the hands of John Fowle of Alborne.

In accordance with common practice at the time, money was often out on loan earning interest and not kept in a box under the bed. Nothing is known of John Fowle: he may have been a struggling young farmer and a friend of the family or he may even have been Joan's fiancé. Her father was certainly a tenant farmer of land in Burgess Hill, though which farm he occupied there is no means of telling. Her estate was valued at £7 and xxjd – a not inconsiderable sum for a young unmarried woman the year that Queen Elizabeth came to the throne.

The poor were usually mentioned in wills of the 16th century and, although from 1601 they were maintained from the money levied on the householders and occupiers of land by way of a local rate, the practice continued until well into the 18th century. It was usual for a testator to bequeath cash as shown in the following examples:

1523. December 24. Richard Iden, Rector of Clayton cum Keymer.

. . . Also I geve and bequeth to every pour man, woman and childe that comyth thither to take dole, every one of them a penny, and that woman that is with child ijd to pray for my soule and for all Christian soules.[5]

1559. January 25. John A Wood of Keymer [Ockley Manor].

To the poor at my burial 5s. Another 5s at my months mynd and another 5s at my years mynd at the discretion of my Executors.

1562. December 16. John Haselden of Clayton.

. . . For the poore men's box xijd.

1564. January 8. Johanne Beach of Kymer, widow.

To the poore of Kymer ijd.

Joan's estate was valued at £7 18s. 0d. which suggests that she could really have afforded much more than a measly 2d. Perhaps she had promised her former husbands (she had at least two) that she would remember the poor in her will and was simply 'going through the motions'.

1570. December 12. Christopher Pyecombe of Keymer, husbandman.

To the poores mens boxe of Kymer iiijd.

Christopher lived at the house later called Grove Farm in Station Road. Since he owned and was farming about 35 acres of land he, too, could have been expected to find more than 4d. as relief for the poor. The total value of his estate is not given but the legacies listed in his will indicate that he was reasonably well-to-do. Two of his daughters were to have £4 each and the other children were reasonably well provided for.

1578. January 21. James Jenner of Keymer, husbandman.

To the poor mens box of my parish ijd.

1579. November 25. Elizabeth Gardiner alias Smyth of Clayton, spinster.

To the poore people of the parish of Stenninge 26s.8d.

To the poore people of the parish of Ashurst 6s.8d.

To the poore people of the parish of Clayton 6s.8d.

Elizabeth was one of at least four servants on the staff of Edward Michelborne of Hammonds Place. Her will was one of the most interesting that has been found. In addition to her generous bequests to the poor she left legacies totalling a further £18 to her cousins and their children. The mention of the poor of Steyning and Ashurst suggests that she may have spent her childhood there before 'going into service' at Hammonds. She seems to have been on very good terms with her master and mistress since both Edward Michelborne and Joan his wife were witnesses to her will and Edward 'her well-beloved master' was appointed her executor. Three other witnesses were described as 'servant' and were clearly also working at Hammonds Place.

1600. September 6. Thomas Anstie of Keymer, yeoman.

To the poore of Keymer 10s.

To the poore of Cuckfield 10s.

Thomas owned and occupied 60 acres of land called Sherrys, later known as Old House farm, near the present high bridge in Rocky Lane on the road to Haywards Heath. He, too, was not over generous to the poor; his daughter Margery was to have £40 as well as 'five payres of good flaxen and hempen sheetes' then highly valued and frequently mentioned in wills, together with the 'cheste the sheetes be housed in'. His three sons had no cause for complaint over their portion.

8. Grove Farm, Station Road, which dates from the early 17th century.

As one would expect, cash legacies for the poor after 1601 tended to be less numerous. This is understandable since those with any property and money to leave were now liable for a Poor Rate. Nevertheless when Thomas Beach a local farmer made his will in December 1609, a few days before his death, he directed that £3 was to be paid to the poor of Clayton and in addition 'to the poor of Hurstperpound and Keymer all such somes of money as the parishes oweth unto me outstanding from last yeare when I was Constable'. This was a generous gesture; constables were frequently required to spend their own money on public business, only putting in a claim for reimbursement on the county or parish as appropriate *after* the money had been spent.

Sometimes a person put certain limitations on his bequest:

    1615. June 20. Thomas Alye of Clayton.
    To five poore women of that parish 12d apiece.

In this example the task of choosing the five women would have fallen to Thomas's widow, Joane, who was the executrix.

Similarly, in 1617 John Nutley of Keymer left 'to every poor wydow of the parish 4d' and John Parker a Clayton farmer left 'to the poorest people of the parish of Clayton 5s to be paid within one month of my death'. Overseers of Parker's will included Rev. William Wane, the rector, and he it was who almost certainly decided who among the 'poorest people' should benefit.

When Edward Michelborne of Hammonds Place died in 1628 he left to the poor: of Clayton £20; of Keymer £20; of 'Cockfeild' £5, and Penshurst £5, payable within one year of his wife's death and also 'the legacies as my father Edward Michelborne, knight, gave to the poor of Clayton, Penshurst and Cockfeild' which suggests that he had been negligent in complying with the terms of his father's will. There was no fear of a repetition of this kind when Edward's kinsman (also named Edward) died in 1685. He left £5 to the poor of Clayton and 40s. to the poor of Keymer and gave instructions that his overseers were 'to sell such of his lands and tenements as would be required to pay and satisfy his debts and legacies'.

The rector between 1683 and 1692, Rev. John Parker, remembered 'the poor of Clayton and Keymer (40s. apiece), Ditchelling (30s.) and Hurstperpoint' (40s.) and in addition, 'the poor of the parish of Kirkby Frely *where I was born* (50s.)'.

Bequests to the poor continued to be made from time to time throughout the 17th century and, indeed, until well into the 18th century, ending finally with a £2 2s. 0d. legacy to the poor of Clayton and Keymer from another rector, the Rev. Laurence Price, who died in 1752.

Instead of leaving cash for the relief of the poor, testators sometimes gave orders that food should be provided. Richard Iden, the rector, went even further in 1523: 'I geve and bequeth to every man within my cures of Clayton, Pyecombe and Kymer, every one of them a busshel of whete'. He makes no provision for the women of his 'cures'; perhaps he was satisfied that they were all adequately provided for from other sources.

1558/9. February 16. Joane Dobbyn of Clayton.

. . . Item I wyll that bread and drink shalbe distributed to the povertye that shalbe at my buryall at the discretion of my Executor.

Item my ꞵynd and wyll is that one busshell of wheate shalbe bestowed upon the poore for my syster Elyanor's soule and all Christian soules.

1558/9. March 16. Thomas Fawkner of Clayton.

And I do gyve to the povertye of Clayton ij quarters of wheate halfe busshell meale to be distributed at the discretion of the overseers of this my wyll . . . Also ij hogges of bacon which I wyll to be bestowed upon the povertie in kynd at the discretion of myne oversears'.

Edward Harfew, a Clayton farmer, in 1573 was very specific. He left 'to the poore of the parish of Clayton one bushell of barley that ys to saye to Stephen Notley one half bushell and Alice, gentlewoman, one other half bushell'. This type of bequest was the exception, however; normally gifts of this nature were left to the poor at large. In this instance both Stephen and Alice may have been particularly well known to him though in that case it seems a little odd that he mentioned 'the poore of the parish of Clayton' at all.

A few years earlier, in 1547, John Beche of Cuckfield said: 'I will xijs be bestowed amongst the pore people of Kymer Strete'.[6] John, though living in Cuckfield when he made his will, had probably been farming land in or near Keymer Street and so knew intimately many of the families living there. The following are one or two further examples of this nature before we leave the subject:

1596. Richard Jeffry of Kymer.

To the poor of Kymer 3s. 4d payable at the tyme of my buriall. Also one busshell of wheate in bread and three cheeses.

1746. Richard Turner of Oldland.

To the poor of Ditcheling and Keymer six bushels of wheat to be divided among the poor of each parish by the church wardens and overseers of the poor.

The latter, in fact, was the only gift of grain noted for the area in the many wills of the 17th and 18th centuries that have been examined. The practice seems to have died out generally about the time of the Poor Law Act of 1601. Richard Turner's bequest was the one exception.

Farm Animals

There are frequent references to farm animals especially in the early years of the period under discussion, when there seems to have been little ready cash available. The following are a few examples of some of the more interesting:

> 1542. William Virgo of Keymer (see page 28).
>
> To Elizabeth Yonge my dawghter ii Kene the which I by my lyves tyme delivered unto her with my own hands.
>
> To Jane Chesman dawghter of John Chesman a kowe and a haffer which John and Thomas Virgo my sonnes shall well and truly kepe for the said Jane untill the day of her maryage.

'Kene' were of course cows and the 'haffer' left to Jane Cheesman was a young cow. It is not known who Jane was. She could well have been William's grand-daughter though it was usual at this time for testators to mention their relationship to beneficiaries as William had already done in the case of Elizabeth. It should be noted that old William had made quite sure that Elizabeth would not be cheated out of her inheritance by her two brothers, by giving her the two cows whilst he was still alive.

> 1551. Richard Geffery of Clayton, husbandman.
>
> To Jone my wife iiij kene of the best . . .
>
> To Elizabeth Onstye I gyve ij yonge kyne, one Redde Shelled,[7] called Larke and one other Redde Shelled called Tytenose . . .
>
> To Margaret Hobbys I gyve a calfe redde and whytt of the backe and syde.
>
> To William Wymarke . . . one cowe the best after my wyffe hath chosyn . . . and ij purr lambes.
>
> To Richard Wymarke . . . a black bullocke of ij yeres old with a white backe.

After one or two other bequests, including two sheep for the poor, and almost as an after-thought, he left additionally: 'To Jone my wife ij calves'. It will be seen that he gave specific instructions as to the disposal of individual animals and even mentioned two of them by name. In his will he also mentions corn, though since the sum total of his goods and chattels was valued at only £21 4s. 6d. it would seem that, if the cattle were valued at only £1 apiece, the corn, farm implements and household goods did not amount to very much, and that his chief assets were his animals.

Then there was John Nutlye who died in 1557. He left to his son Richard, 'a cowe, a calf black wyderyd [withered, i.e., black between the shoulder blades] *with one horn* and a shepe'. Other sons were to receive 'a brown ewe; a calffe and a ewe; and two shepe'. Christopher Pyecombe (see page 29) left to his daughter Elinor 'a red kowe' which her mother was to deliver to her with '*the profytte thereof*' when she reached the age of 18.

In 1590 John Knapp a glover from Keymer left to his daughter Agnes 'a cowe' and to his other daughter Elynor 'one redde cowe being whyte-faced'. From time to time other skilled craftsmen are shown as owning animals strongly suggesting that they were supplementing their income by working as part-time farmers.

> 1614. Richard Beach of Clayton, yeoman.
>
> To Margaret my wife . . . my red and white cowe and my olde white mare.
>
> To Elnor my daughter one redd white-backed heffer that never had calf.
>
> To my daughter Joane Amore two ewes and [their] lambs.

This was the first mention of animals in local wills for several years, not because people had no animals to leave but rather, it is thought, because there was more ready money available and beneficiaries were consequently saved the trouble of selling the animals they had inherited but were given the cash directly. Richard lived at Povey's farm on the west of the town and must have been getting on in years since his daughter Joan was now married with two small sons and living at Scotches farm. He mentions other cattle and goods not already bequeathed and gives instructions as to their disposal.

Occasionally expressions are used that make no sense to us now in the late 20th century. About 18 months after the death of Richard Beach, his neighbour Jerard Burtenshaw (living at part of what was later to become known as Shelleys farm) also died. Most of Jerard's legacies were in the form of cash, but to Nicholas Godley of Keymer he left: 'one young milche cow bullock'. Could this have made sense to the small working farmer during the reign of James I? Could it have meant a young bullock still being suckled by its mother? About a quarter of a century later it crops up again. Thomas Brasier, who farmed part of what is now Clayton Wickham farm, and who died in 1639, left several animals to his grandchildren including 'one heifer bullock being a weanyeare'. Since a heifer is female and a bullock male, one wonders what precisely young Margaret Marten (Thomas's grand-daughter) actually received. It may have been a heifer since her parents were 'to keep it for her benefit' which presumably means that Margaret was to have the income from the milk and its products.

This was one of the last references to animals in wills of the 17th century, apart from two cases involving horses which very rarely get a mention. In 1669 William Turner left to his brother Thomas 'my bay horse' whilst in 1680 Thomas Jenner then living at, and farming, Sheddingdean left to Richard Pilbeam 'my little black ball horse' which must mean pie-bald. In both instances the horses were probably held in great affection by their owners and gratefully accepted by the beneficiaries.

Maintenance of the churches

Maintenance of the church fabric gets a frequent mention in wills of the 16th century, a practice that continued until the end of the century when it seems to have lost popularity. One of the earliest references comes in the will of Richard Iden who in 1524 bequeathed: 'unto the church of Clayton xls and unto the church of Kymer xxs', generous bequests by the standards of the day. Not everyone with goods and money to leave remembered the parish church; some may have quarrelled with the rector, others may have thought that what they contributed in tithes and rates should be quite sufficient.

Bequests varied between 'ijd or iijd' and half a mark (6s. 8d.), though apart from the above we have found only one example as generous as 6s. 8d. This came from Anne A. Wood alias Thurston of Clayton who died in 1572. In addition she left half a mark 'To reparacions of the hye ways' and a further 6d. 'to the high church of Chicester'. As we have seen, Chichester Cathedral, often described as 'the mother church of Chichester', also gets an occasional mention in the 17th century, with an isolated bequest as late as 1638 – a gift of 2d. from the late rector, Rev. John Batner. The latter's will made in 1629 is interesting in that he refers to Keymer as 'Chemar alias Keimar', the first alternative differing little from the entry shown in Domesday Book over 500 years earlier when it was called 'Chemere'.

Personal and other effects

The wills of the period throw considerable light on the way people lived; what they wore; what they owned by way of furniture, kitchen utensils and bedding; and, occasionally, what land they owned or leased, though references to leased land in our particular area are very few. Later, towards the end of the 17th century, there are examples, sometimes in great detail, of personal belongings and individual articles of clothing. Generally, the period from about 1560 to 1700 seems to have been one of increasing prosperity, at least for those with land and capital.

Detailed references to men's clothing in this immediate area are very few and come mainly in the 16th century. The following are one or two examples:

1555. Henry A Wood of Keymer.

To John A Wood my eldest brother all my rayment except my best shyrte; and my best hosse [which must mean hose] I give to Stephen A Wood my youngest brother with my cheste.

1556. Richard Rickman of Clayton.

To my brother John . . . all my best apparell.

1581. John Courner of Clayton, husbandman.

To my brother Henry Courner my best dublet, my best hose, my best hatt and a payre of russett breeches.

1593. Robert Waters of Keymer, minstrell.

To my kinsman Thomas Nutley . . . my best dublett and hose, a paire of highe shoos . . .

1591. John Godley of Keymer.

To Stephen Aly my brother-in-lawe . . . my blewe coate, my best dublett and my best hose.

Henry A Wood was a member of the Wood family who owned and lived at Ockley Manor, a little to the south of the town. He must have been a bachelor since he made no mention of wife or children. Nothing is known of John Courner, John Godley or Robert Waters though we must be grateful that their wills have survived to provide this brief glimpse of what the well dressed young man was wearing in (or near) Burgess Hill 400 years ago. One must also pause to consider how on earth Robert Waters managed to get a living as a minstrel in this truly rural area. Was he a member of a troupe of travelling minstrels? Or did he come to mid-Sussex between engagements, say, in London? And what instrument did he play?

Some of the women, too, left very precise instructions about the disposal of their clothes. Anne A Wood alias Thurston for example mentions: 'my best russet petycote, a chip[8] russet petycote, a dubble vayle, a flaxen vayle, holland kerchiefs, my best frocke', and other petticoats. Margery Bockface of Clayton also bequeathed 'ij of my best peticotes' to Agnes A Kent who was probably the mother of George A Kent, owner of Chappell farm and Blackhouse farm in 1600.

Agnes Attree, who died in 1625, was clearly up to date and wearing what was fashionable at the time. In addition to bequeathing the usual cherished petticoats and 'two wastecotes' along with a couple of kerchiefs, she left to her grand-daughter, Anne Attree, among other things 'one ruff band' which was to remain in fashion for a few years more.

Some women simply referred to 'my wearing apparell' which usually went to one or more of the daughters; some made no mention of clothing at all, possibly because its next user was understood. Take the case of Susan Pockney, who owned houses and land a little to the south of the town in Clayton and who died in 1690. She left to her sons Henry and Richard 1s. each if demanded and to Mary Savage her daughter 10s., little enough when we read that her other (single) daughter, Sarah, and two other of her six sons were to have £10 each. A condition of the legacies to the remaining two sons, who were to share the residue, was that Sarah, their sister, was to be 'allowed to dwell with them' and they were to provide for her ' (provided she will dwell with them) meat, drinke, washing, lodging and apparel till she reached the age of 18 years'. From this it may reasonably be assumed that the residue included the mother's clothing and that it was intended for Sarah when she had grown up.

As previously noted there are frequent references to corn. Wheat, oats and barley, sometimes 'Ote malte', and barley malt are all mentioned from time to time during the late 16th and 17th centuries. Occasionally there is mention of a quern – a hand mill used in the home for grinding small quantities of grain. The local farming community kept cattle and sheep, and all the indications are that mixed farming was widely practised in this area.

Spinning wheels and looms for weaving both wool and linen were currently in use and were handed on when the owner died. Sheets were highly valued and were frequently mentioned, particularly in the late 16th century:

1578. Thomas Parson of Clayton, husbandman.

To Letes [? Lettice] Parson my daughter 40s and one payer of flaxen sheets and another payer of canvas sheets when she shall reach the age of 20.

1591. Edmund Nutley of Keymer.

To John my son £16, four tuns of yard tymber, a chest and two paires of my best sheets.

To Edmund my son £20.

To Alce [?Alice] my daughter £10 and one pair of sheets.

To Margaret my daughter wife of Richard Geare 20s and one pair of sheets.

To Margery my daughter wife of Thomas Dancye 12 lbs of wooll and one pair of sheets.

To Eden my daughter, wife of John Dane £5 and one pair of sheets.

Edmund Nutley lived at Holmbush farm a little to the north of the present town boundary. His youngest son, Thomas, who inherited the farm was also bequeathed: 'a cupbord, a furnis, my best brasse pott, a cheesepress, a malt chest, a table and a bench and forme thereto belonging'. Furniture and household effects will be discussed in more detail later. It is interesting to note that seven children had survived to reach adulthood and that their mother shared the residue of the estate with her youngest son and was therefore assured of a roof over her head for the rest of her life. Nothing is known about John Dane, husband of Eden, but the other two daughters, Margaret and Margery, had married into well known local families. Edmund, like most grandparents of the time, had not forgotten his grandchildren, Joane and Amy Geare, who received 10s. apiece. He makes no mention of his livestock, growing crops, or tools of husbandry (ploughs, rollers, harrows, carts, etc.); these were all included in the 'residue', as so often occurs in wills of this time.

Sheets continued to be mentioned from time to time throughout the 17th century. One of the last comes in:

1699. Thomas Mitchell of Keymer.

To my eldest son John Mitchell . . . one fine holland sheet and pillowcase . . .

To my eldest daughter Mary . . . six pair of fine flaxen sheets and one holland child-bed suite that was her mother's.

Thomas farmed land immediately to the north of Wivelsfield station in addition to other land in the vicinity. Both holland and flaxen sheets were of good quality linen, very hard wearing, that lasted for many years even after constant use. Canvas sheets, very rarely mentioned at this time, were also hard wearing, albeit somewhat rough to the skin.

Furniture, bedding and household goods were frequently mentioned throughout the period but particularly in the last years of the reign of Queen Elizabeth. Pewter platters and dishes were bequeathed at least as early as 1563. Joined presses 'for keeping clothes in'; chests, sometimes described as 'grat' or 'lytle'; beds, sometimes feather beds – all can be found about this time.

Some testators listed their effects in considerable detail. Ralph Calchell who died in 1568 left an estate valued at £19 4s. 11d. He mentions 'whyt meat' and 'baycon', corn growing upon the ground as well as 'ij quarters of wheat *ready thrashed in the howse*' and 'iij quarters of ote malt'. Also:

I give and bequeath to Alice my wife one fether bed and bolster, iiij payer of sheets, one payer of blankets and one coverlett. Also . . . so moch tymber as shall make one tubb and one keler.[9]

Certain of these goods, together with a couple of cows, were to be devoted to the bringing up of Joan and Harry, two of his four children then under 21; and if Alice refused to bring up the children the executors were to have the goods and 'to see that the children were brought up and kept'. The children may well have been Alice's step-son and daughter, Ralph's by a previous wife. He would surely not have suspected that she would have been capable of neglecting her own children. In the absence of parish registers of this date it is

quite impossible further to check the background to this curious proviso. To Harry his son
he left:

> One payre of sheates and the best chest in the house and the best brasse pott, one cauldron of
> brasse, one great spitt and one quarne to grind malt in.

Although he does not say so, one must assume that Alice had the use of these items during
her lifetime, or at least until young Harry became of age or married. There were no such
question marks over what was intended in 1572 when Christopher Pyecombe died. He
specified:

> To Richard my sonne vj ewes when he attains the age of 20 . . . a bedd with all things thereunto
> belonginge, a joyned presse, cubborde, a meele trought, a boulding [used for sifting flour] with the
> table in the hall, the forme benches and shelves fastened to the house there to stand and not to be
> removed, the bedd, cuppard, trought, boulting with the table and standers to be occupied and used
> by my wyfe [Dorothy] during her liffe and then to the use of the sayd Richard.

He also left a 'redd cowe' to his daughter Elnor but specified that the 'profytt' therefrom
should go to his wife until Elnor reached the age of 18. Dorothy was then 'to delyver [to
Elnor] a kow with the profytte thereof'. To Elizabeth 'my dowghter £iiij . . . and a cofer
with locke and key' and 'to Rose my dowghter £iiij and a lytell chest with locke and key'.
Both chests were clearly highly valued at the time.

A century later, in 1681, in the will of Edward Haselgrove, a Clayton labourer, details
are given of what must be the entire contents of the house. Since there is nothing quite like
it in this immediate area it is worth quoting from it in some detail. He lived at Birds Hole,
the cottage adjoining Clayton churchyard, and is one of the very few testators of the 17th
century to be described as 'labourer' – a term that in itself means very little since nearly
every man who was not renting and/or farming land on his own account, or who was not
plying a recognised trade, was almost always described either as 'husbandman' or as
'labourer'. This is what he left:

> To Susan Fleete wife of Edward Fleete, all my pewter and all my brass except my furnace. Also
> my fustian bed, a flock bed and stedle [bedstead], curtains and all thereto belonging with one chest
> of linen standing at the foot of the same bed, with one chest and one table, and one chest standing
> in the parlour, with one brew tub and one baking keeler and all the rest of my wooden vessels and
> four chayres, one flitch of bacon and one mortar and the biggest iron pot and all the rest of my iron
> goods, and one earthen vessell with all my earthen goods and one latten dripping pan.
> To my son Thomas Haselgrove – all my wearing apparell woollen and linen, one flitch of bacon,
> all my working tools, and one litle cupboard in the chamber, and one grindstone with the trough
> and all iron thereunto belonging.
> To my son Edward Haselgrove – ls.
> To my son George Haselgrove – one flock bed and one chaff bed under him, with one flock bolster
> and one chaff bolster, one feather pillow with the sheets and two blankets and one coverlett and
> two boond [bound] chests in the chamber.

He left 20s. to each of his grandchildren who were to inherit when they became 21: in
the meantime each was to have 12d. per year.

Lest it should be thought that he had cut off Edward his son with the proverbial shilling,
it must be said that Edward, being the youngest son, inherited the cottage and the land
attached on his father's death.

It should be noted that Thomas inherited 'all my working tools' and a grindstone. This
suggests that Edward was probably a craftsman. The grindstone could have been used for
sharpening a forester's axe, and tools for clearing undergrowth in the abundant woods that
existed, and to some extent still exist, near Clayton village; or he could have been a hurdle
maker. Either would have been purely part-time occupations; the bulk of his time was
probably spent doing work on the nearby farms. He must have been getting on in years

since he had three grandchildren and, because he makes no mention of a wife, was almost certainly a widower. Susan Fleet was perhaps a kindly neighbour who came in to 'do' for him and perhaps cook him a meal each day. He almost certainly kept a pig or two and cured his own bacon. He had a 'furnace' which means that he also brewed his own beer. The three who witnessed his will were Henry Ford and Thomas Norton, both of whom owned property in Clayton, and John Turner, then owner of Friars Oak and other land in Hassocks. His overseers were his friends John Attree of Freeks farm and Thomas Smith who probably leased land in the village. It will be seen therefore that for a 'labourer' he seems remarkably well connected, though of course his 'connections' may possibly have been a result of his work, whatever that may have been.

This will has been examined in some depth because, although Edward Haselgrove did not live within the present Burgess Hill boundaries, he must have been typical of some of those who did and who left no will. What must be stressed is that the contents of his house seem to be vastly superior to those of men described as 'yeoman' a century or so earlier, when beds and bed linen, livestock and the occasional pewter dish and 'brasse pott' seem to be listed as the most valuable heirlooms to be passed on. An attempt has also been made in this example to demonstrate what can be deduced from a rather more than casual reading of these old documents especially when, from a study of the manorial records, one can identify the house where a given testator lived.

All the indications are that the making of a will was something that was often put off until the very last minute. They are frequently dated only a week or two – sometimes only a few days – before they were proved at the local Probate Court. Richard Wymarke of Freeks farm, for example, made his will on 25 October 1595. By 6 November an inventory had been made and the will proved. Similarly, John Pollington, a local tailor, made his will on 19 July 1632. By 7 August he had died, been buried 'in the churchyard of Keymer', had an inventory taken and the estate settled all in less than three weeks. These are by no means isolated examples.

As noted earlier (page 27) the period between c.1600 and 1700 saw a marked rise in the standard of living. Gold, silver and jewellery were rarely mentioned before the middle of the 17th century though there were just one or two exceptions. In 1557 Joan Lashford a Clayton widow left to her daughter Joan among other things 'my silver hooks and a ring'. Ten years later Richard Fawkner left to his wife 'the residue of my goods, chattels, jewells, real money, dettes, utensylls of husbandry and household not given or bequeathed. . .'. No further references have been found until 1661 when Anne Allcocke, who probably lived at High Chimneys in Keymer Road, left to her son Henry:

> £4 when he reaches the age of 21, one pair of flaxen sheets, one pair of hempen sheets, one flaxen tablecloth, one towel, three peeces of pewter, *my gold ring* and one chest standing at the foot of my bed.

William Turner who lived a little to the south of the present town boundary and who died in 1669 left 'plate' to his daughter Mary whilst his sisters Mary Chatfield and Cornelia Scrase were given 'each of them a mourning ring to weare in remembrance of me'.

The gift of mourning rings was probably not unusual at this time. In 1682 the Rev. Francis Smith, who was rector between 1677 and 1682, left to his brother (in-law) William Read and (blank) his wife: '40s to buy each of them a ring'. Ten years later Frances Luxford, sister-in-law to the then rector, Rev. John Watson, left to her sister Anthe (? Anthea) 'my grandmothers wedding ring, one stone ring [which must mean a ring with a precious stone set in it] and one small silver cup'.

Mary Winchester who died in 1694 bequeathed the usual chests and sheets to her family with 5s. to her son Richard and 1s. to her grand-daughter Barbara, which suggests that she had very little to leave, yet even she had a silver spoon which was left to Elizabeth, another grand-daughter. However all these pale into insignificance when compared with the effects of Thomas Mitchell who was mentioned earlier (see page 35). For a yeoman farmer with very little land of his own he had amassed a small fortune, though in so doing he had made use of £60 that had been left to John and Mary his eldest son and daughter by his mother. This is a complete summary of what he left:

> To my eldest son John Mitchell – £30 in addition to the £30 given to him by my mother Joan Mitchell.
> To my eldest daughter Mary Mitchell – £30 in addition to the £30 given to her by my mother . . .
> To my next eldest son Thomas Mitchell – £30 when he attains the age of 21 or when he marries whichever is earlier.

He also left £30 apiece to his daughter Dorothy, his son James and his youngest son Robert on the same terms as for Thomas. If any of the children were to die before they inherited, their share was to be equally divided among the survivors. These were very generous bequests by the standards of the day, but in addition he left the following, including the sheets etc., previously mentioned:

> To my eldest son John Mitchell – one gold ring, two silver spoons and one 20s piece of gold that was my mother's.
> To my eldest daughter Mary – six silver spoons, one gold ring, one 10s piece of gold.
> To my son Thomas – one silver cup lately given to me by my mother-in-law Mary Holcombe alias Ansty.
> To my loving wife Dorothy – one old 20s piece of gold.

On the face of it poor Dorothy didn't benefit very much. Although she had been appointed executrix she was very ill and Thomas may not have expected her to live. Indeed, he says 'if my wife who is now sicke should die before she proves the Will', that duty was to be undertaken by the trustees and overseers. Her mother, Mary Holcombe, held the small farm called North Inholmes for the term of her life, so presumably Dorothy could be sure of a home so long as Mary was alive. In the event Mary lived until 1704 when the premises passed to Dorothy, then remarried and named Dorothy George.

There are many examples of what appear to be parsimony towards wives. Where there were grown up, and married, children, a widow could reasonably expect to make a home with one or other of them if the husband had made no specific provision for her maintenance. This must have occurred in many of the poorer families who left no surviving will in the 17th century. Frequently a husband left goods and chattels to his wife on the strict understanding that she remained a widow. Sometimes wives were left only such things as they brought with them when they married. This is a brief summary of one or two examples:

> 1590. Robert Davye of Kyemer.
> To Elizabeth Davye my daughter all the goods that were myne before the tyme that I was maryed unto Elizabeth my wife . . .
> To Elizabeth my wife all the goods that weare her own at the tyme I married her whom I doe make my hole Executrix . . .
> 1596. Richard Jeffry of Keymer.
> To Joane my wife £5 p.a. payable quarterly as long as she shall live after my decease, provided she does not marry agayne. If she doe marry again she is to have but the third of my land. Also I give her my bed that I now lye uppon with the bedstead, blankets, coverlets and all other things belonging to that bed. Also four payer of sheets.

It seems reasonable for a man to attempt to safeguard the results of a life-time of hard work and struggle. To leave his entire estate to his wife unconditionally would, at that time, doubtless have left the door open for unscrupulous fortune hunters more interested in what the widow possessed than in her personal well-being. To some extent therefore the conditions imposed may well have been in the interests of the widow, too. A loveless marriage to a man who had little affection for her, or her children, could spell disaster for a young widow.

When James Cooper a local tailor died in 1614, he left his wife reasonably well provided for. After one or two bequests of 12d. each to his nieces, nephews and a god-son, and instructions to his executor to 'bestow at my burial 5s. 8d. and [provide] a coffyn to be buried in', this is what she received:

> To Alice my wife £5 10s.0d. payable within 10 days of my decease. Also my cupbord and a brasse kettle *that was hers*. A linnen wheele and a woollen wheele, and little turned chayre, and one pillow bere [pillow case] and half the sheetes that shee did make and provide in my house in the time of our two lives and all her apparell whatsoever and my great brass pann during her life and after her decease my cousin Thomas Homewood shall have him.

His niece, Thomasine Browne, was given 'one payer of sheetes' and the remainder of the other half of those that Alice 'did make and provide' seems to have gone to two of James's nephews with the residue of the estate which could not have amounted to much. It was very good of James to allow Alice to have 'all her apparell whatsoever'.

Finally there was John Colchinne, a small local farmer, who died in 1616 leaving a widow and seven children, one of whom had married into the Jenner family. She (Elizabeth Jenner) received 10s. which was to be paid within six months of her father's death. Five of the other children, all under 21, were given varying amounts of cash. The other daughter, Joan, received £4 13s. 4d.: Stephen 20s.: Nicholas £14: and Richard the youngest £16. When it is said that he also left 6s. to the poor of the parish and 10s. to each of his friends living in Ditchling (the overseers of his will who were 'to have the finding, placing and disposing of my sonne Nicholas and my sonne Richard'), one would expect to find that adequate provision had been made for his wife. What he said was 'to Joane my wife £10 besides her own goods she brought mee'. Here again it must have been understood that she would make her home with one or more of her children. John and Thomas the elder sons were appointed executors of the will and almost certainly continued to live in the family home, at least until they married. It seems a little strange that his Ditchling friends were to have the responsibility for the younger sons who clearly were meant to be placed as apprentices and learn a trade in due course; perhaps Joan was thought to be incapable of taking on this task. The overseers were also charged with the job of investing the money left to the children under 21, and using the interest for their upkeep until they attained their majority; so perhaps it would all have been beyond Joan's capacity.

Servants

Those who could afford to do so kept a servant or two who lived in and were either treated as chattels or almost as members of the family, depending upon the temperament of the master or mistress. Those who benefited from wills of this period probably fell into the latter category, since there was no legal reason for them to receive anything. There are very few references to servants in the reign of Queen Elizabeth, but from quite early in the 17th century they are mentioned a little more frequently. The following are a few typical examples:

> 1612. To Jane Sowton my mayde – 10s.
> 1615. To Mary Field my mayde – £4.
> To Mary Isted my servant – 20s.
> 1617. To Margaret Balcombe my old servant – the best one of my sheepe and also one third of the flax and hempe growing upon my ground and the old borded bed steddle that standeth in the low chamber by the kitchen.
> To George Kent my boy – a ewe lamb to be kept for him till Lady Day after my decease.
> To Joane Haselgrove my maid – 12d.

This last refers to the will of Richard Beache who was probably the son of Richard Beache of Boddles farm, later to be called Poveys. These were generous gifts and those to Margaret Balcombe and George Kent were clearly the result of some thought. Richard, in common with most of his contemporaries, probably made his will when he was ill and did not expect to live very long. It was dated 30 May 1617 when the ewe lamb he had in mind for young George would have been quite small. He obviously wanted the boy to have one fully grown and therefore it was to be fed and looked after until the following 25 March at the expense of the estate. In the event Richard lived until about February 1621 and it follows that George Kent received what would have been a very young lamb towards the end of the following month.

Living at, and farming, Bedelands farm on the northern boundary of the town about 1670 were two brothers, William and Roger Virgoe, who were to die within a few weeks of each other in 1676. William says '. . . I give and bequeath unto Joane Maebe my servant 20s.' whilst Roger says '. . . to my servant Joane Mate £10'. They are almost certainly referring to the same woman despite the discrepancy in the spelling of the surname. Joan was probably the king-pin on the domestic front, for to her would have fallen the work of catering and cleaning the house. She may have kept poultry to provide a regular supply of eggs; she would most likely have helped with milking the cow (or cows) when the men were busy bringing in the harvest or the hay, and making butter would have been a regular task. In short she would have undertaken all the duties normally carried out by a housewife, for little more than her board and lodging. It is reasonably certain that, whatever the formal conditions of her terms of employment, there must have been times when there was just no money to pay her wages. It must be hoped that after Roger's death she was able to find another post.

Apart from Elizabeth Gardner (see page 29) very little is known about the domestic staff employed at Hammonds Place and the rectory, and the above constitutes the majority of examples of legacies to servants. The Rev. John Parker who died in 1691, however, mentions 'to Ann Brooker my servant if living with me at my death – 20s'. There seems little doubt that many of the more well-to-do yeoman farmers in our area employed indoor staff to help run the house, but left them nothing when they died.

There for the time being we must leave the local, mainly farming, community who by about the year 1700 were enjoying a standard of living higher by far than was ever imagined by their forebears a couple of centuries earlier. Conditions fluctuated from year to year, of course; farming then, as now, was subject to the foibles of the weather – favourable one year, disastrous another, but in general it seems to have been a time of reasonable prosperity.

Maintenance of Law and Order

In the Middle Ages when almost all villagers were, through the manor, firmly linked with the land they were often in effect prisoners within their parishes. By the 17th century this was still largely so, but for quite different reasons. Medieval man was obliged to stay in his village because of the value of his labour to the local lord of the manor. To escape he had to apply for permission to work elsewhere; permission that was probably not always readily given. Now the landless poor, unable to find work within their own parishes, could branch out and seek their fortune further afield; the proviso was that only in exceptional circumstances could they obtain a settlement in the parish of their adoption, especially if it was thought they were likely to become a charge on the poor rate. Thus a man who took temporary work, say, during the haymaking season or harvest, or became a forester during the winter, immediately that work came to an end was packed off to the place where he was born, there to be maintained from the local poor rate.

One can understand the attitude of the local churchwardens and overseers of the poor. No-one in the parish wanted to pay rates for housing and maintaining these unfortunate people. Certainly no-one was going to contribute willingly to the maintenance of poor people from *other* parishes. Local officials went to endless trouble and expense to ensure that only their own poor became a charge on *their* rates. The cost of sticking rigidly to the rules was sometimes equivalent to the cost of maintaining a small family of 'outsiders' for several weeks; but it made no difference. If, on the other hand, the overseers refused to accept a family when ordered to do so by the local justices, they could face a period of imprisonment for not complying with a legal order.[10]

The justices of the peace at this time had wide powers. In addition to dealing with the problems of the poor involving making orders for transfers between parishes; lodging vagrants in the local jail; hearing and adjudicating on a range of minor offences, they also acted as a County Council. In the latter capacity they had powers to order parishes to repair roads and bridges, and mend fences around the parish churchyard. They also had oversight of the county jails, or houses of correction as they were then called. They appointed a treasurer for the rates raised, called 'The Treasurer for Maymed Soldiers and Charitable Uses', and he it was who recommended the level at which rates should be levied from year to year. Magistrates had powers to order special rates in certain parishes as and when a particular need arose.

Local constables could, and often did, arrest a person or persons and take them to a local magistrate who would hear the case and deal with it summarily in his own home: such sentences as may have been imposed were subject to confirmation by the justices at the next Sessions.

Illegitimacy was particularly frowned upon, as much perhaps for its effect on the rates as for moral considerations. The expectant mother was frequently lodged in the house of correction at Lewes and, if the reputed father failed to appear to answer a charge and contribute towards the cost of maintaining the mother and child, vigorous efforts were made to find and apprehend him.

From time to time, when magistrates were advised about changes in the law, it became necessary to pass on the information to the lower echelons of the law enforcement officers. Thus, following a proclamation of the King on 9 December 1699,[11] about '. . . excessive drinking, blasphemy, prophane cursing and swearing, lewdness, prophanacion of the Lord's Day and other dissolute immoral or disorderly practices . . . from the highest or lowest degree . . .', all constables, headboroughs (who were in effect much the same thing), tythingmen, churchwardens and overseers of the poor were ordered to take effectual care in the discovery and prosecution of such offences.

Determined efforts were made from about 1670 to prevent non-conformists meeting and worshipping in private houses 'where people meet to hold non-Anglican Christian services'. Among those fined in July that year was Peter Terry an Anabaptist who was later to live at the premises in Isaacs Lane, now the site of Woodfield Lodge, a little to the north of the town boundary. At the Sessions held at Lewes in October 1670 it was recorded that Michael Marten, then living at Ditchling and farming land in the Keymer area, with Peter Terry and many others, were each fined £2 8s. 4d. for '. . . holding a Religious meeting contrary to the Liturgy of the Church of England . . .'. Although both these men were reasonably well-to-do, the fines do appear to be unreasonably excessive. Similar cases cropped up from time to time until 1688 when the Toleration Act was passed. Thereafter dissenting ministers were required to 'deliver into open court a certificate under their hands of their officiating as Ministers or Teachers in a congregation or assembly of protestant dissenters to be held for religious worshipp . . . According to an Act for exempting their Majesties protestant subjects dissenting from the Church of England from the penalties of certain laws'.

But if this helped the low-church dissenters the Act did little for the Catholics.

As early as 1655, when Cromwell issued a Proclamation 'for putting in execution the laws statutes and ordinances against Jesuits and Priests and for the speedy conviction of Popish Recusants', Catholics had been subject to persecution similar to that carried out during the reign of Queen Elizabeth. From this time magistrates were required to obtain from suspected Papists a formal renunciation of certain basic tenets of their faith in the following form:

> I [name] doe Abjure and Renounce the Popes supremacy and Authority over the Catholique church in general and over myself in perticular. And I doe believe that there is not any Transubstantiation in the Sacrament of the Lord's Supper or in the elements of Bread and Wine after consecration thereof, by any person whatsoever. And I doe believe that there is not any Purgatory and that the Consecrated hoast, crucifixes or Images ought not to be worshipped neither that any Worshipp is due to any of them. And I doe also believe that Salvation cannot be merited by works, and all Doctrines in affirmation of the sayd poynts I doe abjure and Renounce without any Equivocation, mentall reservation or Secret Evasion whatsoever taking the words by me spoken according to the Common and Usuall meaning of them. Soe help me God.

It was little wonder the justices were warned that many of those examined might refuse to take the oath or indeed fail to attend a hearing when summoned.

By 1689 constables were ordered to submit returns of 'papists or suspected papists . . . in accordance with an Act of Parliament Entituled An Act for the better securing the Government by disarming papists and reputed papists', which suggests that the Government was still very nervous about a possible Catholic revival.

Many dissenters supported the Duke of Monmouth when the Catholic James II came to the throne after the death of his brother, King Charles II. Among those listed 'who supported James Scott late Duke of Monmouth and his traitorous associates abetted by the malcontent dissenting and phanaticall partye . . .' were, perhaps not surprisingly, Michael Marten and Peter Terry along with four other Keymer men all of whom lived in the parish a little to the north of the town boundary. Great efforts were made to seek out and arrest these people. Constables were ordered 'to make diligent search . . . and to apprehend them and carry them before some Justice of the Peace to be bound with sufficient sureties for their appearance at the next Quarter Sessions'. In October 1685 most of those summoned for supporting the Monmouth rebellion had not been apprehended, for 'they doe abscond and lurke from place to place to prevent their beinge apprehended'. One cannot escape the impression that the local constables were not trying too hard to find the offenders. Villages were still quite closed communities and it would have been difficult for a criminal to find shelter and food without help from the inhabitants. It follows that they should have been apprehended fairly easily. In the event the majority seem to have been pardoned which may reflect to some extent the views of the local magistrates or alternatively a dearth of witnesses. In any event the offenders had probably done little more than say publicly that they were 'for' the Duke of Monmouth or 'against' the King.[12]

Among the officers elected at the annual parish Vestry meeting, in addition to the churchwardens and a number of overseers of the poor, were the waywardens or, as they would be called today, the surveyors of highways. When a complaint had been made to the justices that a certain parish road had been neglected and was overdue for repairs, it was this officer who was usually summoned to the court and ordered to explain why the parishioners had failed in their duty. Thus in October 1687:

> Richard Neale, an inhabitant of the parish of Clayton comes here in court in his proper person and asks to hear an Indictment of Record against the Inhabitants of Clayton as to why they had failed to repair the common highway . . . leading from Newhouse Gate . . . to Fryes Oake . . .

Richard Neale was at that time farming 50 acres of land called Fowles to the south of Royal George Road. He pleaded not guilty to the charge and deposited recognisances of 20s. which was refunded a few months later when he could demonstrate that repairs had been effected. This kind of case cropped up from time to time throughout the 18th and early 19th centuries, not very frequently in our area for it was in the villagers' own interest to ensure that the roads were kept in a reasonable state of repair. The road to Friars Oak was part of what is now the A273, a vital link between Clayton village and the church and the parishioners living in Hassocks and Burgess Hill to the north.

As suggested earlier, servants sometimes had difficulty in getting their wages. In the last resort they could, and sometimes did, seek redress through the local magistrates. In 1692 two servants of Thomas More Esq. of More House, Wivelsfield succeeded separately in bringing actions against him through the court:

> January 1652. Andrew Durrant complained that Thomas More of Wivelsfield owed him xvjs due to him for wages. A warrant was issued against Thomas More to bring him before some Justice of the Peace to pay the same or show cause to the contrary.

> October 1652. Thomas More Esq., was ordered to appear before some Justice of the Peace to show why he did not pay William Alderton his late servant 20s for wages and £iij. ixs for charges and expenses when he lay sicke in London while he was Thomas More's servant.

Although More House, a moated farmhouse about two miles north-east of Burgess Hill, is well outside the town boundary this important freehold property was then held of the manor of Clayton.[13] Because of this, and since there are very few similar examples nearer home, it is included here.

One cannot help but feel a good deal of sympathy for the unfortunate servants. Andrew Durrant's 16s. 0d. probably represented up to six months' wages if he was 'living in', and Mr. More was probably several months in arrear in paying William Alderton's £1. If William had been kept waiting previously one wonders how he was able to find £3 9s. 0d. for his expenses whilst he was ill in London. Eighteen months later Thomas More was in trouble again when he was ordered 'forthwith to pay to Edward King of Cuckfield vjs for work done by him for the sayd Mr. More'.[14] Edward King was probably a blacksmith or a carpenter who had the contract for the work at More House farm and, like the servants, had to take Thomas More to court to get his money. In all three cases the amounts were quite small even for those days, so was there some other reason why the three men went to these lengths to embarrass Mr. More? Did it all hinge on a clash of political views during the unsettled early years of the Commonwealth, or was Mr. More genuinely short of ready cash at the time? It is thought that it may have been the latter since there were two similar cases in our area in July 1655:

> Upon complaynt by John Cotty late servant of Thomas Marshall of Keymer that there is due and owing to him xxs for halfe yeares wages. It is ordered that unless he shall pay the sayd 20s or show good cause to the contrary to some Justice of the Peace he shalbe bound over to the next Sessions to answer for his refusal.

The other case was a claim by William Scrase of Wivelsfield, weaver, who was owed 4s. 6d. by Thomas Holford, a Cuckfield clothier. Here we have an example of a local cottage industry with William Scrase weaving cloth which he sold to a man in the adjoining parish. Again, it is surprising to find a man suing his customer for such a small sum.

Quite early in the austere and joyless days of the Commonwealth there was a clamp-down on 'unruly alehouses' resulting sometimes in wholesale closure. All those in Lindfield in 1652, for example, were closed with the exception of 'that run by John Fuller'. This was to be a recurring problem throughout the second half of the 17th century. In July 1674 we find that:

> It appeared to the court that there were too many alehouses than was necessary or needful in the parish of Hurstperpoint. It is ordered that the following be suppressed and putt down: the house of Richard Rosam . . . called and known by the signe of the *Royall Oake*. It is further ordered that he doe forebeare to sell or utter any Beere or Ale within the said house. And . . . that the signe of the *Royall Oake* . . . be pulled down and taken away.

In the first example the Puritans were taking action to suppress anything that remotely resembled loose living and irreverence. In the second, after the Restoration, the pendulum had swung too far the other way and beer-houses were closed because of lack of self-discipline by those who used them.

Sentences were often very harsh for some relatively minor offences; others seem remarkably lenient by today's standards. This aspect of local affairs will be discussed in more detail in the next chapter. Meanwhile, this is a cross section of some of the treatment meted out to offenders in the second half of the 17th century:

> January 1654/5. Edward Jenner convicted of wilful injury to be sett on the pillory in the market place at Lewes and to have both his ears nayled.
> January 1657/8. Samuel Marten of Keymer, brickmaker, indicted for shooting and killing a mare.

Samuel's case was deferred to the next court in April 1658 when he pleaded 'not guilty and submitted to a fine by protestation . . . 5s'. This means that he avoided the need formally to stand trial (and possibly be found guilty) and therefore could not appear as 'found guilty' in the court records. Considering the charge he seems to have got off remarkably lightly.

There are frequent references to offenders being whipped, sometimes publicly, either in the market place at Lewes or at the 'carts tayle'; sometimes the order specifically said 'to be whipped until his/her back be bloody'. In some instances (not in our immediate area) the inhabitants of a parish were ordered to repair the stocks and whipping post where punishment would be administered by the local constable. Offences ranged from simple vagrancy to sheep stealing, or just being idle and refusing to work when ordered to do so:

> October 1682. Ann Bennett, an idle girle, committed to the house of correction in Lewes, there to remaine for the space of a weeke and receive correction twice and then discharged.

Presumably to 'receive correction twice' meant that the unfortunate Ann was whipped twice during her one week in prison. This was not unusual at the time.

In July 1693 Joane Jenner,[15] was 'indicted for felony and stealing diverse goods' and was 'to be whipt at the whipping post and then to be discharged'. She had stolen a loaf of bread (2d.), 1lb. of pork (2d.) and 1lb. of butter (2d.), possibly only because she was half starved. But that did not matter. She had committed one of the most serious of crimes: she had taken another's goods and must pay the penalty. The prices quoted should not be taken too seriously. Clerks of the Peace sometimes deliberately deflated the value of goods to keep the crime under the heading 'Petty larceny', where the value of goods was set at 10d. or less.[16] Above that the offence became grand larceny, and subject to more severe sentences.

There was to be little change in the coming century and a half; if anything, sentences for some offences became even more harsh especially for second or third time offenders. There is as yet little or no evidence of the first stirrings of public conscience regarding the poor. It seems never to have occurred to magistrates, or to anyone else for that matter, to ask *why* a prisoner should have to steal; and *why* a man, frequently with a wife and several children, was forced to take to the road; and *why* he had lost his home. If the full evidence had been recorded and made available for study now, it is quite likely that in the majority of cases involving theft and vagrancy the causes could be traced to sheer ill fortune, such as illness or an accident, circumstances entirely beyond the control of the individuals concerned.

It was still a period when people were too busy securing their own financial future and that of their children to waste time on 'weaklings', who ought to be capable of supporting themselves and their families; and in any event there was always the poor relief. Did not the 'haves' contribute to the poor rate for this very purpose? 'Let 'em get on with it then, we've done our bit', and in the last resort there was always the house of correction or transportation to the North American Colonies for those who, to keep body and soul together, were forced to resort to stealing.

This was the attitude that prevailed in 1700 and was to continue with little change until well into the 19th century.

Chapter Four

The Embryo Town in the 18th and early 19th centuries

In this chapter, an attempt will be made to continue the previous theme through the whole of the 18th century and into the first quarter of the 19th century – up to 1828, in fact, when the Keymer commons in Burgess Hill were enclosed. As stated in the previous chapter there was to be little change in social conditions after the end of the 17th century; the main differences were that the better off were continuing to improve their standards of living and their social status, whilst the poor were becoming poorer. The ever widening gap between the 'haves' and the 'have nots' was to continue throughout the period and beyond. Yet despite the increasing pressure of a steadily rising population, there is no evidence of the fierce scramble for land that had occurred in the middle of the 17th century. There were, of course, the occasional cases at the manor court of encroachments and illegal grazing on the commons, but these were not so numerous as they had been during and just after the Civil War. In fact throughout the whole of the 18th century, with one or two exceptions, our immediate area shows a certain degree of stability.

Engrossment

As one might expect there was virtually no change in the area of land being farmed between c.1600 and 1828. There were, as we have seen, a few grants of small parcels of common land, some of which had been acquired initially by illegal encroachment, but the farms on the periphery of the commons remained unchanged. What changes there were, were mainly due to a process known as engrossment, whereby a few holdings came into single ownership through purchase, marriage, or inheritance, and became composite farms. Among these were the present West End farm.

In 1532 there is mention of copyhold land called Wylmottes, Graylinges and Hobbs, later to be converted into a freeholding called Northlands. Adjoining this to the east and abutting Fairplace Hill were two more ancient holdings called Perryfields and Perryfields Mead, leased in 1531 by Thomas Woodde to Thomas Alchorne. The five holdings extended westwards from Fairplace Hill in the east, north to the stream (a tributary of the river Adur) and slightly to the east of the present farmhouse. The farmhouse itself was called Floods Hatch and was part of a 30-acre property held of the manor of Wickham. To the west, and extending to the boundary between Clayton and Hurstpierpoint, were three more separate holdings called Collyns and Westuppsmede, Franklyns and Breakspears Croft, and Swyle land all in separate ownership in the 16th century and all part of the manor of Wickham. In addition there was the cottage and seven acres called Coopers Croft. By 1750 at the latest all had been acquired by the Webb family who, later through the female line, were to hold them until 1840 as two farms, Floods Hatch to the west and The Fairplace or Howels to the east. So far as can be ascertained these became a single farm about the middle of the 19th century. Thus it will be seen that by the middle of the 18th century what had once been ten holdings varying in size from about seven acres to 30 acres and once supporting five families was now owned by one man – an absentee landlord who leased the premises to local farmers.

Similarly, four parcels of land held by Richard Parsons in 1600, together with Love's

Acre then held by the Vincents, had been amalgamated as early as 1642 when they came into the hands of Thomas Jenner. The now composite farm was acquired in 1690 by Henry Shelley of Horsham more or less by accident. He had lent the previous owner, Peter Marchant of Ditchling, £200 at interest which Peter had failed to repay by the due date. Consequently the premises reverted to the mortgagor and remained in the hands of the Shelley family at least until 1883 when they were enfranchised,[1] and disappear from the records.

Three small premises called Lottmotts, in Keymer Road opposite the turning into Folders Lane, remained in separate ownership until the Marten family of New Close and Burgess Hill farms acquired them one by one between 1762 and 1789. The land was then merged with Burgess Hill farm whilst the cottages accommodated its farm workers.

Immediately to the south of Lottmotts also in Keymer Road, was a small seven-acre holding called Cowpers (or Coopers) which was merged with Batchelors farm from 1673,[2] when both were acquired by Edward Luxford of Ockley Manor.

Finally there was Bedelands farm to the north of the town. In 1600 there were two original properties described as: (1) 'cottage and 32 acres called Le Bedellands' and (2) 'cottage and 12 acres called Coopers'. Both were then owned and farmed as a single unit by Roger Vyrgoe who died the same year. By 1624 a parcel of land variously described over the years as 8 acres, 12 acres, 5 acres, and 4 acres (the manor court seems to have been thoroughly confused as to the area) had been taken in from St John's common and called Wakelins Inholmes. This, too, was incorporated into what later became Bedelands farm. In this case the engrossment had occurred very early; though there is no doubt that Bedel lands and Coopers were once held by two entirely separate families.

These are all the engrossed premises known within the Burgess Hill boundaries, and having described the process in some detail we must go on to say that in one or two cases the exact opposite occurred.

In the early 17th century when John Rowe compiled his admirable 'rental' of the manor of Keymer, Cants farm extended from Janes Lane to Birchwood Grove Road and included a long triangular piece of land that ran from a little west of Wivelsfield station to the southern part of Junction Road. Some time before 1750 the southern 80 acres, later to be known as Doubledays, was hived off and sold. Also sold during the 18th century were 26 acres lying to the north and later called Frankbarrow. Thus the original Cants farm of 200 acres and more was reduced to roughly half its size.

Much the same thing happened with Woodwards farm, a 60-acre freehold lying to the south of Folders Lane. Acquired in 1612 by Richard Aucocke from Sir Richard Michelborne, who in that year purchased a quarter of the manor, it was sold in 1646 to his two sons, Richard and Edward, each having approximately 30 acres. Later, the northern half became known as High Chimneys and the southern part Purtons – named after Nicholas Purton who had purchased it from Edward Aucocke and who died in 1689.[3]

Mortgages

People with any surplus cash either bought land or lent it in the form of mortgages at a modest rate of interest. Where a mortgagor defaulted the money lender could sometimes find himself owning property that at the outset he would never have thought of purchasing directly. Some attempt had been made in Tudor times to place a ceiling on interest rates and later the level of 5% set in 1713[4] was to remain in force for over a century. Even then with fluctuating interest rates, depending upon supply and demand, there was to be no significant change until modern times.

Those with money to lend mainly lived locally: Cuckfield, Lewes, Hurstpierpoint and Lindfield, for example, with Keymer men topping the list. They were drawn from a broad

9. High Chimneys in Keymer Road formerly called Woodwards. The original 60-acre farm became two separate holdings – Woodwards and Purtons – in 1646.

cross section of society; some were described as gentlemen or esquires; others as yeomen, or tradesmen such as cordwainers (shoemakers), coopers, innkeepers, brickmakers, and so on. Among the latter was John Marten of Keymer, who in 1692 lent £15 to Sarah Marten 'to be repaid at the porch of Keymer church on 5 October next'. Amounts varied enormously between a few pounds as shown in the example above – as little as 44s. in one instance – to the £840 advanced in 1715 by Leonard Gale, the well known ironmaster from Crabbett Park in Worth, to the then owners of Brooklands farm – Isaac Attree and Mabel his mother. By the early 19th century when land had increased considerably in value Ned Noakes was able to raise £3,000 on his two farms later called Old House and The Rookery, both a little to the north of the town boundary. In 1705 even an innkeeper (William Batchelor of Le Tyger, Lindfield) was able to advance £440, this to a tenant of the manor of Keymer holding land in Balcombe. Nathaniel Turner, who kept a butcher's shop in the house on St John's Common later called The Gattons, was also able at various times between 1706 and 1721 to lend amounts ranging from a modest £20 15s. 0d. to £126, the latter by no means a trivial sum for a small tradesman 270 years ago.

Money was lent for various periods, mostly for one year but now and then for only a few months; sometimes just to tide a man over until the harvest was ready or his cattle and sheep became of marketable size; sometimes to buy more land or improve existing premises. From time to time almost the whole of the purchase price of a property was borrowed. In this respect the history of the *King's Head* is interesting:

1798. Acquired by William Potter of Keymer, victualler.

1803. Mortgaged by William Potter for £416 18s. 6d. to James Newnam of Portslade, brewer.

1807. Surrendered by William Potter to Richard Hobden of Lindfield (a mortgage of £400 was still outstanding).

1810. Surrendered by Richard Hobden to William Pagden of Tunbridge Wells (subject to an outstanding mortgage of £400 with James Newnam).

Between 1810 and 1820 James Newnam had been declared bankrupt although the outstanding mortgage had been repaid. By 1820, however, William Pagden was obliged to mortgage the inn for £350 to Nathaniel Hall of Henfield. The money had not been repaid ten years later when William died and the mortgagee, Nathaniel Hall, was admitted to the premises. By 1839 Hall himself was in financial trouble; he owed £640 to a John Pagden and £350 to Richard Tamplin. Together they ordered him to sell the inn which was acquired by Charles Stepney, who was almost certainly already living there either as Hall's manager or as his tenant. Stepney had already purchased (for £10) 13 rods of land that had been allocated to the inn under the Enclosure Act of 1828. Now he was obliged to borrow £800 from John Ireland, a Balcombe wood merchant. This sum was still outstanding in 1852 when he died. His trustees, Richard Norman and Joseph Glazebrook, then sold the premises to John Pronger, a local builder, and after allowing for repayment of the mortgage there was just £30 to be divided among Stepney's five nephews and nieces, beneficiaries under the terms of his will. Thus the £800 borrowed in 1839 represented roughly the total value of the premises.

In 1694 Fowles farm was sold by John Challenor to Richard Neale, who was probably already the tenant farmer there. He acquired a dilapidated property. Since 1680 Edmund Challenor and later John, his son, had been constantly in debt to Timothy Burrell of Ockenden in Cuckfield for various sums between about £170 and £280, yet even so when Richard Neale took over the premises he was immediately presented at the court and ordered to repair the dilapidated buildings. He, too, was obliged to borrow from Timothy Burrell – £210 to help pay for the farm and presumably to carry out the necessary repairs.

There is no point in quoting further examples. The borrowing of money whether to enable a man to purchase a house, or to expand his business, or to pay pressing debts, has always been a feature of our economy and, of course, continues to this day. In the time of which we are writing it was all done on a very much more personal basis; in most cases both lender and borrower were known to each other or, at least, were both well known by the intermediary who put them in touch.

Encroachment on the Commons

From time to time a parish throws up men who used to be termed 'characters'. Two such were the Samuel Martens, father and son, discussed earlier; another was Walter Welfare who acquired and worked Valebridge mill from 1695 until his death in 1725. He seems to have lived a normal, orderly life until 1714 when something occurred that apparently changed his attitude in local affairs and from which time he was in constant trouble. Here is a list of his misdemeanours:

1714 (March). He had grazed sheep and horses and had used up herbage on the commons and wastes of the manor to the loss and prejudice of the tenants.

1714 (June). He had continued to graze his animals on the manorial waste where he had no right or licence. The homage asked that 10s. be levied on his goods and if he offended again he would be in mercy £5.

1715 (February). He had continued to graze his animals on the manorial waste and was

10. Fowles Farm as it was in the early years of this century. Once a 50-acre copyholding, the land was sold in 1913 when it ceased to function as a farm. The farmhouse, however, still stands.

in mercy £5 as allowed at the previous court. He had also cut down quantities of bracken and broom on Valebridge common and was in mercy 5s.

1715 (July). He had continued to pasture his animals on the common and the homage prayed that 10s. be levied from him and 40s. for any other offence of this nature.

He had encroached and enclosed a parcel of waste on Valebridge common and was given until the next court to lay in open on pain of 5s.

The same Walter Welfare had continued another encroachment on Valebridge common and was ordered to lay open before the next General Court on pain of 40s.

1715 (November). The penalties imposed on Walter Welfare for grazing his animals on the commons without right or licence had not been levied. The homage asked that they now *be* levied so that the liberties and privileges of the customary tenants be preserved against him and other encroachers.

1717. He had not laid out his encroachment on Valebridge common as ordered at the last court and was in mercy £5. Also he had cut down and carried away several quantities of bracken and broom from the aforesaid waste and had grazed his sheep there so he was in further mercy £5.

1718 (October). He had continued several encroachments on St John's and Valebridge commons and had continued to graze his animals on the said commons without a licence. He was given until Christmas to remove the encroachments on pain of £5.

1718 (November). As he was in mercy at the last court for sustaining several encroachments on St John's and Valebridge commons, the homage presented that the greater part of the enclosed land and his cottage there called Getlittles was taken out of the waste within the memory of several persons still living.

1720. He had not laid open the lands enclosed and encroached on Valebridge common. The Beadle was ordered to summon him to the next court to show why the penalties imposed had not been enforced. He had also cut down without licence quantities of bracken, broom and heather on the lord's waste and the Beadle was ordered to summon him to the next court to show by what right he had cut them down.

As if this were not enough Walter also appeared before the justices in Quarter Sessions at Lewes in April 1721 accused of stealing a spade and a small gate together worth 10d. from John Hurst of Wivelsfield. On this occasion, we should hasten to add, he was found not guilty and discharged.[5] The fact that John Hurst was later proved to be the heir to Bedelands farm and a potential beadle of the manor, however, may not be without significance (see below).

The beadle of the manor was, by long established custom, the holder of Bedelands, the farm a couple of fields to the south of the water mill. To him fell the unpleasant duty of collecting the fines imposed by the manor court. For more than a century, the office of beadle had been held by the Virgoe family the last of whom, William, died in 1712. Thereafter there was a hiatus whilst the next of kin was traced and, although we know that the manor was not left without a beadle, Walter himself no longer had this tiresome official 'living next door'. In the event William Virgoe's next of kin was found to be: 'John Hurst of Wivelsfield, tanner, youngest son and heir of Joan Hurst, deceased, who was the youngest daughter of Richard Virgoe who was the youngest brother of Roger Virgoe late of Keymer, deceased, who was the grandfather of William Virgoe, deceased, late customary tenant of this manor'.[6] All this took five and a half years (to October 1717) to establish and, once the premises were his, John Hurst sold them to Walter Carpenter, a Ditchling butcher, who filled the office of beadle until 1735 when he, too, sold out. So did Walter Welfare take advantage of the disappearance of the beadle from practically off his doorstep to add to his holding or did he have a violent quarrel with the lord of the manor or his steward? If so, was this long list of offences carried out with revenge and hatred in his heart? We shall never know for sure, for the background to a long standing dispute of this nature is never noted in official records.

The entry for November 1718 is of particular local interest in that it concerns land that adjoined a cottage and two acres that had been taken in from St John's Common about 1650. Since the entry refers to its having been enclosed 'within the memory of several persons still living', it seems probable that the two sites had both been encroached during the upheavals of the Civil War and that, whilst the tenancy of one had been regularised through the court, the other had slipped through the net. One wonders whether the irregularity would have come to light at all had not Walter Welfare made such a nuisance of himself. By 1749 the two sites had become merged into one and referred to as 'Holcomb's Cottage or Getlittles', later (from 1869) called Firtoft, remembered today in the pleasant residential close of that name.

After Walter's death his widow, Mary, carried on at the mill for 25 years before handing it over to her youngest son, also named Walter. In 1731 she, too, was in trouble at the manor court. Because she had allowed the mill to become dilapidated and had refused to do repairs and pay the rent 'which had not been paid for many years', it was seized into the lord's hands by Walter Carpenter, the beadle. The manorial rent for the mill was 3s. 4d. a year, not, one would have thought, beyond Mary's means. Of course, she was not thrown out of the property; how she got together the money to pay the back rent and repair the mill is not clear, but she was still the owner and living there in 1749. Walter II seems to have behaved himself but *his* son, Thomas, was on three occasions before the court:

1771. He had encroached on Valebridge common by erecting two haystacks formed round and was ordered to remove them.

1791. He was presented for enclosing part of the waste of the manor near Valebridge mill and was ordered to lay it open to the waste.

1792. He was ordered to remove an encroachment on Valebridge common by the next court upon pain of a fine [amount not specified].

No more is heard before he died in 1797 and one assumes that he had complied with the orders. His grandson, Thomas Welfare Ford, who succeeded him and who lived until 1857, created no such problems; indeed he seems to have been a model citizen.

Apart from the offences of the Welfares who created so much trouble on and off throughout the 18th century and other occasional encroachment on the commons, there was nothing like the free-for-all there had been about the middle of the 17th century. There were some problems, of course, particularly when 'outsiders' helped themselves to bracken and furze or pastured more animals in summer than they were able to feed on their customary lands during the winter. In an attempt in 1716 to put the record straight the homage presented:

> . . . that divers persons not having right of common do daily make incroachments surcharges and trespases upon the commons and waste grounds . . . and that the right of commonage hath immemorially belonged to the copyhold tenants of the said manor of Keymer not being cottagers and that no other persons are intituled to any right of common.

The homage, comprising seven substantial copyholders, were not strictly accurate. As we shall see, a little over a hundred years later when the Keymer commons were enclosed several cottages and even one or two freeholders received an allocation of the common after claims had been submitted and thoroughly examined.

The Brickmaking and Pottery Industries

There were only two cases recorded of encroachment on the Keymer side of the commons in connection with the clay-based industries in the 18th century:

1. Seeking his fortune in Burgess Hill some time before 1747 came Sampson Bagnall and Susan his wife from the parish of St Andrew's, Holborn.[7] They seem to have little success for in July of that year they were ordered back to Holborn. Nevertheless, what Sampson saw he clearly liked; and whilst he was here he may very well have acquired some skill as a potter. Twenty years later, in 1768, he and his wife were back, this time with two grown-up sons, Sampson aged 21, and James aged 20. Together they set up a kiln and dwelling place on the common and 'enclosed divers parcels of land adjoining'. He was soon in trouble with the manor court and was ordered to pull down the buildings and lay open the enclosed land under penalty of 20s. This was in September 1768. He and his wife and the two sons managed to hang on until April the following year when they were again ordered to be removed to Holborn, where the parish officers this time appealed against having to accept them. This brought the Bagnalls a respite for six months, but in the end they had to go, leaving behind a kiln and, no doubt, a shed or two, and of course the cottage. The site was still recognisable in 1812 when 'half an acre of land, parcel of the waste of St. John's Common or Starford Heath whereon the Potter's Kilns formerly stood' was granted by the lords of the manor with the consent of the homage to John Eager, a local farmer, at a yearly rent of 2s. 6d. The site, no longer identifiable today, lay to the north of Station Road on the present market place in the Clifton Road area.[8]

2. In 1745 George Taylor was fined 5s. for digging clay on the lord's waste at Starford Heath.

George Taylor, brickmaker, had acquired the Slutswell site in 1738 and continued to manufacture bricks there until his death in 1747. His son James inherited the site on his father's death, but whether he continued the brickworks is not certain. What is known is that in 1762 he sold it to William Marten of New Close farm, who became the owner of Burgess Hill farm in the same year. The site probably ceased to operate as a brickworks from that time.

In 1789 William Taylor, probably a distant relative of George, acquired the brick, tile and pottery works to the south of Station Road[9] from Robert Gallop, whose grandfather Robert Leech had bought them from Thomas Marten, a member of the family mentioned in Chapter Two. So far as is known this site continued to manufacture bricks, tiles or pottery without a break from about 1670 to 1940, the only one of the original three in Burgess Hill to do so. By 1794 William Taylor found himself running short of suitable clay and, instead of helping himself as his namesake George had done half a century earlier, he applied to the manor court which recorded:

> Leave was given to William Taylor of Keymer, brickmaker, to dig Brick Earth upon the waste of this manor called St. John's Common, he paying the Overseers of the Poor of the parish of Keymer 25 shillings per annum to be by them laid out in the purchase of a warm coat for the oldest Poor Man of the parish not receiving the Alms of the Parish and so that the same object does not receive it two years successively, and in default of such payment the leave so given to cease and become void.

This example is unusual in that the parish, the manor, and local industry had all co-operated in an effort to solve local problems. William got his clay at a not unreasonable price; the overseers of the poor were relieved of one fairly substantial item of expenditure; and the lords of the manor, Thomas and James Cooke, leather cutters from London, very generously agreed to forgo an item of manorial income in an effort to help one of the deserving poor. It will be seen that those elderly men already in receipt of parish relief were not eligible to apply for a 'warm coat'; nor could the 'same object' apply two years running. Nevertheless despite the limitations (and both are entirely reasonable) this isolated example does suggest an awakening of public conscience towards the unfortunate poor in this still brutal age. The action of the lords of the manor was unique in our immediate area. Poor-houses and lands, the income from which was devoted to relief of the poor, all paid the usual nominal rents, heriots and entry fines when trustees died or changed, for manorial profits were usually safeguarded right up to the end. No other instance of a lord or lords voluntarily waiving manorial income in favour of a local good cause has been found.

On the Clayton side of the common in the early years of the 18th century the situation was rather less stable. The brickworks at 'Dunstalls' was extended between 1705 and 1711, when Thomas Dunstall died and the premises were inherited by his son Rev. John Dunstall. It all began with a presentment in 1705, when:

> A day was given for Thomas Dunstall to lay open part of the waste of St. John's Common being the place where his brick kiln now stands and which was lately enclosed by James Sanders and John Turner.[10]

Thomas Dunstall was presented again in 1707 and 1708 but nothing was done until his death when 'a brick kiln and two acres part of the waste of St. John's Common' was granted to Rev. John Dunstall. Even with the additional land (the original one acre site had been extended to two acres in 1666 and to seven acres by 1716 when there were two brick kilns) there was still a shortage of suitable clay. It is found therefore:

> 1713. James Parker had dug and removed earth from St. John's Common and was in mercy.
> 1716. George Taylor and Rev. John Dunstall had dug earth and clay and made Clay Pitts on St. John's Common to the damage of the tenants. Each was in mercy 10s.
> 1729. George Taylor and James Parker had dug clay on St. John's Common and had made clay holes. Each was in mercy 10s.

James Parker and George Taylor were already well established brick makers. As previously noted, Taylor's kiln was a little way to the south, at Slutswell. James Parker was almost certainly managing Dunstall's works, which he acquired in 1730 and held for the next 21 years. He was constantly in debt and finally sold the premises to Joseph Coulstock, a maltster from Hurstpierpoint. Brickmaking on this site seems to have continued until the early years of the 19th century when there was a break, although the industry was revived there for a period in the early part of the present century.

In his privately published manuscript entitled *Development of Burgess Hill and its Potteries (1828-1978)* F.M. Avery states that William Norman, a Chailey potter, had established a small works in 1812 on land to the north of Station Road. This was most likely the site granted to John Eager on which Sampson Bagnall had tried to establish a pottery in 1768. By 1818 William had died, leaving the now developing business to his two sons, William and Richard, who in 1825 acquired a large site of some 13 acres a little to the west, previously called Butchers. When land was offered for sale in 1828 to help defray the cost of the Enclosure Award, the two brothers purchased about 15 acres lying to the north and west of Butchers at a cost of £493 10s. 0d. It was on part of this newly enclosed land adjoining London Road that the Normans resited their works which continued without a break until 1930, when their successors sold the site to the Burgess Hill U.D.C.

Local Money Lenders

Reserves of hard cash were sometimes to be found in the most unlikely households. Quite frequently people with only the barest necessities in the house were able to save and have substantial sums out on loan. Take, for example, the case of Elizabeth Brooker, who kept a small alehouse in Fairfield Road and who died in 1728. When the assessors came round on a warm summer's day at the end of July that year, this is what they recorded:

> Inventory of Elizabeth Brooker of Clayton, widdow. Taken by Peter Marten and William Heasman on 25 July 1728.

Wearin aparrell and money in pockett	£ 0.15s.0d.
In the lowroom one bed and all thereto belonging	£ 1.10s.0d.
The rest in that room, two tables and other small things	£ 0.17s.6d.
In the brewhouse one furnice and brew vessells one still and barrells, one steal mill and other small things	£ 4.03s.6d.
In the drinkroom the beer and the barrells and the bottles	£ 2.07s.0d.
In the kitchin one teable and form, one jack, brand irons and pot hooks, a firepan and tongs pewter and other small things there	£ 2.13s.6d.
In the chamber one bed and all belonging to it and the linnen and other small things	£ 3.04s.0d.
Without doors – foorms and faggotts	£ 0.14s.0d.
Money due to her upon bonds and bills	£ 247.00s.0d.
Other things unseen and forgoot	£ 0.05s.0d.
	£ 263.09s.6d.

Her total assets, excluding the money out on loan, came to a paltry £16 9s. 6d. There was virtually nothing of any value indoors or outside. She did not, apparently, have a chair upon which to sit at her 'teable' in the kitchen – only a backless form. Yet she had £247 0s. 0d. due on bonds and bills. Elizabeth was formerly the wife of Richard Bennett who, as mentioned on page 18, was granted the cottage originally in 1694. Her second

husband William Brooker had died less than three months earlier leaving an estate worth
£236 18s. 6d. of which £230 was money out on loan. In the circumstances Elizabeth may
well have inherited the bulk of the money out on loan from William. Even so the amount
had been increased by £17 0s. 0d. in a matter of only 12 weeks. The wills of both Elizabeth
and William have survived. William is described as 'of Clayton, victualler' and his will is
very brief and to the point. He left 5s. to the poor of Clayton 'to be disposed among them
by my executrix [his wife] within one month'; the residue after payment of debts and legacies
he left to Elizabeth. It is little wonder that with assets well in excess of £250 Elizabeth was
able to leave:

To my eldest son Richard Bennett £15; and to my grand-daughter Mary Simmons £20.

Eight grandchildren by her daughters received £5 apiece as did three of her daughters.
William Small, a grandson, was to have £40, and his sister Mary Small was bequeathed
£30 in addition to 'a feather bed and all belonging to him, three pair of tow sheets of the
best in my house, three largest dishes of pewter, four pewter plates and the middle iron
porridge pot'. Mary's mother, also called Mary, was to have 'an old mare', whilst Elizabeth
Simmons, another daughter, had 'my clock and case'.

The gifts of cash totalling in all about £164 were clearly intended to be paid from the
money out on loan, and one can only speculate on the possible financial embarrassment
the calling in of the loans would have had upon the borrowers. The most surprising aspect
of Elizabeth's affairs is the discrepancy between what the assessors recorded in her inventory
and what she specified in her will. She must have possessed 'an old mare' and 'a clock in
its case' and the iron pot, so why were they not itemised in the inventory? Did she, on her
deathbed, somehow manage to spirit these valuable items away or had they already been
taken over by those members of the family who were intended to have them?

There are many similar examples of seemingly poor people having substantial sums of
money on loan; old Thomas Wickens, for example, who lived at Grove farm in Station
Road and died in 1721, seems to have occupied only one room, judging by the contents of
his inventory. Apart from the bed and its curtains, a couple of blankets, one chaff and
feather bolster, a pair of sheets, a 'rugg' and a chest, there was nothing of his in the house.
Outside he did have three horses which he may have hired out to his family or neighbours,
and a saddle; and that is all. Yet his wearing apparel and ready cash were valued at £5
and he had £50 out on loan. Although described as a yeoman, he had probably given up
farming and handed over to John his son with whom he seems to have been living at the
time of his death.

Then there was Anne Smith (widow of William Smith, a Ditchling farmer) who died in
1724 in a cottage now demolished but once in the present Keymer Road. Her bits and pieces
in the house, clothing and ready cash were valued at roughly £20, but she had £84 under
the heading 'money on bonds and bills', probably the life savings of her husband and
herself slowly accumulated by dint of hard work and penny-pinching over many years.

Richard Neale who died in 1711 at Fowles farm was also farming land at Alborne and
Berrylands [not yet identified]. His total movable assets were valued at £878 2s. 3d., a
princely sum at the time, yet of this no less than £623 7s. 3d. was shown as 'ready money
and money at interest'. Joan Haynes, a widow who died in 1730, probably spent her last
days living to the south of the town boundary with one of her children, since her only
chattels were a bed worth £3 0s. 0d. Her wearing apparel and money in her purse was
assessed at £6 12s. 6d. and 'money on security' no less than £112 0s. 0d.

It seems that there was no serious shortage of money early in the 18th century – at least
not so far as the small yeoman farmer and some of the small tradesmen were concerned.
People probably saved as a cushion against 'a rainy day', which for them would have been

a season when the harvest virtually failed or when the cattle or sheep were subject to disease. The great problem must have been trying to recover the money from the borrowers when it was most urgently needed, since they too would have been in the same predicament.

Early Eighteenth-Century Shops

It may come as a surprise to many local readers to learn that there were no fewer than four retail shops in the embryo town in the early 18th century; one was the butcher's shop of Nathaniel Turner, mentioned earlier.[11]

In the house in Mill Road once owned by Avis Budd (see page 18) between 1711 and 1734 lived John Marten, described as 'taylor and shopkeeper'.[12] 'Shopkeeper' nearly 300 years ago meant just that; for although he was basically what today would be termed a draper and haberdasher, his shop and the chamber over the kitchen, then used as a stockroom, contained merchandise as diverse as 'four testaments', sugar, tobacco (49lbs), soap, cloggs, and 'pattings', which must mean pattens for use as over-shoes during the winter when mud was several inches deep. Ten gallons of 'strong waters' were valued at £1, along with five gallons of brandy (15s. 0d.); one could get drunk quite cheaply in those days. Raisins and currants were also stocked as were 'brooms, tar and apples (5s.)'. Three hundred weight and one quarter (28lbs) of cheese were assessed at £3 9s. 0d. and he had 'earthenware' to the value of £2 5s. 0d. It is known that some men in the area had shotguns and it was interesting to note that John Marten had in stock: '8lbs of gunpowder (8s. 0d.) and 15lbs of shott (2s. 0d.)', reasonably cheap for those fortunate enough to possess a gun.

Some of the materials listed in the inventory make strange reading today. '30 pieces and a remnant of Ferret (£1 10s. 0d.); 17 pieces of Quality, broad and narrow (£1 4s. 0d.); and 3 gross of shirt buttons and cruel (3s. 0d.)' all need some explanation. Ferret was a stout cotton or silk tape; quality, a kind of worsted tape for binding mats and carpets; and cruel a thin worsted yarn. 41lbs of lump sugar and a pair of hand cards were valued at 3s., the latter being the implements used for carding wool prior to spinning.

Some of the weights and measures used at this time and now long forgotten include the 'ell' (45 inches). John Marten had: '33 ells of brown canvis (£1 4s. 9d.)'. Also listed are '13 ells of doulace (a coarse linen) valued at 10s. 10d. and 3 yards of fustian (a short napped cotton cloth) – 2s. 3d.'. Worsted was measured in pounds as well as in yards, e.g. '4 yards of wosted at 8d. . . . 2s.8d; 10 pounds of wosted and 5 wosted caps . . . £1.10s.6d'. His stock included '400 needels' but strangely, only 'six pair of stockings', the latter assessed at 5s. And there is listed: lace, flannel, linen, tapes, buttons and buckram, as well as various types of cloth – linen cloth, broad cloth and Rushia cloth – all items one could expect to buy in a good quality store at the present time.

It would be inappropriate to leave John Marten without a reference to his house and its contents. Like so many dwellings built about the turn of the 17th century, the kitchen seems to have been the focal point for its occupiers. There the day-to-day domestic arrangements were planned and executed by Elizabeth his wife, who seems to have managed with very little in the way of utensils. There was a table, a 'fourm', a stool and six chairs, the usual fire irons, a pestle and mortar and a warming pan. There were 28lbs of pewter (valued at 14s. 0d.); two dozen trenchers (wooden plates) and wooden dishes and earthen plates were also mentioned, which suggests that John and Elizabeth may have used the latter for their normal meals, bringing out the pewter when they entertained visitors. Cooking involved the use of iron pots of which she had four, a couple of skillets (a sort of saucepan on legs) and two brass kettles.

Adjoining the kitchen were a pantry (containing among other things 'a sive, a fry pan and eight crocks'), and what was termed the 'Back room'. This may once have been used as a parlour but John and Elizabeth kept there only two tables, 'a fourm, one reel, beans and peas and six sacks'. The (? dried) beans and peas may well have been part of the stock for the shop, whilst the reel was once used with the spinning wheels now stored outside in the stable. They must have slept in the 'Back chamber', which had two beds 'all as they stood', five pairs of sheets, 14 pieces of linen, three chests and a box. The main bedroom, called the Kitchen chamber, mentioned earlier, contained 'a bed all as it stands' and six chests along with shirts, sheets and pieces of linen which, as previously suggested, were almost certainly stock to be sold in the shop.

There is no indication of where John did his tailoring. He may well have had working space in a corner of the shop, which appears to have been a single storey addition to the house. He was probably a good business man since there was only one 'Desperate debt' of £6 0s. 0d. and this, although shown as part of his assets, had probably long since been written off insofar as all attempts to recover the money had been abandoned.

11. Nos. 44-46 London Road where Elizabeth Ford kept her shop in 1738.

Elizabeth Ford, who lived at the old houses once called Chapel Cottages still standing on Fairplace Hill (and now 44-46 London Road) and who died in 1738, also kept a shop not unlike John Marten's. Whereas John's goods and chattels were valued at £82 17s. 3d., Elizabeth's, although described in much less detail, totalled £217 0s. 0d., reflecting perhaps the value of a greater quantity of, and higher quality, goods. Her stock included 'bodes' (which must mean bodices) and stays; silk cords, 'hanchiffs, cambricks and moesling (i.e. muslin)', most of which suggests that she catered for the more well-to-do farmers' wives who had a little money to spare for a few frills and furbelows. Yet sandwiched between some of these near 'luxury items' we find 'hops and cheese (£12); candels, pattens, cloges [clogs], worsted and yane [yarn] (£8) and round frocks [for farm workers], cheese cloathing and hop bagen', all of which demonstrates that the so-called luxury trade could not be sustained without recourse to stocking some of the more workaday items.

'In the Wearhouse' were £15 worth of 'tobacco, salt and ode [other] things', whilst outside were accommodated: a mare, a sow and 'two tobes pich' (two tubs of pitch). Her £10 worth of 'Book Debts' were itemised as: 'Good £5 0s. 0d., Dubious £3 0s. 0d., and Bade £2 0s. 0d.'.

The horse would have been her only means of transport at a time when the road system was almost non-existent, and she would have used it to ride to the market at Lewes, or perhaps Horsham, when she needed to replace her stock. On those days it seems highly likely that she rode out and walked beside the heavily laden mare on the return journey. The £26 shown as 'money and wearing apparel' probably comprised mostly cash set aside to buy stock for the shop. The appraisers, James Allin and Thomas Baker, confined their statement of her assets to the barest minimum and gave no details of the contents of the 'Kitchen and other rooms' nor of what was in the 'two chambers'; all they said was that the contents of the former were valued at £6 0s. 0d. and the latter at £16 0s. 0d. There is no evidence to suggest that the shop continued after Elizabeth's death, nor for that matter before she became a widow in 1729 when William, her husband, died. She may well have invested the few pounds that he left in sufficient stock to start a small business and from there went on to become a reasonably successful trader.

The fourth shopkeeper was one Thomas Mugridge who lived in London Road on the plot of land,[13] part of which was later to become the site of Norman and Burt, the well-known local builders who flourished in the 19th century through to about 1975. Thomas died in 1736 having also acquired the 'Cottage and work house' originally erected by Henry Peckham (see page 16). Since both his will and inventory have survived quite a lot is known about Thomas Mugridge or Muggeridge.

By trade he was a fellmonger, a dealer in animal skins; not just any old rabbit and cattle skins obtained from local butchers and farmers but also buckskin and 'beaver scins'. His 'shop goods' in addition to the beaver skins included 'men's and boys' briches (buck and doe) and ship briches', which could possibly refer to breeches made of sheep skin. There were 31 pairs of these garments and some gloves in the shop when he died. Upstairs in the 'Chichern Chamber' were: '98 brocken buckscins', which must mean broken buckskins (£28), along with a 'bead and stettle and healing [bed, bedstead and coverings or hangings], a small flock bead and stettle and all thereto belonging, a pair of andirons, three cheeses, some linen and other small things', in all valued at £34 19s. 0d. There were three other bedrooms each of which contained a bed: the 'Chamber ore stayers [over the stairs]' also contained three chests and there was a 'clock on the staircase' valued at £1 1s. 0d. The 'Chamber ore the shop' had four chairs valued at a shilling apiece, whilst 'in a smale room ore ye stayr and a closet' there was in addition to the 'wool bead and a small stettele', a side saddle and pillion, another saddle, a chest, and 'some pocket scins' worth £2. The latter had probably once been offcuts, left over from the making of breeches, now carefully salvaged and set aside for making pockets.

He and Mary his wife, like so many of their contemporaries, brewed their own beer in the 'Brewhouse' which contained keelers, tubs, barrels, a copper and 'an old brass kettle'. In the 'Chichern' were dishes and plates of pewter, 'a dusen trenchers', four brass skillets, a couple of iron porridge pots and the usual cooking utensils and fire irons; there was also a warming pan to take the chill off the coarse sheets during the winter months. Curiously, the assessors made no reference to a table though they recorded seven chairs; perhaps it was included in 'Things unseen and forgot – 9s. 0d'.

The outdoor stock comprised: two 'meares' [mares] worth £8 the pair; some hay (£3), a grindstone (2s. 8d.) and 'an ingen and allom in tubs' valued at £1 10s. 0d. 'Ingen' was the current spelling for 'engine' which was almost certainly used in the process of tanning, possibly a kind of mill to grind bark. Alum was used to make leather hard and stiff when it was called 'tawed leather'.[14]

In his will Thomas left to Mary his wife 'all the rents of my houses, lands and premises during the term of her natural life and all my goods and chattels except my wearing apparel and . . . the residue . . . after my debts and legacies and funeral expenses are paid'. She was also appointed executrix.

They had two daughters: Sarah, married to John English, who was bequeathed 'my Great Coat'; and Mary still unmarried and 'now dwelling with me'. Two grandchildren, Mary and Thomas English, were to have a guinea apiece when they attained the age of 21, and after the death of their mother the two women were each to have a half share in the estate. Mary died in 1744, about eight years after her husband, and the two daughters duly inherited. Mary the daughter was now married to Nicholas Dunton, a local carpenter, and, since he had been one of the witnesses to old Thomas's will, one cannot escape the impression that he may have been aware of Mary's prospects and begun paying her court from then on.

Some twenty years before his death Thomas had taken on an assistant, John Copper, who in 1717, along with Thomas himself, was summoned to give evidence at the next Quarter Sessions at Lewes against Abraham Clement of Wivelsfield, who had been charged with assaulting Roger Davis of Cuckfield and of biting off his ear.[15] It seems that Abraham Clement, formerly 'an officer for the duty on leather', had gone to Thomas's shop to have some work done when he heard that his successor, Roger Davis, was due to visit Thomas that very day and that he (Davis) had an old score to settle. In due course Roger appeared

12.   The Post Office and Stores opposite the *King's Head* – the oldest shop in the town.

and Abraham was instructed to wait upstairs whilst Thomas and Roger completed their business; but Abraham came down before his enemy had gone and they at once began quarrelling, in the course of which Abraham took Roger 'by the neck cloath' and blows were exchanged. Thomas did his best to separate the two men but Roger would have none of it. He 'strip'd of his cloaths' and challenged Abraham who didn't really want to fight, but the battle continued and Thomas, in a sworn statement before a magistrate, declared that he saw Roger's ear drop down between the two fighting men. The case was heard at the next Quarter Sessions in July when the court decided that since Roger Davis had apparently started the fracas he should put up with the consequences, and that Abraham Clement should be exonerated and discharged.

The oldest shop in the town today is the one opposite the *King's Head* in London Road. The house, now called Fayre Place, was acquired in 1725 by John Bodle, a butcher from Hurst, who may have rebuilt the original cottage erected in the 17th century by John King (see page 18). It was still called Bodles in the middle of the 19th century. By 1780 it had come into the ownership of Mary Cave of Fletching, wife of John Cave, shopkeeper, who in 1803 sold the premises to John Gard, a local shopkeeper, who may well have been using it as a shop for some years. It seems to have continued as such to the present day without a break, probably from the late 18th century, but certainly since 1803.

The values quoted in this section make little sense when juxtaposed with those of today, but as a broad guide one can say that compared with the purchasing power of the pound in June 1985, £1 in 1700 would be roughly equivalent to £40, and from 1730 to 1750 approximately £45. Between 1770 and 1790 the values dropped to about £33 and then to £29; whilst during the Napoleonic wars it fluctuated between about £14 and £21 with a generally upward trend to 1914 when it stood at about £26.[16]

Butchers

There is little information about Nathaniel Turner, the local butcher mentioned earlier. He was not a property owner and does not appear to have had an inventory taken or left a will, at least not one that was proved locally. He may well have thrived in business for a few years, during which time he was able to act as a small time money lender (see page 48), and then have fallen on hard times.

Walter Carpenter, the butcher from Ditchling who acquired Bedelands farm in 1717, sold his land in 1735 and when he died about three years later he was also selling linen goods, the details given in his Inventory showing little evidence that he was making very much from the butchering side of his business. The total value of his goods and chattels was only £59 14s. 2d. and this included £5 10s. 0d. owing as 'Book Debts' and £20 7s. 2d. for the stock of linen goods. Ditchling at that time was a much more densely populated area than Burgess Hill. If Walter Carpenter was finding it difficult to prosper it seems more than likely that Nathaniel Turner may have been forced out of business altogether, died intestate and worth very little anyway. The house on the Clayton part of St John's Common, occupied by Nathaniel Turner, almost certainly served as a butcher's shop from early in the 18th century. There is a reference to Richard Christopher, of Clayton, butcher, who probably lived there around 1708 and much later, about 1758, Arthur Gatton, also spelt Garton,[17] was running a butcher's shop from the same house which was later named after him.

Smithies

Although there are frequent references to many craftsmen and trades people in the parishes of Clayton and Keymer it has proved well nigh impossible to establish precisely where they all lived and worked.

However, it is known that the site adjoining the *King's Head* to the north, called Smeeds, was a smithy at least as early as 1659 when it was acquired by William Smith, and it appears to have continued as a smithy in one form or another until early in the present century when, in addition to the forge, the premises also contained a wheelwright's shop, a saw house, timber sheds and an engineering shop. Yet the name, which first appears in the manor records in 1604, suggests that there may have been a smithy on the site at least as early as the reign of Queen Elizabeth. Bearing in mind that 'th' and 'd' were once interchangeable, it is a short step from Smeed to Smeeth to Smith.

An early 18th-century occupier of Smeeds was John Knight who died in 1713.[18] In addition to his trade as a blacksmith he also worked as a part-time farmer for, included among his goods and chattels, were a couple of horses, 'a wagon, a plow and two harrows'. He also had a cow and a heifer, four sheep and two lambs on land close by, in addition to five ewes and two lambs 'at Shermanbury'. On the ground were three acres of wheat and one of oats together with an unspecified area of clover and nonsuch. The contents of the smithy were listed in considerable detail and because it is the only 18th-century example in Burgess Hill it seems appropriate to quote them in full. This is what the appraisers, Thomas Wood, Richard Bull and Walter Burt found when they visited John's shop on 2 June 1713.

In the Shopp

Item Two steel anvils, five sledges, four hand	
hammers and two nailing hammers	£ 6.10s.0d.
83 horseshoes	£ 0.18s.0d.
A vise [vice] and hand vise	£ 2.00s.0d.
Two nailing blocks and one beakhorn	£ 0.12s.0d.
20 plates, 15 linces	£ 0.07s.6d.
Bellows, a strackmail toole	£ 1.10s.0d.
New iron and coale	£ 0.07s.8d.
Tools and iron against the wall	£ 2.00s.0d.
Other tools and iron by the south wall	£ 0.12s.0d.
Files, pincers and shoeing tools	£ 0.05s.0d.
Old iron and some harness	£ 0.15s.0d.
Beam blades, weights and grindstone	£ 1.13s.0d.
A trough, a chest aprong [apron] & tongs	£ 0.18s.0d.
A box mould and box of drawers	£ 0.04s.0d.
Wool	£ 0.05s.0d.
Things unseen and forgotten	£ 0.05s.0d.

Some of the items require a few words of explanation. A beak-horn may have been a small anvil with tapered ends (see O.E.D. Beakiron). Linces was another word for dials which suggests that John Knight may have tried his hand at clockmaking. A strackmail tool may have been an implement used when fitting iron rims to wooden cart or wagon wheels which can still be seen from time to time in country craft museums. Indeed almost all the items listed about 270 years ago could be found in a blacksmith's shop of the mid-20th century before farm horses were finally superseded by the tractor.

The inventory included 'In the Parlor – a linnen wheel, a woollen wheele and reel', along with hand cards and many other things, and since there was 5 shillings worth of wool in the 'Shop' it seems certain that spinning and probably knitting was carried out in the house at this time.

Unusually for a small businessman of the early 18th century, no mention was made of money owed to the estate by way of debts, good, dubious *or* bad; neither did John have any money out on loan to others.

The only other smithy known to have been within the town boundaries in the 18th and early 19th centuries was the site in Fairfield Road originally granted to Henry Peckham and acquired by Thomas Jeffery, blacksmith in 1793. His son James added to this small holding in 1827 by acquiring 21 rods adjoining, then part of the roadside waste. This land is now (1986) the site of the garage and petrol filling station on the corner of London Road and Fairfield Road then described as 'the lane leading to Hurst'.

Milling
Before the 19th century milling of flour was carried out at Hammonds Mill, Valebridge Mill and Pophole (or Pookshole) Mill lying at the foot of the Downs to the north of Underhill Lane in Keymer.

By 1624 John Rowe records the existence of two windmills on Valebridge common though a detailed study of the court records shows that there was never more than one. In 1606 Edmund Attree, then the owner of Brooklands and Birchetts farms, was granted an acre of land on Valebridge common with the intention of building a water mill thereon with mill dam and 'fludgates' and was granted a licence to flood six acres of waste to provide a mill pond (with fishing and gaming rights reserved to the lords). He was to repair the bridge over the water course at the highway from time to time.[19]

In 1612 Edmund Attree was granted permission 'to build one windmill on the waste called Valebridge common a little way from his water mill' provided that no damage resulted to the animals belonging to other tenants. If there were damage he was to repay the tenants the full amount of their loss or risk forfeiture of the site. The windmill on Valebridge common seems to have fallen into disuse by about the end of the 17th century; the last entry in which it gets a mention comes in 1692. On the other hand, between 1666 and 1677, there are references to two water mills, one of which probably adjoined Isaacs Lane (O.S. Ref. TQ315222). There are no further details about the latter and the author would welcome any additional information that may exist in documents still in private hands. He cannot believe that this mill had a life of only 11 years.

Although Gregory in his *Story of Burgess Hill* states that the post mill on St John's Common bore a date of 1769 it now seems doubtful whether it was erected so early. It first appears in the Land Tax returns in 1797 when it was shown as owned by Mr. Cooke, then one of the lords of the manor. It seems reasonable to assume that he would have been taxed on the new mill at the earliest possible date and it is now reasonably certain that 1796 is much more likely than 1769. The miller's house, now divided into two dwellings, can still be seen in Mill Road which itself was named after the post mill that was working there when the road was first fenced in 1828.

Inns
Apart from the Brookers' alehouse mentioned earlier and two isolated references in the Quarter Sessions records also in the early years of the 18th century, when in 1724 Sarah Gower of Keymer, victualler, was charged with assaulting her sister-in-law, and again in 1731, when William Hillary of Keymer, victualler, was presented for keeping a disorderly house, there is no firm evidence of the establishment of a permanent inn in Burgess Hill until the last half of the 18th century.

The cottage lying to the rear of 73 London Road was described in 1738 as 'Messuage and one and a half acres of land called the *White Hart* lying at St. John's Fairplace in Clayton' when the then owner, Henry Morley, mortgaged it for £36 8s. 0d. to John Oliver of Hurstpierpoint, miller. The name *White Hart* certainly suggests that it was in use as an alehouse or a beer shop, but there is nothing to confirm that the house was used for this purpose before that date. Later, some time after 1763, when the then owner Ann Reynolds

13. The cottages, once the home of the miller, in Mill Road. Built towards the end of the 18th century, the original building has now been converted into these two attractive cottages.

14. The *King's Head Inn*, London Road, before it was modernised in the 1930s. Established in about 1780, it is by far the oldest inn in the town.

had married John Daniel, its use as an inn may have been revived since John was described as 'of Clayton, victualler'.

On the other hand the *King's Head* seems to have become a permanent inn from about 1780. In 1736, then called 'Cottage and Orchard late Pilbeams', it was acquired by Thomas Baker, described as 'of Clayton, yeoman', which suggests that he was getting his living by farming and had probably bought the premises as an investment. Be this as it may, when he died in 1763 he was described as a 'victualler', having almost certainly established an inn or public house on the site. On his death Thomas left the premises to his daughter Elizabeth, wife of Elliot Allcock, also described as a 'victualler'. Shortly after Elliot Allcock died in 1771, his executors leased the premises for 11 years to John Daniel, who paid an annual rent of £9 p.a. for 'a Messuage or tenement being late an Inn or victualling house known by the name or sign of the *Red Lion*'.[20] This description suggests that for a few months after Elliot's death it may have ceased to be an inn and that John Daniel may have found his cottage, a little way down the road, to be too small or in the wrong place and had decided to move and to transfer his business to a more suitable spot.

The new turnpike road from Brighton to Lovell Heath (Lowfield Heath) near Crawley (planned to run across St John's Common) had been authorised in 1770 and, although it was not in fact to reach our present London Road for another 9-10 years,[21] John Daniel may well have foreseen the enormous advantages of having an established inn along the route from London to Brighton and was anxious to get in on the ground floor. After the deaths of Elizabeth and Elliott Allcock about 1771, the premises passed to Elizabeth's sister Sarah, who later married John Sutton, a Rottingdean carpenter. In 1789 they leased: 'a Messuage or tenement being an Inn or public house (together with a stable, garden and orchard thereunto belonging) called or known by the name of the *King's Head* . . .' to the executors of the late Isaac Grover, a brewer from Brighton. They in turn sub-let the premises to Thomas Daynes, father of Michael Longmer Daynes, who became very well known in the developing town later in the 19th century. The inn was permanently called the *King's Head* from 1782,[22] by which name it is still known today.

Other Trades and Occupations

The only known 18th-century plumber and glazier was William Ford, who lived at the premises later called Chapel farm between 1756 and 1797.

Thomas English, who died in 1809, was a well-to-do timber merchant who built up a thriving business in the last half of the 18th century. He applied, successfully, to the manor court in 1761 for a grant of land from the common, the half-acre plot that he was allocated lying on the west side of London Road opposite the junction with Leylands Road. Here he built himself a house and in 1788 sold off about a quarter of the land on which he had already erected a cottage. The buyer (his new neighbour) was John Corney, a wheelwright who continued on the site until his death in 1829.

The earliest known bricklayer (who today would be described as a builder) was William Brand who died at Lottmotts in Keymer Road in 1728. His inventory has survived and shows in great detail the contents of his house. Outside there were 'oats in the barne, faggots, a rick of clover hay and some clover standing upon the ground', but there is no mention of ladders, bricks, lime, sand, etc. – all the things one would expect to find in a small builder's yard. Perhaps at the time of his death he had given up 'bricklaying' and was living on what his 10-acre holding could produce. Later in the 18th century, William Brooker, who was married in 1790 and who lived to celebrate his golden wedding, similarly described as a bricklayer, also established a thriving building business. Among the houses still to be seen today that were built by him are Nos. 73 and 75 London Road and the Pentecostal church in Leylands Road.[23] There were undoubtedly others that have still to be identified.

The principal brickmakers have already been mentioned. John Parker, who was here in the early 18th century, was described as a tile maker in 1704 and a brick-burner when he made his will in May 1713. There is no evidence that he was running his own business on one of the commons at this time.

One of the three known carpenters in the infant town was Thomas Holcombe alias Ansty, who lived at North Inholmes farm and who died in 1688. Another was Nicholas Dunton who, you may recall, married Thomas Mugridge's daughter Mary and through her inherited a half share of Thomas's estate. For many years after the death of Thomas's widow, Mary Mugridge, in 1744 the two daughters, Sarah English and Mary Dunton, held old Thomas's two properties in undivided moieties, an arrangement which seems to have worked satisfactorily until 1753 when the Duntons acquired the other moiety of the site in London Road (adjoining the present *Brewers Arms*), and the Englishes took over the whole of the site in Fairfield Road later to become a smithy. Lastly, there was Thomas Chandler, who in 1822 acquired part of the site once owned by Thomas English.

In 1733, Thomas Baker was trading as a carrier from premises in Junction Road (now the site of Denmark House) one of only two carriers mentioned between 1600 and 1830.

One of the most essential articles of clothing in the 17th and 18th centuries, and indeed later, was a good stout pair of boots. It is not surprising, therefore, to find no fewer than 10 men working at the trade in our area during the period under review. One of those working in Burgess Hill as cordwainers (as they were then called) was William Lashmere who in 1672 acquired a cottage on what is now the site of the *Weald Inn*. He seems to have run into financial difficulties about 10 years later, for in 1682 he defaulted on a mortgage for £15 9s. 0d. and the premises passed to Thomas Norton, a well-to-do farmer from Hurstpierpoint. William, however, may very well have continued making and repairing boots in the same house; the main difference was that he now had to pay Thomas Norton the current economic rent. The only other cordwainers known to have lived and worked in Burgess Hill were Thomas Ford, who had married Walter Welfare's grand-daughter and who lived at Chapel Cottages in Fairplace Hill at the end of the 18th century, and James Eager, who acquired the cottage now the site of the *King's Head* and who died about 1728. There may have been others.

In an attempt to improve the texture of our heavy clay and to make cultivation a little easier a small lime burning industry was established in the 17th century. In 1657 John Marten, 'lyme-burner', was living in Freeks Lane and probably assisting James Saunders on or near what was later to become the Dunstall's brickworks site. As already noted the 10 acres of newly assarted land on the Keymer side of the common, granted to Samuel Marten in 1663, contained a 'Lymè Kill',[24] though it is not known how long lime was produced there. The fact that it was produced here at all suggests that Burgess Hill was becoming recognised as a potential centre for trade and industry other than just bricks, tiles and pottery.

The foregoing comprises almost all the local tradesmen known to have lived within the present town boundaries. There could have been others 'of Clayton or Keymer' whose names appear fleetingly in legal and other documents and whose precise addresses are unknown. In many instances it seems highly doubtful that their places of work and/or residence will ever be known since legal documents (if any) relating to sub-leases of the 17th, 18th and early 19th centuries have long since been lost or destroyed.

Among those who lived somewhere in one or other of our parent parishes and whose addresses are not known are: '1753. George Hedgehog of Clayton, gardiner.'

In addition to those previously mentioned, three more servants are recorded at various times: in 1643, Rachel Thorne; 1788 Allan Daw; and 1803 Nathaniel Howe, a negro. One or more of these may have been in service at Hammonds or at the rectory near Clayton church, but there is no positive information.

In 1798 William Squire, a soldier, was buried in Clayton churchyard, having possibly died of wounds following service in the armed forces during the Napoleonic Wars. The Clayton parish registers also record the burial of one 'Bulbecke, a tynker' in 1621, but he may have been merely passing through and not a permanent resident.

Thomas Daynes, mentioned earlier, was described as a 'Vintner' in 1788 when he acquired the premises on the Clayton part of St John's Common, later called the Gattons, which suggests that he may have been running a high class 'off licence' and supplying wines and spirits to the more well-to-do at this time.

Weavers are mentioned from time to time. The earliest reference found concerns John Englyshe who died in 1563. His will suggests that he had little to leave apart from a couple of cows and some odds and ends of furniture and a little pewter. A little over a century later John Scrase, who died in 1685, and whose childless wife had predeceased him, was able to leave £30 each to his nephews and nieces,[25] whilst his eight cousins shared the residue 'except my weaving tackle [which] I doe bestow on Walter Sturt for £5 which I owe him', which does not say very much for the value of the loom(s).Walter Sturt was also a weaver who died in 1701. His children, Hannah and Walter, were to have £20 apiece when they reached the age of 21; the residue went to his eldest son William. It will readily be seen that both John Scrase and Walter Sturt were considerably better off than their predecessor John English.

Finally, just two further examples: Drew, or Drury Waters lived at Peppers in Leylands Road which, in fact, he owned. Described as a husbandman, he seems to have eked out a living for himself, his wife and children, Mary and Drury, by producing what he could from his five acres of land and renting other land nearby, possibly the adjoining holding called North Inholmes. In 1707, about three years before he died, he was apparently trying 'to earn a bit more on the side' since he, together with Francis Leny of Keymer and two others, was charged with trading as 'a kidder, lader, carryer, buyer and seller of butter, cheese, eggs, poultry and other dead victuals . . . contrary to statute'.[26] The outcome of the case that came before the Justices of the Peace at the Quarter Sessions is not recorded, but the example does show how difficult it was in the early years of the 18th century for people to turn their hands to something new in an attempt to earn an honest living. On the other hand, had Drew and his cronies made a formal application for a *licence* to trade as dealers in the commodities mentioned in the indictment, they may well have received a sympathetic hearing. Their offence was that they failed to observe the correct procedure.

That some enterprising men *could* set up in business successfully is suggested in the following extract from the diary of Thomas Marchant of Hurstpierpoint: 'November 1714. Went . . . to Osbourne at St John's Common to see after fish but to no purpose.' It seems highly likely that Osbourne was a fishmonger who had a stall or shack on the common where he sold his wares. To replenish his stock each day would have meant a long and tiring journey on horseback, or by pony and trap, over the Downs to Brighthelmstone and since Mr. Marchant went 'to no purpose' we may assume that either the fisherman had met with little success the previous night, or that Osbourne had been delayed.

Older people may recall that some men were still scratching a living by small-time dealing, as illustrated in these two examples, right up to the outbreak of the Second World War in September 1939. They are quoted here to demonstrate the growing importance of Burgess Hill as a trading centre from the early years of the 18th century, although another century and a half were to elapse before it really began to come into its own.

The Manor Pounds

It is proposed to round off this chapter with a brief section on the manor pounds which have not so far been given more than a passing mention. There were three, once located either with immediately adjoining the town boundary, demonstrating how Burgess Hill had become an important centre of our parent parishes from very early days.

The pound, a small fenced enclosure to contain straying animals, was an important feature of manorial administration in the days of the open-field system of agriculture; though rather less so insofar as Burgess Hill and its adjoining farms were concerned during the period under review, since all its land except the commons had been enclosed and fenced before 1600. Nevertheless the manors of Keymer and Clayton continued the age-old practice of maintaining their respective pounds albeit not without some difficulty:

Keymer. The homage presented:
    1720 that the lord's pound was in a ruinous state owing to his failure to do repairs.
    1729 that the pound was in a state of disrepair.
    1777 that the common pound was out of repair and that the lord of the manor ought to repair the
        same.
    1820 that the manor pound had fallen down.

That is the last time the Keymer pound is mentioned. It had been situated on land at the rear of the *King's Head*. Eight years later, when the Keymer waste was enclosed, no provision was made to reinstate it and it must be assumed that the need for a pound within the manor had completely disappeared.

The situation insofar as Clayton was concerned was slightly different:

    1821 the homage presented that there was no pound for this manor and that one should be erected
    on the south side of the common near to the turnpike road.[27]

The fact that there is no mention of a pound in the Clayton court records before 1821 suggests that until that time the tenants either had had the continued use of one from time immemorial, or that it had fallen down many years previously and no one had pressed for a replacement. A hint of its former location is given in the tithe survey of 1838 which records 'Pound Field' as part of Fowles farm then owned and occupied by Thomas Avery. Pound field lay to the south of the present Royal George Road and if it took its name from the manor pound, which it almost certainly did, then we may reasonably assume that the pound lay on the southern boundary of the common near to, or actually adjoining, this field which itself lay in the vicinity of modern Orchard Road. The tenants in recommending that a replacement should be erected on the south side of the common probably visualised a new pound on or very near the same site as the old. Thirty-five years later when this part of the common was enclosed the Commissioners made provision for a new pound and allocated one square perch for this purpose; it was sited not on the south but the north side of the common a little to the east of West End farm house. Its purpose may well have been to contain animals straying over newly enclosed land the hedges of which were still very young and incapable of keeping stock either in or out. How long it continued as a pound is not known and the site itself has long been incorporated within the curtilege of West End farm.

The third pound, that for the manor of Ditchling, lay on the west side of Ditchling common next to the house called Hopkins Crank, which was described in 1754 as: 'parcel of land containing one acre and one rood formerly parcel of the waste adjoining Ditcheling Common Pound on the south and to Freckborough Hedge on the west'. This pound served all premises held of the manor of Ditchling, including those now in Burgess Hill, but lay just outside our present eastern boundary – the Freckborough Hedge mentioned in the foregoing description.

Finally there was Stone Pound at Hassocks which lay about a mile and a half to the south of the town boundary and was probably the oldest and most interesting of them all.

It almost certainly began life as the pound for the manor of Wickham. This was based on the Ham and Coldharbour farm (the demesne lands) and included several small holdings in the near vicinity: *Friars Oak* (formerly Frize Oak), Friars Oak farm (formerly Fryers), Wilcombe Crofts, Pinwish, Matchland, Plump John's (now Friars Oak villa) and a cottage called Bookers.[28] Wickham could well have been a direct successor to the Roman settlement at Hassocks on the sandy ridge of land that runs east-west through the area about a mile to the north of the foot of the Downs. Indeed, there are sound reasons to assume that the land there has been cultivated with no significant break from Neolithic times, and that some kind of enclosure may have been in use before the coming of the Saxon settlers in the fifth and sixth centuries. The earliest reference comes in 1773 when 'William Marchant one of the inhabitants of the south part of the Hundred of Buttinghill' appeared before the Justices at Lewes 'to hear an Indictment of Record against the said inhabitants why they did not repair a certain pound called Stone Pound in Clayton . . .'. Mr. Marchant, on behalf of the people of Buttinghill, was found 'not guilty' when the case was eventually heard nearly three years later. From this it seems that the pound no longer served just the manor of Wickham but the whole of the south part of Buttinghill Hundred which included Clayton, Keymer, Hurstpierpoint, Cuckfield and Bolney. It probably went out of use finally about the middle of the 19th century, though the name lingers on as Stone Pound crossroads to the present day.

It is hoped that this review of some aspects of life in the 18th century will throw new light on the immediate area and help dispel the hitherto generally expressed view 'that it all began in the 19th century'. Burgess Hill must have been in the course of establishing an identity from the 17th century, for shopkeepers do not set up in business in the centre of a green desert.

In the next chapter we will try to show how the poor fared in the 18th and early 19th centuries and how the gap between them and the comparatively prosperous yeomen and tradesmen widened still further.

Chapter Five

Poverty and Affluence

The changes in social conditions that occurred during the 18th and early 19th centuries were not quite so marked as those described in Chapter Three. For those with capital it was a period of consolidation – a matter of not only hanging on to what they already had but also of adding to existing assets wherever possible, for example, by purchase or by marriage. A well-to-do widow could be certain of being surrounded by a number of hopeful suitors once the respectable period of mourning was over. In the same way daughters who had inherited property, whether a simple cottage and garden, or a fair sized farm, could be equally sure of attracting eligible men from far and wide whatever her personal charms or lack of them.

For the poor it was, generally, a time of abject poverty – a never-ending struggle to find enough to eat; to find fuel for cooking and heating; to find money for clothes and footwear; and most importantly to keep a roof over their heads. Conditions were tolerable whilst a man could be assured of permanent work; the great problems arose when he was laid off, often during the winter months when a regular income was more important than ever. Let us therefore examine their plight in more detail.

Housing of the Poor

As mentioned briefly in a previous chapter, from 1722/3 parish officers (the churchwardens and overseers of the poor) were authorised to buy or rent workhouses. They were also authorised to contract with enterprising businessmen to 'lodge, keep, and maintain and employe the poor'.[1] Here in Burgess Hill this latter requirement had been tried out at least as early as 1695 when John Marten the brickmaker and Martha his wife (then living in Station Road) took into their service Anne Earle 'a poor girl of the parish of Keymer'.[2] John and Martha also undertook at the same time to pay 40s. a year on Easter Day for the next two years for the use of the poor of Keymer. It would be improper, even libellous, to suggest that John and Martha had purchased a slave; yet however kind they may have been, it seems highly likely that to young Anne her new post smacked of little less than bondage.

On the other hand it is known that the parish officers purchased cottages to accommodate their homeless poor. According to John Rowe, by 1624 or earlier Keymer parish had acquired a cottage and five acres of land called Bulnors for which they paid the lord of the manor a rent of 3s. 10d. a year. This lay to the west of Lodge Lane in Keymer village but by 1733, when it was mentioned in the official records for the first time for a century or more, the cottage had gone and the area of the site had been reduced to only three acres, which was let to a tenant for the rent it would bring. It is interesting to note that this freehold site was allocated nearly one acre of the common when it was enclosed in 1828.

Keymer parish later acquired four more sites all of which lay in or very close to the town boundary. The earliest, anticipating the Act of 1722/3, was a cottage and one acre described as 'in or near Lye Lane'. This in fact was a large, roughly triangular plot, covering all and more of the site of the present Manor Court residential flats and the children's play area on the adjoining Janes Lane recreation ground. It was originally granted in 1655 from lands once part of Cants farm and was surrendered 30 years later by the then owner William

69

Clifford to Edward Luxford, Richard Turner, and John Plummer, the churchwardens and overseers of the poor for the benefit of the poor of the parish.

In 1734, some 11 or 12 years after the passing of the Act, two more cottages were acquired. One was the site of the pair of mid-19th-century houses in London Road, now numbered 76 and 78. To the rear of these still stands a brick cottage which could well have been built about this time. The second was on the common adjoining London Road and is now part of St John's Park. If you stand in Lower Church Road near the children's playground and face north you will see a footpath leading at an angle north-westwards to the left to London Road, and at a similar angle a row of trees once part of the boundary hedge leading right to the north-east. At the limit of these two arms draw an imaginary line parallel with Church Road and you will be able to picture the roughly triangular site of this poor house and its adjoining garden.

The fourth adjoined the old mill pond at Valebridge. This was acquired in 1807 and later became the site of a former house called Jesters, now the delightful residential close of that name.

All four of these poor houses were retained until 1844 when, following the opening of Cuckfield workhouse, they were sold to private buyers.

In Clayton parish nothing seems to have been done until 1804 when a house and garden in Clayton Street, once called Easons, was acquired by the parish officers. This seems to have accommodated Clayton's poor until 1837 when the churchwardens and overseers purchased one and a half acres of land adjoining Gattons and built a cottage (later called Cromwell Cottage and now demolished) and four dwellings (later called the Barracks, also now demolished) to house the growing numbers of poor then being attracted to the area. These, too, were sold in 1844 when Cuckfield workhouse became operational.

In addition to the above, some of the poor of Hurstpierpoint were once accommodated in Burgess Hill. Between 1790 and 1840 they were housed in a cottage that once stood in the present farmyard of West End farm, close to the old and dilapidated wooden granary on staddle stones that still stands (just) today.

All the poor were made to work, for poor houses were not rest homes; and the parish officers had authority to spend public money on the purchase of materials and equipment to keep the idle homeless (including the children) fully occupied. About this time printed forms signed by two of the Justices were issued to newly appointed overseers of the poor which set out in precise detail the scope of their responsibilities and the penalties for neglect of duty. The following example is self explanatory.

> By virtue of the Statute made (in the three and fourtieth year of the Reign of our late Sovereign Lady Queen Elizabeth)[3] for the relief of the poor: These are to Will and Require you whose names are here under-written. That You, together with the Churchwardens of your Parish for the time being, do according to the same Statute take order from time to time [for this year to come] for the setting to work of the Poor within your Parish (as well married as unmarried) that all able to work, and have no means to maintain themselves nor use no ordinary and daily Trade of life to get their living by. And also for the placing out as Apprentices all such children within your said parish as are fit to be put forth, whose parents are not able to keep and maintain them. And also for the raising of a convenient stock of Flax, Hemp, Wool, Thread, Iron and other necessary Ware and Stuff in your said parish for that purpose and also for the providing of necessary relief of all such Poor within your said Parish as are Lame, Old, Blind, Impotent, and Unable to work, wherein if you be found negligent, or shall fail to meet once a month to confer together for the purpose aforesaid, then You are to forfeit 20s apiece every month that you shall be found remiss or careless therein. And therefore see that you fail not in these Premisses at your perils. Dated . . .[4]

This official notification says it all. It seems highly likely that many of our local men, when elected at the annual vestry meeting, accepted the office only after strong protest and with great reluctance. There may have been some who enjoyed wielding the local power

15. Cromwell Cottage, Colmer Place, built in about 1837 as a Poor House. It was demolished in 1978.

16. Wooden granary on staddle stones at West End Farm (since demolished to make way for a new road).

they had been given; but it was a time-consuming job and entirely unpaid, though out of pocket expenses were reimbursed, often long after the money had been spent.

Vagrants

For the poor who had no home and took to the road there was no hiding place. Those found sleeping in barns, under haystacks, or in the shelter of the hedge-rows were quickly apprehended by the parish constable and taken to the nearest Justice of the Peace. Here they were given an opportunity to explain their circumstances. Clearly, the first priority was to identify the parish where the offender or offenders were born since, ultimately, it was their parish of birth that would have the financial responsibility for their maintenance until work could be found for them. But this was not always a simple matter to establish as the following statement shows:

> January Session 1743.[5]
>
> The examination of Jane Robinson a vagrant taken upon oath before John Board Esq one of his Majesty's Justices of the Peace for the county of Sussex the 25 day of March 1742.
>
> This examinant saith that she is about the age of twelve and under fourteen years of age, that her mother died about nine months ago of the smallpox at London and that she believes that Henry Robinson her father is likewise dead, or if not dead his abode or place of residence is not known to this Examinee who says she has neither seen nor heard from him within a year last past, that she knows not the place of the last legal settlement either of her said Father or Mother, that she has often heard her Mother declare that this Examinee was born in the parish of Little Hampton in the county of Sussex which she likewise believes to be true, and being born a vagrant has never been in any service nor knows not that she has acquired for herself any legal settlement.

Jane, perhaps not surprisingly, could neither read nor write and endorsed the above statement with the usual cross – 'her mark'. The local constable was ordered to take her into his custody and convey her to Littlehampton 'and there deliver her to some Churchwarden or Chapel warden or Overseer of the same parish to be there provided for according to law'.

That was the attitude 240 years ago: get rid of her as one would an unwanted animal as quickly as possible, for every day she remained, unwelcome and unloved, she was costing the locals money to feed and house her and to keep her decently attired. It will not have escaped the reader's notice that the statement was taken in March 1742 and that it took nearly ten months for the case to come before the court. Such delays were not unusual at this time and sometimes people charged with quite minor offences languished in jail for several months before their cases were heard. Two years later John and Mary Wood and Thomas their son, who had been committed to the House of Correction as vagrants in Clayton by William Poole Esq, one of the magistrates, after being in jail for over two months awaiting trial, were ordered 'to be whipped and then discharged'; though presumably the son, unless he was of fairly mature years, would have been excused this indignity.

In contrast to the utterly callous and cold-blooded treatment meted out in these two cases, the face of Justice could at times be almost benign by comparison. The following is an extract from an account showing the money expended on food and clothing for a poor, homeless prisoner who had been committed to jail and placed in care:

> Elizabeth Goodman being bigg with child was comited ye 5th day of June 1747 by William Poole Esq to be taken care of and was delivered of a female child ye 1st day of August last.

For keeping her from ye 16th of July to ye 1st of August is 2 weeks and 2 days at 3s.6d per week is	£0.08s.0d.
From ye 1st of August to ye 29th August is 4 weeks for her lying in	£2.00s.0d.
Payd for a payre of second hand stayes	£0.03s.6d.
More for a payre of new shoes	£0.03s.6d.
For a payre of new hose	£0.00s.9d.

More for keeping her and her child from ye 29th
of August to ye 8th October is 5 weeks which is   £1.08s.9d.
Payd to Mr. John Woodgate for things had out of
his shop for the use of her and her child   £0.10s.3d.

All this came to a total of £4 14s. 9d., a far from insignificant sum for the times. Her food allowance was only 3s. 6d. a week which means that nursing and medical care during the four weeks 1-29 August came to no less than £1 6s. 0d. At the time she was admitted she apparently had no shoes or stockings and it would be interesting to have had details of the 10s. 3d. spent in the shop of Mr. Woodgate. Perhaps it was to cover the cost of the baby's layette.

Elizabeth and her child spent several months in the House of Correction at Lewes during which time she was given a second-hand cloak costing 1s. 8d. and a pair of clogs (6d.). We last hear of them in July 1748 when the account for their keep was settled (nine days at 6d. per day) and five shillings was given 'to help her out of ye county'.

A year or two later 'Sarah Coleman from Kimer' was admitted to the same House of Correction at Lewes in similar circumstances but fared less well. In January 1752 and again in April that year the accounts for her subsistence were recorded as 'bread for Sarah Coleman . . . committed for Bastardy her time now out which from ye 16th of January to ye 3rd of April when she dyed is eleven weeks and two days [total 12s. 9d.]. Funeral charges for Sarah Coleman who 'departed this life ye 3rd of April early in ye morning . . . £1.2s.9d'. There is no mention of the illegitimate child she gave birth to. If it was still-born, which seems likely, there would probably have been no need to record the fact in the official records. Had it survived, the parish officers would certainly have been ordered to assume responsibility for its upkeep.

The removal of vagrants to their places of birth was usually ordered by the local Justice of the Peace, who signed an impressive printed document which was then countersigned by a fellow J.P. A typical local example comes in 1753 when Sarah Smith was found in Clayton without means of support and upon the complaint of the parish officers was ordered to be removed to her place of settlement – Cuckfield. A copy of this order signed by Thomas Sergison of Cuckfield and Edward Treadcroft who probably lived at Bolney is reproduced on page 74 by kind permission of the County Records officer E.S.R.O. Lewes.

Throughout the whole of the 18th century and well into the 19th similar orders were issued throughout the county. The numbers varied according to the time of year – they tended to be more numerous in winter than in summer – and upon the current economic climate at any given time.

The following brief extracts give some idea of the distances some of these unfortunate people had to be transported when they were ordered home.

    1763. Martha Furlough single woman, from Clayton to Birpham [near Arundel].
    1768. William Harland and Mary his wife from Twineham to Clayton.
    1769. Sampson Bagnall, Susanna his wife and their sons Sampson and James from Keymer to St. Andrews Holborn.[6]

Others from parishes just outside our area, e.g. Ditchling, Cuckfield and Hurst, sent or received people from as far away as Trotton near the Hampshire border, London, East Grinstead, Old Shoreham and Kent.

Persistent offenders against the vagrancy laws were usually sent to the House of Correction at Lewes and there 'whipped until their backs are bloody' and then discharged. That was the simple way out. It was much easier than setting up a committee of, say, local justices and parish officers to find out *why* people could find no permanent place in which to settle, where they could establish roots, *and where* they could expect to be cared for when the lost their jobs and/or homes, often through no fault of their own. There may have been some

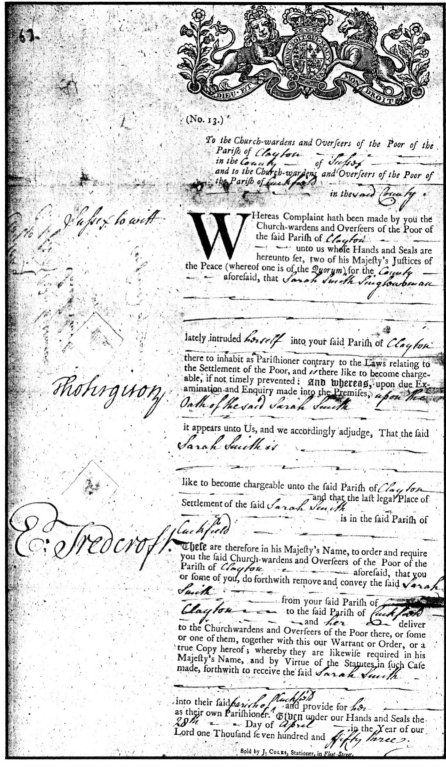

(No. 13.)

To the Church-wardens and Overseers of the Poor of the Parish of *Clayton* in the *County* of *Sussex* and to the Church-wardens and Overseers of the Poor of the Parish of *Cuckfield* in the said *County*.

Sussex, to wit.

WHereas Complaint hath been made by you the Church-wardens and Overseers of the Poor of the said Parish of *Clayton* unto us whose Hands and Seals are hereunto set, two of his Majesty's Justices of the Peace (whereof one is of the *Quorum*) for the *County* aforesaid, that *Sarah Smith Singlewoman*

lately intruded *herself* into your said Parish of *Clayton* there to inhabit as Parishioner contrary to the Laws relating to the Settlement of the Poor, and *is* there like to become chargeable, if not timely prevented: **and whereas**, upon due Examination and Enquiry made into the Premises, *upon the Oath of the said Sarah Smith*

Thohrgison

it appears unto Us, and we accordingly adjudge, That the said *Sarah Smith is*

like to become chargeable unto the said Parish of *Clayton* and that the last legal Place of Settlement of the said *Sarah Smith* is in the said Parish of *Cuckfield*

E: Tredcroft.

These are therefore in his Majesty's Name, to order and require you the said Church-wardens and Overseers of the Poor of the Parish of *Clayton* aforesaid, that you or some of you, do forthwith remove and convey the said *Sarah Smith* from your said Parish of *Clayton* to the said Parish of *Cuckfield* and *her* deliver to the Churchwardens and Overseers of the Poor there, or some or one of them, together with this our Warrant or Order, or a true Copy hereof; whereby they are likewise required in his Majesty's Name, and by Virtue of the Statutes in such Case made, forthwith to receive the said *Sarah Smith*

into their said *Parish of Cuckfield*, and provide for *her* as their own Parishioner. **Given** under our Hands and Seals the *28th* Day of *April* in the Year of our Lord one Thousand seven hundred and *fifty three*.

Sold by J. COLES, Stationer, in *Fleet Street.*

17. An Official Order for the Removal of Sarah Smith from Clayton to Cuckfield in 1753.

who had no intention of working for a living if they could avoid it and perhaps some of these deserved to be punished. But there must have been many like Jane Robinson who genuinely didn't know where they were born and where they could turn for help in a time of dire need.

The cost of removing vagrants was met from the county rate which until well into the 19th century was called 'The Tax for Conveying Vagrants and other Uses'. Earlier in the 18th century it had been called 'The Tax for Maymed Soldiers and Charitable Uses' – the maimed soldiers being those who had fought on the Continent with Marlborough during the War of the Spanish Succession.[7] In January 1713, for example, the treasurer was ordered to pay the churchwardens and overseers of Brighthelmstone £5 11s. 10d. money laid out by them in relieving 180 seamen, late prisoners in France 'in theire return to their Habitations'. No other references of this nature nearer our immediate area, have been found.

There we must leave these poor, wretched, unfortunate people. There was to be little change until 1834 when Union Workhouses were established and after which time the active homeless poor were obliged to tramp every day from one workhouse to the next in order to get an evening meal and a bed for the night – a situation that was to change very little for the next 100 years.

Crime and Punishment

For the times, when people were so poor that they frequently went hungry and cold, the 18th and early 19th centuries were not apparently a period of great lawlessness. Indeed, local people by and large seem to have been remarkably law-abiding.

One of the most common offences was assault, for in the closed atmosphere of village life there were times when tempers flared quickly and arguments tended to be settled by recourse to fisticuffs. This situation seems to have been thoroughly understood by the justices who frequently passed relatively mild sentences for offences which today would be classified as grievous bodily harm. The following are one or two examples:

July 1768. Arthur Garton [later called Gatton] of Clayton, butcher, was charged with making an assault upon Thomas Welfare at Keymer on 15th May and then and there did beat, wound and ill-treat him so that his life was greatly despaired of.

At the same court Richard Miles of Keymer, labourer, faced a similar charge of assaulting William Welfare of Keymer.

April 1763. Bartholomew Smithers of Clayton, yeoman, and William Oram of Keymer, yeoman, ordered to appear at the next sessions to answer charges by Philadelphia Awcock of Keymer alleging assault and a breach of the peace.

The outcome of none of these cases was recorded; but a little later there are five similar cases almost all outside the Burgess Hill area but quoted here to illustrate the point:

April 1781. Thomas Dennett, late of the parish of Preston, gentleman, being indicted for an assault on Richard Morley pleaded guilty . . . and his fine is set at £0.0s.vjd.

October 1788. For an attempted rape on a ten year old girl William Stevens of Lewes was sentenced to one month in jail and to two whippings. And whilst he was in jail he was to have only the 'House of Correction Allowance' [which probably means he was given just bread and water].

July 1789. Mary French wife of Henry French of Hurstperpoint, labourer, and Mary French also of Hurst, spinster, were jointly charged with assault on Barbara Butcher of Hurst so that her life was greatly despaired of. Mary the elder was found not guilty. Mary the younger [presumably her daughter] was fined 6d.

July 1792. Thomas White late of Ditchelling found guilty of assaulting James Fenner and fined 6d.

There were five similar cases of assault heard at this court,[8] and all defendants paid 6d. for a fine. Finally:

October 1801. John Burton of [Fowles farm], Clayton, yeoman, found guilty of assaulting Susanna Potter wife of John Potter at Clayton and fined 5s.

The small fines for assault, sometimes followed by binding over to keep the peace, probably reflect the tolerance shown by the magistrates in cases of this nature and although the would-be rapist was given what today would be considered a reasonably severe sentence, it was trivial when compared with sentences meted out for theft. Again most of the earlier examples are outside the Burgess Hill area:

October 1783. George Gower of Cuckfield, labourer, found guilty of stealing a pair of leather breeches valued at £1.1s.0d. and one cloth jacket valued at £1.1s.0d. . . . sentenced to seven days imprisonment and to be whipped at the market place at Lewes between the hours of eleven and one o'clock.

January 1785. Frances Mills of Plumpton, widow, found guilty of stealing a sheaf of wheat worth 6d . . . sentenced to 14 days hard labour and a private whipping.

October 1786. Philip Moorey of Clayton, labourer, and Sarah Geering late of Clayton, found guilty of stealing 15 geese worth 30s the property of John Pellen. Sentenced to six months imprisonment and at the end of that time to be publicly whipped at the cart's tail through the town of Lewes and then discharged.

April 1790. Abraham Chatfield of Cuckfield, labourer, found guilty of stealing a bushel of wheat valued at 5s. Sentenced to be transported for seven years.

These four examples are all what today would be considered petty offences. Yet all attracted severe prison sentences and all except Abraham Chatfield received whippings, some in public to add humiliation to the excruciatingly painful punishment. It was enough to put people off stealing for ever which, of course, it was meant to. Abraham was probably a second or third time offender to warrant such a savage sentence for so trivial an offence.

Half a century later, when the town was first beginning to develop and when it was packed with navvies working on the new railway, little had changed except that whipping seems to have been replaced largely by solitary confinement. For example:

1841. Frederick Gumbrell of Clayton, labourer, found guilty of stealing a gelding worth £2.0s.0d. the goods and chattels of Charles Webber . . . sentenced to transportation for 15 years.

Benjamin Cheeseman of Keymer, labourer, charged with stealing one flannel frock (4s) and one waistcoat (10s) the goods and chattels of Joseph Eckles. He pleaded guilty and was sentenced to four months hard labour except the first and last fourteen days which were to be served in solitary confinement.

Thomas Cottingham of Keymer, labourer, charged with stealing one rail pole (2d) and one piece of wood (2d) the goods and chattels of Philip Jenner. He pleaded guilty and was sentenced to 14 days imprisonment with hard labour.

Thomas Wood of Keymer, labourer, charged with stealing seven copper coins called pence the monies of William Berbury. He pleaded guilty and was sentenced to six months hard labour except the first and last fourteen days which were to be served in solitary confinement.

Frederick Gumbrell's theft of a horse, too, may well have been a second or third offence to attract a sentence of 15 years' transportation. His sentence almost certainly meant banishment since, even if he served his full 15 years, he would have had no money to pay his fare back to Sussex from Australia or Tasmania or wherever in the Antipodes convicted felons were being sent at that particular time. The other sentences for stealing goods mostly of trivial value were clearly meant to be a deterrent and, faced with sentences of this magnitude, would-be thieves must have given any plan involving theft very careful thought indeed.

Cases of trespass, too, were usually treated fairly leniently. John Peckham living at and farming North Inholmes made a thorough nuisance of himself early in 1715 when 'by force and arms' he entered upon the premises of Mary Richardson of adjoining Bedelands farm much to Mary's annoyance. Yet when the case was heard at Lewes several months later and he was found guilty of the offence he was fined a paltry 10s. 0d.

By 1822, when public whipping was beginning to die out and fewer private whippings were ordered, a new form of punishment was introduced. It was decided that, since prisoners were usually given sentences of hard labour, their energies should be harnessed and utilised so as to produce income. Accordingly the magistrates agreed in April 1822 to install the recently invented treadmill to drive mill stones for grinding flour. With stones of 3ft. 3ins. in diameter revolving 120 times a minute and requiring only 15 men to work them, two bushels of wheat could be ground every hour or, as they estimated, about 64 bushels a week.[9] This diabolical punishment was regularly meted out until about 1840 when the treadmill and machinery at Lewes were disposed of. Meanwhile the plant had been let to local millers who paid an appropriate rent for the facilities it provided.

On very rare occasions a man could escape imprisonment and a whipping for a petty crime by volunteering for service in H.M. forces, especially if the country happened to be at war at the time.

> January 1793. James Williams, labourer, was found guilty of stealing food and liquor by false pretences and was sentenced to two months imprisonment and a whipping. But on condition of his entering on board one of His Majesty's ships of war to be immediately discharged.

One wonders if James made a wise decision. Two months was not a long sentence and he would have been flogged aboard a war ship for a quite minor infringement of naval discipline. In prison his personal safety would have been assured and he would at least have had a roof over his head and regular meals. Afloat he would have spent long hours on watch, sometimes in appalling weather and always wet and cold in northern waters during the long months of winter. And even if he survived he could not possibly have foreseen that more than twenty years were to elapse before the final defeat of Napoleon. There must have been times when he bitterly regretted his decision to enlist.

To end this section here is a local example of the way in which a man, who in a moment of weakness committed a petty crime, could embark on the downhill road to ruin.

In October 1790 Thomas Peckham of Keymer, labourer, was charged with stealing a goose worth 2s. 6d., the property of John Ford. He was found guilty, sentenced to six months' imprisonment with hard labour and to be whipped twice – once publicly at the market place in Lewes before being admitted to prison, and again at the end of his term before being discharged. John Ford was at that time the occupier of Batchelors farm in Keymer Road and Thomas was probably an employee, or at least a neighbour. The upshot was that, as a result of his crime, Thomas lost his home, for about nine months later, in July 1791, when he is next heard of, he had been committed to the House of Correction at the Cliffe near Lewes for vagrancy and ordered to be whipped at the market place there the Saturday following his trial. He had served his sentence, and had scratched some sort of living for a few weeks after his release; but it was no use. He had lost not only his home but also his livelihood and the respect of his former friends and acquaintances in the parish. Nobody, it seems, was prepared to give him a second chance and in the end he lost his self respect and possibly even the will to live. He could look forward bleakly only to a life of abject poverty and finally to a pauper's grave to which he would go unlamented and unmourned. And for what? A goose worth half a crown!

Minor Civil Cases

Local government during this period was dominated by the landed gentry and prosperous middle classes in their role as Justices of the Peace. They were a vital channel of communication between central government in Westminster and the parishes whose affairs were regulated by the churchwardens, overseers of the poor and the constables, or headboroughs as they were sometimes called. Before County Councils were set up in 1888 the activities of the parish officers were supervised by the local justices. They gave their sanction, for example, to the raising of a local rate and they approved the appointment of the surveyor for highways. Justices were also responsible for the maintenance of county bridges, the building and oversight of prisons, licensing of alehouses and theatres, removal of vagrants and supervision of the highways. They had powers to punish a person for failure to contribute towards the repair of roads when ordered, and they could make maintenance orders against individuals if parish officers failed to do so. In this section are quoted one or two examples of sentences affecting this area.

Anyone who had the means to do so was expected to maintain his own kith and kin, for instance:

> July 1724. Ordered that William Burt of Keymer, 'being a person of good ability' pay to the Churchwardens and Overseers of the Poor of Keymer 1s.6d. a week towards the relief of Ann Burt his mother now chargeable to the said parish.
>
> April 1757. Ordered, upon complaint of the Churchwardens and Overseers of the Poor . . . that Stephen Laugham[10] of Keymer, yeoman, is a person of ability and ought to contribute to the relief of Thomas Laugham his son a poor person now chargeable to the parish. An order for 1s.0d. a week was made so long as Thomas continued to be a charge on the parish.
>
> April 1789. William Brigden, yeoman, was ordered to pay 2s.6d. per week for the maintenance of his three grandchildren, Frances Berry aged 11, Sarah Berry aged 7, and Richard Berry aged 5 then a charge on the Churchwardens and Overseers of the Poor of the parish of Wivelsfield so long as they remained a charge on that parish.

There is no further information about William Burt who seems to have been content to let his ageing mother fend for herself; and very little about William Brigden except that he was then living in Cuckfield and that he was expected to help support his daughter's children. Stephen Laugham on the other hand was the owner (in the right of Martha his wife) and occupier of extensive farmland a little to the north of the town called Isewoods later, as now, known as the Rookery. He also held in his own right copyhold land in Mayfield. Why he could not have found employment for Thomas, his son (who appears to have been single) on his 120-acre farm is not known. Perhaps Thomas was handicapped in some way that made arduous work in the fields and yards impracticable; but even if times were bad for farmers, Stephen must still have been relatively well off compared with the genuine poor of the day, many of whom had no home and no regular income at all. It must be assumed that a shilling a week was considered adequate to keep body and soul together, as was the half-crown that William Brigden paid for the maintenance of his three young grandchildren and the 1s. 6d. that provided support for Ann Burt.

From time to time parish officers might find themselves faced with a bill for medical treatment and the nursing of a visitor to the parish. On 1 October 1712, for example, Sarah Marten, daughter of John Marten, who had set out from Keymer a few days earlier to visit her mother then living in Brighton, fell sick of the smallpox and 'being very ill of the same and not in a condition to remove without endangering her life she having noe friends or relations of Ability to provide for her became an extra ordinary charge to our said parish of Brighthelmstone as followeth viz:-'

> To the widow Bridger to take her into her house, nurse her and supply her with necessarys during her said sickness for four weeks time at sixteen shillings per week.   £03.04s.00d.
>
> Two days board after pretty well recovered   £00.02s.00d.
> To cloths to send her home in (her own being

so bad not fitt to putt on and was all cast away).   £00.15s.00d.
    To horse hire and charges in carrying her to
Kymar.   £00.04s.00d.
    The whole amounting to four pounds five shillings. Witness our hands this thirteenth day of
November Anno D: 1712.

This was a very heavy item of expenditure at a time when Brighthelmstone was so
overburdened with relieving her own poor that many of the less badly off parishes across
the whole of East Sussex, from Portslade to Brede, were ordered to levy a special rate to
help Brighton in its time of need.[11] The £4 5s. 0d. that it cost to take care of Sarah represented
almost the entire income of a 1d. rate for the parish of Keymer; and more than the £3 15s.
6½d. that Clayton could raise by the imposition of a penny rate in the 18th century. Today,
with our efficient National Health and Social Security Services which we now tend to take
for granted, it is difficult to imagine the plight of Sarah Marten. It appears that she was
sent home, on horseback in November, after only two days' convalescence.

Maintenance of Roads and Bridges
Responsibility for these vital means of communication rested primarily with parishes
although the county, through the justices sitting in Quarter Sessions, were directly responsible for some of the more important bridges, e.g. Exceat in the Cuckmere valley, Cooks
Bridge near Lewes, and so on, levying, when necessary, a special county rate for their
upkeep.

    Because none of our local bridges was maintained by the county, complaints about them
came before the justices only very rarely when, for example, there was doubt as to who was
responsible for repairing them, or when those known to be responsible had failed to keep
them in good repair. The only bridge in this area that created any problem in the 18th
century was the one at the foot of Fairplace Hill. Here, in 1709,[12] four substantial
copyholders of the manor of Clayton were indicted as follows:

> Whereas Richard Neale, John Attree, Richard Turner and Thomas Norton . . . stand indicted for
> not repairing of a certaine Horse Bridge called St. John's Bridge lying at St. John's Common . . .
> And whereas a Wayne Bridge has been thought more convenient . . . the said Richard Neale, John
> Attree, Richard Turner and Thomas Norton have consented to and built a Wayne Bridge which has
> been done by agreement of the copyhold tenants of the said Mannor and the Inhabitants of the said
> parish of Clayton on this condition that from henceforth the coppyholders of the said Mannor of
> Clayton shall at all times hereafter att theire owne costs and charges Repaire, Amend and Maintaine
> the said Bridge and the Clappers lying att the end of the said Bridge, And that the Inhabitants of
> the said parish of Clayton shall att all times hereafter repaire, amend and Mayntayne the highway
> att both ends of the Bridge and Clappers . . .

This arrangement was agreed by the justices in their role as the authority for the provision,
repair and maintenance of roads and bridges for the county of East Sussex. The four
copyholders who footed the bill for a very much improved bridge owned respectively:
Fowles farm, Freeks farm, land in Clayton village, and parts of West End and Clayton
Wickham farms. None of them would have needed to use the bridge very frequently, some
perhaps less than once a week, yet these public spirited men decided not only that an
improved bridge, able to bear the weight of loaded wagons and not just horses with very
light loads, was in the best interests of the local community, but also found the money to
pay for the initial cost. The main beneficiaries would have been those living to the north of
the bridge in what is now Cuckfield who needed to go to Brighton; to use the smithy at
Smeeds, and perhaps the one or two existing shops and other facilities located on the
common at this time. The freeholders at what are now called Bridge Hall and Woodfield
Lodge, too, would have derived considerable benefit from the new bridge; yet it seems they
were not approached for a contribution towards the cost, nor were they expected to do so.

There is no evidence that similar problems arose over Eylesford Bridge and the bridge near Hammonds that we mentioned in Chapter One.

Occasionally a parish had to be forcefully reminded of its responsibilities for repairing the roads. In 1728 Thomas Warden, one of the justices, at the July Sessions 'presented upon my own knowledge the inhabitants of Clayton for not repairing the highway ... leading from Saint John's Common to the Stone Pound being about the space of one mile and a half'.[13] One can imagine Mr. Warden making his way from Cuckfield to Brighton along an almost impassable road which even in summer was so deeply rutted that he may have been tossed out of his carriage or whatever horsedrawn vehicle he was driving at the time, or at least been severely shaken and bruised. He was sufficiently infuriated to ensure that the matter was raised at the earliest session thereafter. Nevertheless, as a general rule such cases locally were rare. The next to be recorded came in April 1769 when:

> We the Constables of the Hundred of Buttinghill ... do present a certain peace of the King's Highway in the parish of Keymer leading from St. John's Common to Whale Bridge Common for the space of 20 rods [about 100 metres] and upwards being very dangerous for his Majesty's subjects to go or travel thereon and that the same ought to be repaired and amended by the Inhabitants of the said parish of Keymer.

This presentment made on 5 April 1769 was signed by Allan Avery and Thomas Tulley, constables of the Hundred, names that would become familiar here in Burgess Hill about a century later though there is no evidence that either of these particular constables lived in the immediate area. The stretch of road referred to was part of Lye Lane in the vicinity of the present Wivelsfield Station. About this time modern Junction Road, when it was mentioned at all, was called 'the highway leading from Keymer village towards Heywards Hoth'. The reference to Whale Bridge at this late date is interesting.[14]

Later, in 1826, when the turnpike road near Hammonds Place was straightened and improved the justices decided to stop up 'a public highway leading from St John's Common through certain lands called Hammonds farm or Hammonds Place farm belonging to and in the occupation of Robert Podmore Esq. towards and near a certain mill ... called Hammonds Mill about 260 rods in length' together with a public bridleway that linked this road with the turnpike road and ran close to the then ten-year-old mansion house called Clayton Priory. Mr. Podmore was given the opportunity to purchase the land thus made redundant at its current market value. Part of the site of this road, which was also mentioned in Chapter One, is now a public footpath and provides a pleasant walk through the fields, some of whose boundaries have not changed for centuries.

Rates of Pay and Transport of Goods

There was strict control of wages and carriage of goods in the early 18th century. Workers were not allowed to demand more than the rates laid down; neither was an employer permitted to pay more, however outstanding any given employee might be. The following is a brief extract from those published in April 1733:

> No chief servant of a Smith shall take by the year with Meat and Drink above £6.5s.0d.
> And the second sort not above £5.10s.0d.
> The best ... gardener, bricklayer, glazier, brickmaker, tilemaker, lime burner, wheelwright ... shall not take by the day from the Annunciation [25 March] till Michaelmas with Meat and Drink above 10d.
> Nor without Meat and Drink above 17d. Nor between Michaelmas and the Annunciation with Meat and Drink above 10d. Nor without Meat and Drink above 16d.
> The best Dairy Maid or Cook Maid shall not take by the year with Meat and Drink above £3.
> The second sort not above £2 and the third sort not above 20s.

The above are only a very few examples of the rates quoted in this long and detailed document. Everyone could be fitted into one of the categories given or, where there was any doubt, be classed as general labourers or servants.

The cost of transporting goods, too, was subject to very strict controls. For example every hundredweight to and from London to 'Hurstperpoint, Ditchelling . . . and places of like distance' by wagon in summer (1 May to 1 November) cost 3s. An additional 6d. was payable for transport over the same distances during the winter. The same rates applied to goods carried by packhorse. Small items, too, are shown in considerable detail: e.g. every pig, goose or turkey cost 3d; a cock, hen, duck or rabbit cost 1d; a flitch of bacon 2s. and so on.

Rates were also laid down for the transport of vagrants as follows:

For vagrants by Dung Cart from Maytide to Michaelmas by the mile	6d.
From Michaelmas to Maytide	1s.0d.
For every single horse from Maytide to Michaelmas	2d.
For every single horse from Michaelmas to Maytide	3d.
If on foot by the day for the officer	1s.6d.
If on horseback [for the officer]	3s.0d.
For the allowance for every Vagrant by the day	6d.

The above illustrates the relatively enormous expense involved in getting rid of unwanted vagrants. It would have cost Keymer, for example, 4s. to convey a single vagrant from, say, the *King's Head* to Cuckfield in winter, little short of a week's pay for an experienced brick or tile maker. A number of instances have been found where a parish sometimes faced crippling expense in order to be free of the responsibility of maintaining some poor soul who could prove no right of settlement. The cost, it seemed, was relatively unimportant in these cases. There was a principle at stake and that principle had to be observed regardless of the cost. Transport by dung cart was deliberately designed to inflict the maximum humiliation on these unfortunate people who would have been exposed to the scorn, catcalls and hoots of derision of all who happened to be on or near the road when they passed by, for few bystanders would have expressed sympathy for their predicament in this callous and brutal age.

Illegitimacy

Affiliation orders made by the justices at this time normally set the weekly amount required to support a child at 1s. 6d., e.g.:

January 1732. It was ordered that Ralph Sayers of Lindfield, clocksmith, father of a female bastard child born to Frances Parker of Clayton, single woman, should pay £9.4s.6d. to the Churchwardens and Overseers of the Poor of Clayton for maintenance at the time of her lying-in and 1s.6d. a week so long as the child shall continue to be a charge on the parish, and £6 towards putting the child out Apprentice.

July 1776. William Lewry of Keymer was adjudged to be the father of the bastard male child of Sarah Ead of Cuckfield, single woman and ordered to pay £2.6s.0d. to the Churchwardens and Overseers of the Poor of Cuckfield for arrears of maintenance of the child, plus 2s.0d. weekly so long as the child was a charge on the parish. Margaret [which must be a scribe's error for Sarah] was ordered to pay 6d. a week to the Churchwardens and Overseers of the Poor of Cuckfield so long as the child be chargeable to the parish in case she should not nourse or take care of the child herself.

William Lewry (or perhaps his son) was then farming Brooklands which had been acquired in 1728 by the then lord of the manor, Abraham Addams, who had probably rebuilt or adapted the old house into the imposing building we see today. Sarah appears to have been a simple minded country girl about whose ability to care for her baby the parish officers had grave doubts, hence the requirement to pay them 6d. out of her allowance of 2s. 0d. a week as a form of insurance.

The incidence of illegitimacy was not high by modern standards – about 3%-4% of total births compared with about 19% nationally in 1985,[15] and it is evident from the entries in some of the local parish registers that only a fairly small proportion of cases ever reached the courts. Most settlements seem to have been made without the need for unmarried mothers (or their parents) either to sue, or to be a charge on the parish. It is thought, admittedly without any hard evidence, that in many cases the unfortunate girl's parents made themselves responsible for their unwelcome grandchild's upbringing.

This seems an appropriate point at which to end this brief review of the plight of the 18th-century poor. There was to be little change until well into the 19th century when the great Victorian reformers began to initiate action to stop some of the more brutal excesses of employers and others in authority, and when for the first time some effort was made to understand the problems of coping with the less fortunate members of society. Even so, yet another century was to elapse before the coming of the modern welfare state.

The Well-to-do

If the plight of the poor left much to be desired how did the yeoman farmer and smallholder and local tradesman fare? Considerable light can be thrown on their circumstances by studying carefully their wills for, as previously noted, most of those with any movable assets left a will. A general indication of the value of the estates of some of those who left no will can sometimes be obtained by reference to the administrations, which have been summarised on indexed cards and can be seen at E.S.R.O. These give the name of the deceased, the name of the persons to whom letters of administration were granted, and sometimes the value of the estate either as an exact sum or expressed in round figures as, for example, 'under £200, under £2,000', and so on. In some instances, however, no figure is given at all. Similarly some, but not all, wills contain a reference to the value of the goods and chattels of the deceased, whilst surviving inventories which cover mainly the period 1710-40 still exist for many 18th-century locals and these, too, can provide a graphic description of what could be found both in the house and out of doors.

From what can be deduced from these sources it appears that, locally, the early part of the 18th century tended to be a time of great prosperity. As stated in the previous chapter, some of our local butchers and alehouse keepers had considerable assets in the form of money out on loan. Other tradesmen, too, enjoyed a reasonable standard of living at this time. Take the case of John Easton, a retired blacksmith, who died in the spring of 1728. His goods and chattels were valued at no less than £496 4s. 4d. and that figure excluded 'my messuage and freehold land commonly called Cants alias Fragbarrow containing by estimation 26 acres', which he left to his eldest daughter Anne Easton along with 30 acres and another parcel of land called Griggs or Giffords in Wivelsfield. Mary, the second daughter, was left 'the Longcroft or by whatsoever it is called containing 3 acres in Cuckfield adjoining to Moister Green', together with a house and smith's forge and one acre of land at Cowfold and another cottage and 'smith's shop erected on the lord's waste with 12 rods of land in Slaugham adjoining the King's highway leading from Handcross to Warninglid'.[16] Cants alias Fragbarrow was the northern part of Cants farm later called Frankbarrow in Junction Road which was sold off about this time and which was mentioned earlier.

His movable goods and other assets were considerable.[17] His wearing apparel and ready money totalled no less than £122 4s. 0d. and he had £110 out on loan. 'Money on the Books', which presumably means money due for work done, was given as £53 12s. 8d., whilst arrears of rent (£74 14s. 6d.) and desperate debts (£40) accounted for another £114 14s. 6d. His animals, which included two horses, a cow, four sheep and a lamb, and some heifers, along with a rick of hay, wood, faggots etc. were valued at £28. And we must not think that he and his wife and three daughters were living in near poverty-stricken conditions indoors as were the Brookers mentioned earlier: far from it. The house was as well equipped as any noted during the period 1710-40 when so much detailed information is available. The kitchen had everything – including a clock, two 'gunns' and three flitches of bacon all in addition to the usual tables, chairs, pots, kettles and fire irons which were valued at £6 16s. 2d. Included in the detailed list of things in the three bedrooms were nine silver spoons, a bodkin and seven gold rings valued at £10 the lot, clearly the treasured possessions of John's wife, Mary, who also had an excellent stock of bed and table linen much too numerous to describe in detail here. Unusually for an artisan, tucked away in an entry which includes 'a close stool, four chamber potts, a joynt stool and a press to hang clothes in' are no fewer than 28 books with no indication, unfortunately, of their titles or authors.

Nearly a century later, in 1823, when a well known local blacksmith died, his goods, chattels and credits did not amount to £20. The smith in question was Thomas Jeffery (grandfather of Charlotte who later married Mr. C.D. Meads) and who lived on the site of St John's Fairfield. It is true that Thomas's son, James, who died in 1845 having meantime acquired additional land and expanded the business in a developing area, was able to leave movables and credits to the value of little under £450; but this, after allowing for inflation, was still far less in real terms than the £496 of John Easton – roughly half, in fact. And James Jeffery had nothing like so much real estate as John Easton had acquired.

If the apparent prosperity of the 1720s had continued, one could reasonably expect that a man owning and farming 50 acres in about 1750 would be equally well or much better endowed with worldly goods than a humble blacksmith. Yet when, in July 1749, John Marchant and John Clarke made an inventory of the goods and chattels of John Osborne of Fowles Farm,[18] there was very little of value either indoors or out. The grand total, and this amounted to only £250, included £109 16s. 0d. out on loan. Most of the remainder comprised his animals and what was called 'husbandry tackling' which must have included ploughs and harrows, carts, and a wagon. His three horses were valued at only £3 *in toto* which suggests that they were a pretty poor lot and likely to expire of old age or exhaustion at any time. The value of all the effects in the house were assessed at a mere £24 10s. 0d. The *best* bedroom contained only 'a bed and all thereto belonging, two chests, a trunk, a gun, five sheets, four napkins and eight cloaths' (whatever they might be) valued at £4 10s. 0d. The kitchen seems to have been the best equipped room in the house but, apart from 15 pewter dishes, a clock and a warming pan, the remainder were a few workaday items without which a housewife would barely be able to manage. John's 'wearing apparel and money in his purse', on the other hand, was valued at £44 10s. 0d., a not inconsiderable sum for the time.

In common with many family men at the time John Osborne seems to have favoured his grandchildren much more than his own daughters. Ann, who was single and probably kept house for him after the death of her mother, was left a trifling 5s.; yet Ann and Hannah Osborne, her nieces (daughters of her brother George who was to have the farm), were left £30 apiece which was to be paid when they reached the age of 21 or when they married, whichever happened first. Another two nephews and a niece, the children of Hannah and Edward Godley, were to have £30 apiece on the same conditions. So concerned was John about the future of his family that he specified in his will that 'whereas it is thought that Hannah Godley is quick with child . . .', that child and any future children she might have were all to receive £30 each as above.[19] If Edward Godley died leaving Hannah a widow she was to have £5 a year payable every six months. Poor Ann who seems to have carried the burden of running the home had to be content with her miserable legacy of 5s. She probably ended her days as general dogsbody to her brother George and his wife and family, occupying the 'Garrett' which contained only 'an old bed and lumber' that had been valued at £1 by the appraisers.

The general trend throughout the second half of the 18th century, and indeed well into the 19th, seems to have been that the average small farmer and tradesman did little more than maintain the standard of living that had been reached during the later part of the previous century. For a few the standard may even have declined. On the other hand, the more energetic and enterprising business man could amass a small fortune in the course of an active lifetime as will be seen shortly.

Legacies to Dependants

Almost without exception husbands made provision for their wives during the period under discussion. Here are a few examples:

> 1741. Edward Haylor [who lived at Tibballs near Hammonds].
> To Sarah my wife all the household goods and an annuity of £4 whilst she remains unmarried and the use of my customary messuage, barn and lands called Barbers.
> 1758. John Bennett [who held Bedelands farm and other land locally]
> To my wife Ann Bennett an annuity of £10 to be paid quarterly on condition that she relinquishes all right, title or claim out of the copyhold lands held on the manor of Keymer to the Executor of the Will [their youngest son George]. Also the use of the household goods and chattels during her lifetime.
> 1769. Robert Leach of Newtimber [who held the 'Meeds' site].
> To my dearly beloved wife Elizabeth £15 per annum to be paid quarterly by my Executors.

Hugh Vincent (of Bedelands Farm) who died in 1773, left 'to my loving wife Elizabeth all my customary messuage and lands called Bedle Lands, Coopers and Wakelins Inholmes', until their sons Thomas and Hugh came of age. She was to have the rents, income and interest from his personal estate so long as she remained unmarried. If she remarried the income was to go to two other sons and his 'friend and neighbour George Taylor, Brickmaker', who were the executors. In the event of Elizabeth's remarriage she was to receive just £5 – the remainder of the personal estate to be divided among the children.

In 1797 William Ford of Chapel Cottages in Fairplace Hill left 'To my loving wife Elizabeth Ford an annuity of £12 from the portion of tithes in Cuckfield called Westbaileys for the term of her natural life', together with the free use and occupation of the house and garden where they both lived. The annuity was given in lieu of all her manorial widow's rights that she might claim or be entitled to out of the freehold and copyhold premises that William held. If Elizabeth did claim her age-old rights, the annuity was to cease.

Similarly in 1804 George Bennett of High Chimneys formerly Woodwards left 'to Elizabeth my dear wife my freehold messuage, barn, buildings, farm, lands and premises lately purchased from Mr. Whichels with copyhold tenements held of the manor of Keymer' together with £1,000 and all the household goods, plate, linen and furniture as belonged to her previous to their marriage. The remainder of the household goods were to be divided between Elizabeth and his nephew Richard Bennett.

This last will[20] demonstrates the way in which a man of relatively humble origins (John Bennett mentioned above was his father) could, by a lifetime of dedication to the land, end his days a relatively rich man. The 'land lately purchased from Mr. Whichels' was in fact High Chimneys mentioned in a previous chapter; the copyhold land was 'Butchers' sometimes called Poveys, and other land adjoining on St John's Common later to become part of the site of Norman's Brickworks. In addition, he had for many years – between 1780 and 1799 – farmed Ockley manor. At the time of his death the country was involved in the wars against Napoleon and much of his wealth was probably amassed at about the turn of the century when the prices of corn, cattle and sheep were much higher than normal.

There are many similar examples but we will quote just one more since a widow sometimes needed more than just some measure of financial security.

In 1816 John Eager of Keymer, yeoman left 'To my wife Susannah my copyhold messuage, cottage and estate called Potters Kilns on St. John's Common'. His friends Nathan Holford, who farmed Freeks, and Henry Mitchell of Cuckfield were asked to help Susannah 'in the management and carrying on of the farm and lands wherein I now live, and I hereby intreat the said Nathan Holford and Henry Mitchell to lend her such aid and assistance'.

John was a small tenant farmer – the lessee of Leylands Farm in Leylands Road; he also owned the site called Potters Kilns originally enclosed by Sampson Bagnall, mentioned in the previous chapter. He was by no means a wealthy man since his goods and chattels did not amount in value to £200. He may very well have underestimated Susannah's business abilities for 12 years later she was farming Fragbarrow in Ditchling and, when the Keymer commons were enclosed, she was successful in her application for an allocation in respect of the Potters Kilns site for which she was awarded 38 square poles (nearly quarter of an acre). In addition, when plots were offered for sale to raise money for the expenses connected with the same enclosures, she was able to find £45 in ready cash with which to acquire over three acres of land to the east of Mill Road, bounded by Grove Road to the east and north, which suggests either that she may have had a good deal more business sense than John gave her credit for, or that his old friends were exceptionally conscientious with their 'aid and assistance'.

As previously noted people occasionally remembered servants in their wills. In 1723, for example, Thomas Davy, who owned a cottage near West End farm and a house and some 25 acres of land to the north of the town boundary, left everything (except one legacy of £20 to a relative) to his housekeeper Elinor Brickwell. In this case, however, we know that Elinor was a very special servant, because when he died six years later and she claimed her inheritance they had married and she was Elinor Davy.

> 1749. Rev. Laurence Price [then rector of Clayton cum Keymer].
> To the servants living with me at my decease £6.6s.0d. payable within three months of my death to be equally divided amongst them.

There are one or two other examples in the early 19th century but reference must be made to just one more which actually comes after the end of the period:

> 1853. Elizabeth Barbara Shaw widow of the late William Shaw of Keymer, Brickmaker.
> 'To my servant Ellen Knowles if living with me at my decease – £10'.

In addition she was to have the income from 'my freehold and tithe free farm called Baldwins in Keymer containing $12\frac{1}{4}$ acres which I purchased from the Executors of Thomas Dominick Whiteman Esq . . .'.[21] However 'if Ellen married or cohabited with any man', the farm was to go to Elizabeth's nephew John Wood and Elizabeth his wife and Ellen's income would cease. In this instance a faithful servant was apparently rewarded with a pension which was to cease if she married or set up home with a man who was prepared to support her.

Only one reference to legacies to god-children has been noted in the Burgess Hill area:

> 1744. Thomas Marten of Keymer, brickmaker.
> To my god-daughter Anne Sanders daughter of Richard Sanders of Cuckfield – £6.
> To my god-daughter Philadelphia Parker daughter of Frances Parker – £6.
> To my god-son Thomas Parker son of William Parker – £6.
> To my god-daughter Mary Hubbard daughter of John Hubbard of Clayton – £1.1s.0d.
> To my god-son John Steel and god-daughters Elizabeth Hayward and Mary Richardson 5s. to buy them bibles.

Then, as is sometimes found today, the responsibilities of god-parents seem to have been undertaken fairly lightly. Many, perhaps most, of those who had money to leave must have had god-children so why were those children not more frequently remembered in a testator's will? The answer may be that Thomas seems to have died childless, since he mentions no children nor grandchildren, and his brickworks in Station Road were left to a kinsman of the same name living at Alborne. Perhaps his inability to have a family of his own made his god-children very special to him and consequently they came in for the paternal affection that would normally have gone to his own offspring.

As noted briefly a little earlier, John Osborne appeared to favour his grandchildren much more than his own children. There are several similar examples of this at this time.

When George Taylor, the brickmaker, died in 1746 and was living at Wivelsfield at a place charmingly called Windle Socks alias Ballard, he left his real estate partly to his eldest son John, and partly to his youngest son James. George the middle son received nothing though *his* son, also named George, was left £40 and his two daughters, Mary and Ann, each had £30. One of John's daughters, Susanna, was to have £5; and Mary the youngest £55, but no mention was made of the middle daughter or daughters. So why were they and George ignored?

Mary Clarke of Smeeds, who died a widow in 1780, also made some provision for her grandchildren. Ann Worsfold a grand-daughter who lived at Ewhurst was bequeathed seven acres of freehold land in Twineham called 'Guns' on condition that she (Ann) paid £10 to another of Mary's grand-daughters named Catherine Potter within six months of Mary's death. Catherine was also to have two guineas immediately and her brother, John Potter, had three guineas. The residue of the estate went to Thomas Packham, her daughter Elizabeth's husband. Elizabeth herself, although she subsequently became technically the owner of the property, was not mentioned in Mary's will at all. One would have expected that Mary would have left her one or two trinkets at least.

Later, when John Burton of Fowles farm died in 1835, the bulk of his estate went to Thomas Avery his grandson. John had two daughters: Barbara wife of Richard Burtenshaw who was bequeathed some freehold land in Bolney and Hurstpierpoint; and Sarah, married to Allen Avery. Sarah was to be allowed to live in the house where John Burton had lived and 'to have the use of part of the household goods and furniture and to live free of all rents, taxes, etc.'. A great grandson, John Burton Scrase (a grandson of Sarah and Allen), was to have three freehold houses in Spring Gardens, Brighthelmstone. A condition of the legacy to Thomas Avery – which comprised Fowles farm and Barbers (in all about 70 acres) and a cottage called Nortons now the site of the *Weald Inn* – was that he should pay to John his brother, and to Amy, Eliza and Martha his sisters, £300 apiece within 12 months of John Burton's death. To do so Thomas was obliged to borrow £1,150 at $4\frac{1}{2}\%$ interest from John Wood of Ditchling, a figure that seven years later was increased to £1,500. In fact Thomas was never out of debt for the rest of his life; there was a sum of £1,500 still outstanding when he died in 1887.

These are not isolated cases but it should be emphasised that there are more examples in the early 19th century than there had been earlier.

Before leaving this interesting glimpse into people's attitudes over the period covered in this chapter, we will close with one or two observations which suggest that human nature has not changed much over the last 200 years.

When old Sarah Verrall made her will in 1769, some five years before she died, she began by saying: 'I . . . being in good bodily health and sound of mind and memory . . . being desirous of settling my worldly affairs so as to avoid all unhappy disputes and differences that may otherwise arise about the same . . .', then goes on to instruct her joint executrices (her sisters Mary and Martha) that, after payment of all debts, funeral expenses and the cost of proving her will, the residue of her personal estate was to be equally divided between them. The preamble suggests she was expecting trouble from the two, possibly quarrelsome, sisters and since she was a woman of some means – the farm called Scotches and a cottage in Fairfield Road went to her youngest daughter Sarah Tulley – it is strange that she did not appoint as executor an outsider with authority to act as arbiter between Mary and Martha. How, for example, were the two women to decide how three gold rings, or a single watch, or five dresses, or any *odd* number of articles should be equally divided? Mary was married to John Hart, an Eastbourne weaver; Martha was the wife of William Townsend, a labourer from Ripe near Lewes. One can imagine them descending upon Sarah Tulley at Scotches farm and setting about the task of sharing out their sister's personal effects. In the event, it may of course have all been settled amicably; or perhaps Sarah Tulley helped by acting as referee. In yet another case the outcome is left to the imagination.

Elizabeth Bennett, who lived at High Chimneys in Keymer Road, died in 1815, a few weeks before the Battle of Waterloo. As previously noted her husband, George, had already predeceased her, leaving her very comfortably off. She left part of the household furniture and effects to 'Richard Bennett of the Anchor House in Keymer, nephew of my late husband who looks after my farming interests . . .', the other part went to her niece, Mary Elizabeth Noakes, wife of Ned Noakes who farmed many acres of land to the north of the present town. The residue including ready money, debts owing, money realised from the sale of farming stock, corn, hay, etc. was to be invested after payment of her funeral expenses and one or two minor legacies, and the income used to pay her sister Mary Laugham 'now living with me' £16 per annum. The residue of the interest was to go to Mary Elizabeth Noakes '*to be paid into her own hands apart from her husband* or future husband for the term of her life'. The trustees were instructed to ensure that the Noakes's children were adequately cared for if Mary died before they reached the age of 21. This does not appear to suggest anything particularly untoward on the face of it, but on the evidence available it appears that Ned Noakes was something of a scatterbrain. He had acquired Old House farm, a 60-acre holding in Rocky Lane, in 1799 and Mary inherited the Rookery in 1807 on the death of her father John Laugham. These, together with other holdings in the area, made up a substantial estate of more than 200 acres.[22] All this affluence seems to have gone to Ned's head in that he began to emulate the lifestyle of a landed country gentleman. On one occasion,[23] in his capacity as constable of the Hundred of Buttinghill, he failed to appear before the justices and had failed 'to do and perform such matters as to his office appertains'. For this he was fined 5s. He was constantly in debt and by 1820 he and Mary had sold the Rookery for £3,800 to Stephen Bine of Saddlescombe. Ned was also unable to re-pay £1,200 he had borrowed from Joseph Baker of Bolnore in respect of Old House, so he lost that, too. In the circumstances it is little wonder that Mrs. Bennett was anxious to secure the future of her niece and the Noakes's children. She clearly doubted whether Ned Noakes could be relied upon to do so.

The examples quoted in this chapter are all typical of what was happening, not only in the immediate area, but also throughout the whole of Sussex and probably in other parts of the country. An attempt has been made to present a balanced view and every effort taken to avoid the bias that would have arisen had only the very best and the worst in the range of cases that came to light in the course of the research been quoted. There must have been many men like Ned Noakes, and others previously mentioned, up and down the county. They were all children of their age having, in general, scant regard for the unhappy state of those on or near the bottom rung of the human ladder. It would not, for example, have cost John Ford very much to put in a good word for Thomas Peckham who, you will recall, had stolen one of his geese. He could well have shown that there were extenuating circumstances; and even if such evidence had not secured a verdict of 'not guilty', it may well have saved the unfortunate Thomas either the whipping or such a long term of imprisonment. Furthermore, John's action could have helped to rehabilitate him in the eyes of his former neighbours and friends.

It is a sad reflection, too, on a society in which more is known about the poor and the petty wrong doers of the area through entries in the official records, than about the thousands who trudged their way through life; who led honest and hard-working lives, who kept themselves in work and out of trouble, and who are just names in the parish registers; and who, when they died and were buried in the churchyard of one of the local parish churches, do not even have a headstone to record their former presence.

But there we must leave our 18th- and early 19th-century predecessors with their narrow, parochial outlook, their quarrels and petty offences, the whippings and the torture of hard labour on the treadmill. Changes *were* on the way as will be seen from the chapters that follow.

Chapter Six

Enclosure of the Keymer Commons

Such a wealth of information is available about the enclosure of the Keymer commons that it has a chapter to itself. We make no apology for the large number of quotations from various sources; all are relevant to the main theme.

The 19th century witnessed momentous changes both nationally and locally. The country was rapidly shaking off the last remnants of the Middle Ages and, with the end of the long drawn-out Napoleonic wars and the social upheavals that followed, the demand for reform became ever more insistent. It was not just that the rising middle classes were agitating for votes: the industrial revolution was in full swing and other forces were at work. The great wave of enclosures, for example, that had been gathering momentum since Tudor times reached our own parish of Keymer early in 1827 when the first steps were taken towards the enclosure of its commons.

It should be understood that commons were 'owned' by the lord of the manor *and* his tenants, and therefore any proposal to enclose them meant that all tenants with rights of common could expect to receive a share roughly in proportion to their holdings. Thus a tenant with a 30-acre farm would normally expect to receive an allotment roughly twice as large as that of his neighbour who held only 15 acres. It did not always work out like that, as we shall see, but this in broad outline was how the enclosure procedure was expected to work.

By the early 19th century 'common rights' were mainly confined to grazing, though the taking of turf and bracken seems also to have been exercised from time to time.

The open arable fields had long been enclosed – certainly from Elizabethen times, possibly earlier. Where they had once existed, at the foot of the Downs in Clayton and Keymer, near Clayton Wickham and in the vicinity of Keymer Street, nothing now remained except one or two fields, mostly near the parish boundary with Hurstpierpoint, which, measuring about a furlong in length and with hedges forming an elongated curved S, reminded men of medieval farming practice.

The large field adjoining Clayton churchyard on gently rising ground on the lower slopes of the northern escarpment of the Downs was called Church Laine on the tithe map of 1838 and it seems that the original name clearly lingered on long after the strips of arable had been enclosed and indeed had, for the past 100 years at least, been incorporated into the lord's demesne. Similarly, right up to the middle of the 19th century, was a field a little to the south of Keymer Street called The Gores, a name almost certainly derived from an awkwardly shaped parcel of land unsuitable for communal cultivation. That is almost all there is, locally, to remind us of the former open fields, except a possible reference in the will of John Savage who held land in Clayton village and who died in 1596. In this his wife was to have among other things: '. . . her dwelling in my worst house for the term of her life with the use and occupation of the several pieces of land viz: one peece lying in Claiton fylde and ii combes and one piece lying below Clayton church'. Clayton field was once a communal field though it is difficult to say where it was situated. It could have been near to, or adjoining, John Savage's own land about a quarter of a mile east of the church; its exact location remains to be established.

Within the town boundary there remains just a hint of a possible survival of the open fields on Janes Lane Recreation ground. Here, if the relatively modern 'kink' in the road where parking of cars is now allowed is ignored, one can just make out the elongated S line previously mentioned. Moreover the distance from the present Valebridge Road to the ancient parish boundary is roughly a furlong (220 yards). Elsewhere the pattern of the layout of former fields, *and* those still existing, leads one to conclude that most had been wrested piecemeal from the virgin forest many centuries earlier, probably between Saxon times and, say, 1300.

Since there were no open arable fields within either Clayton or Keymer early in the 19th century, it follows that any mention of enclosure, or inclosure as it was properly called, was confined entirely to the commons of which there were four within the manor and parish of Keymer: St John's, Valebridge, part of Haywards Heath, and a long, narrow stretch of roadside waste called Broad Street Green, part of the present Keymer Road, which lay a little to the south of the turning into Folders Lane and which extended as far as the ancient track that leads via Oldlands to Ditchling.

St John's common in Keymer lay mainly to the east of London Road and covered an area bounded very roughly by London Road, Station Road, Mill Road and the western part of Leylands Road, with several more acres on either side of Freeks Lane. Here it was frequently called Freck common in the official records of the 17th and 18th centuries whilst the remainder of St John's common was often referred to as Starford, or Studford, even Sturford Heath. The map gives a rough guide to the extent of the Keymer commons and how they relate to the town today. The blank spaces represent the ancient enclosures mentioned in Chapter Two.

Proposals to enclose the Keymer commons had been made as early as July 1634,[1] when 18 tenants put their names to a document agreeing to the enclosure. The lords were to have one-third and 'the tenants the remainder, reserving sufficient ways and roads wherever they are used', which means presumably that the share of the lords was to be one-third of the gross area, whilst that of the tenants was to be two-thirds of the net area after land required for roads and other rights of way had been set aside. Among the signatories were John Rowe, who held Burgess Hill farm; Richard Dumbrell of Leylands farm, Nicholas Jenner of Sheddingdean and Roger Virgo of Bedelands farm. Nothing was done; but about three years later it was recorded:

> April 1637 . . . that at this court it is agreed by the lords and all whose tenants of this manor whose names are underwritten that St. John's common alias Sturford, and the waste called Valebridge common, and one parcel of common at Haywards Heath, shall be inclosed. And that the lords of this manor shall have a third part thereof in several to their use. And any tenant that ought to have common of pasture upon them shall have a fitt proportion or share of the other two parts according to the value of their tenancy that are holden of this manor.[2]

Only 12 signatures were obtained and, although these included John Rowe and Richard Michelborne (who at this time was buying up every acre he could lay his hands on), there were two or three men who held very little land indeed, which suggests that the majority of the tenants were not very impressed with the terms. Again nothing was done and there the matter rested for 80 years. In 1716 it was recorded:

> The lord and lady [William Northmore and Anne his wife] consented that the copyhold customary tenants might have liberty to enclose 2/3rds of the commons (in proportion to their holdings). The homage agreed that the lord and lady should have the other 1/3rd to hold and enclose provided the tenants were permitted to enclose and hold the 2/3rds.

On this occasion no attempt seems to have been made to secure the agreement of the tenants as a whole. The homage at this court consisted of seven substantial tenants but they do not appear to have been representative of many of those lower down the social scale.

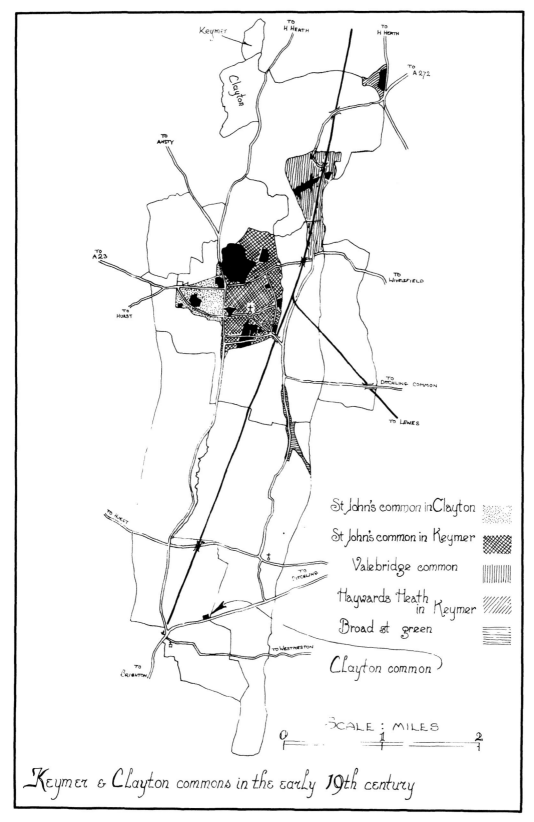

Keymer

TO H HEATH

TO H HEATH

Clayton

TO A 272

TO ANSTY

TO A 23

TO WIVELSFIELD

TO HURST

TO DITCHLING COMMON

TO LEWES

TO HURST

TO DITCHLING

St John's common in Clayton

St John's common in Keymer

Valebridge common

Haywards Heath in Keymer

Broad st green

Clayton common

TO WESTMESTON

TO BRIGHTON

SCALE : MILES

0   1   2

Keymer & Clayton commons in the early 19th century

Map 2

It has already been seen that manor courts went to some lengths to protect the tenants' rights in the 17th and 18th centuries. When John Rowe produced his classic record of the rents and customs of the manors of which he was steward, he recorded:

> The copiholders . . . have and ought to have in the common pastures, sheepedownes, commons and waste common of pasture for their sheepe and cattell respectively appendant to their lands and tenements and may take brakes [bracken] and bushes thence to be imployed on their copiholds. Such as surcharge the commons with greater number of cattell than by their tenure is justifiable, and all others that usurpe uppon the commons, their cattell ar to be impounded and themselves to be presented and amerced.[3]

There was to be little change until about the end of the 18th century. Until that time the commons were almost certainly regularly used by some of the tenants for grazing, and as a source of bedding for their animals when straw was in short supply. They probably provided a source of fuel, too, in the form of turves and dead wood that could be taken 'by hook or by crook'. If the withdrawal of these facilities resulted in hardship for the tenants it was little wonder that there was a singular lack of enthusiasm for the earlier schemes, particularly as the tenants' share was to be so small.

By the 1820s the situation had changed. The agrarian revolution of the late 18th century brought with it the four-course crop system which ensured a reliable supply of animal feed from turnips, swedes and mangolds now regularly grown as winter feed. The commons had never provided anything more than indifferent grazing from the coarse grass and tiny saplings which sprang up year after year. It was no longer economic for a couple of boys to drive a farmer's cattle or sheep several miles to spend a day on the common and then drive them back each night. The livestock could not have been left unattended for fear that they might stray, or fall into one of the pits left by those who had extracted clay for brickmaking and which had not been filled in; and there was always the possibility of rustling. No. The boys could be better employed on weeding, or scaring the birds from newly planted corn, or doing a few of the innumerable light jobs that arose in the course of each farming day.

Many of the larger landowners lived some miles from the commons; and it seems doubtful whether any of those manorial tenants living in Balcombe and Worth had driven their cattle south to graze there for many years. To them the commons were of no practical benefit whatever. We know that digging of clay was still going on and that it was to continue right up to the time of the enclosure. The two activities were not compatible. The farmer would have been concerned about possible injury to his animals; the clay diggers would have found inquisitive cattle or sheep just a nuisance.

Far-sighted businessmen who had bought land in the manor as an investment may have foreseen a need for future building sites. To them the loss of the commons meant very little. Their farms could still be let without common rights with no difficulty. But the potential value of building land near the important turnpike road was quite another matter. Here was a possible little gold mine if the demand for building sites 'took off'. They might even see the beginning of a new town in an area already a centre of activity for its parent parishes. The possibilities were tempting to say the least.

The upshot was the passing of the enclosure act, the preamble of which reads:

AN ACT

for
Inclosing Lands in the Manor and Parish of Keymer in the county of Sussex.
[Royal Assent 18 April 1828]

Whereas there are within the Manor and Parish of Keymer, in the county of Sussex certain Commons and Waste Lands;

And whereas the Reverend Henry Bayntun, clerk, is Lord of the Manor of Keymer, and as such is entitled to the soil of the said Commons and Waste Lands;

And whereas Caroline Chatfield, Stephen Bine, Thomas Dominick Whiteman, and other persons are owners and proprietors of Lands, Tenements and Hereditaments situate within the said Manor in the several parishes of Keymer, Balcombe and Worth, or some of them, in the said County of Sussex, and in respect of such Lands, Tenements and Hereditaments have Rights of Common of Pasture, or other Commonable Interests in the said Commons and Waste Lands;

And whereas the said Commons and Waste Lands yield but little profit, and in their present state are incapable of any considerable improvement, and it would be highly beneficial to the Persons interested therein if all Rights of Common of Pasture and other commonable rights and interests in and upon the said Commons and Waste Lands were extinguished, and the same Commons and Waste Lands were divided and inclosed, and specific Parts or Shares thereof allotted to the several Persons interested therein according to their respective rights and interests; BUT such extinguishment division and allotments cannot be effectually made without the authority of Parliament . . .

Thus commences one of the most important documents ever likely to affect Burgess Hill in its entire history. After references to the General Enclosure Acts of 1801 and 1821 which set out the clauses normally included in Enclosure Bills and acceptable to Parliament the Act then gives the names and addresses of the three commissioners appointed to 'divide, allot and enclose' the commons and waste lands and to 'carry the Act into execution'. The Commissioners were: George Smallpiece of Compton near Guildford, James Hodson of Birling in the parish of East Dean, Sussex, and Robert Clutton of Hartswood, Surrey. All were described as Land Agents.

The Act empowered the Commissioners to appoint a Clerk and a Surveyor and placed a 'ceiling' on the sums that could be claimed for expenses. Each commissioner and the clerk were to receive not more than three guineas (£3 3s. 0d.) per day; the surveyor was to have 1s.6d. an acre for 'surveying, measuring, mapping or planning' the land but could not claim more than two guineas a day.

Illegal enclosures and encroachments 'except such as have been enjoyed for twenty years . . . without interruption' were to be 'deemed part and parcel of the commons and waste lands to be divided, allotted, inclosed or disposed of. . .'. The commissioners were authorised to extinguish all rights of pasturage and common after giving formal notice in writing (such notice to be displayed on the outer doors of the parish churches of Keymer, Balcombe and Worth), and offenders could be fined up to 10s. for every horse or head of cattle, or 2s. 6d. for each sheep or swine, found on the commons after the agreed date. Existing roads and paths could also be stopped up, though not until new roads had been made.

Land could be sold to defray the cost of the enclosure either by auction or by private contract and the lord of the manor was to receive one-sixteenth of the land that remained after the sale(s) and after sufficient land had been allocated for public highways and roads.[4] Those receiving an allocation of common were required to 'inclose, hedge, ditch, bank and fence' it within such time as the commissioners should direct. All land sold or allocated to freeholders was to be freehold; that to copyholders to be copyhold.

The foregoing were a few of the main provisions in this detailed Act that covered some 40 pages of text with another 12 pages comprising a comprehensive index.

It will be seen that the Act specifically mentions three important tenants of the manor. Miss Chatfield was the youngest daughter of the Rev. Henry Chatfield, rector of Balcombe who died in 1819 and was a substantial copyholder of the manor with several hundred acres of land in Balcombe parish. Stephen Bine of Saddlescombe had the large holdings to the north of Burgess Hill later called the Rookery; whilst Thomas Dominick Whiteman held nearly 100 acres of land in Keymer village lying on either side of Keymer Street between Spittleford bridge and Keymer church.

W.E. Tate says: 'often the Bill carries on its final page the name of the local attorney who acted as clerk to the commissioners, sometimes also that of the London Parliamentary agents who in fact solicited it'.[5] It is interesting to note that on the final page of the Keymer Act are mentioned: 'Attree, Brighton – with Clutton, Carter and Fearon, Temple, Solicitors', and 'Doringtons and Jones, Parliamentary Agents, House of Commons'. As will be seen shortly, Mr. Attree of Brighton was appointed clerk to the commissioners; Clutton, Carter and Fearon were Miss Chatfield's solicitors. When in 1827 she lay critically ill in London she appointed John Fearon as one of her two attornies. The other was William Clutton of Buckland, Surrey, an estate agent who may have been related to Robert Clutton, one of the three Inclosure Commissioners who was also her cousin. There seems such a close link between all these names as to suggest that Miss Chatfield's solicitors were involved in the proposals that resulted in the passing of the Act from a very early stage supported, perhaps, by Messrs. Bine and Whiteman.

The very first reference noted came on 2 April 1827 when the following appeared in the *Sussex Advertiser*:

Manor of Keymer

Notice is hereby given that a Meeting of the Tenants of the said Manor and of Parties having rights of Commonage over the wastes hereof will be held at the *Talbot Inn*, Cuckfield on Friday the sixth day of April next at Twelve o'clock precisely for the purpose of taking into consideration and deciding on the propriety of applying to Parliament for an Act to *enclose the Waste Lands* of the said Manor.

Brighton.   ATTREE AND COOPER
March 24th 1827.   STEWARDS

It seems highly likely that this official announcement came as no surprise to the three major landowners all of whom may have previously been in touch with the stewards of the manor.

The Act also specified that the commissioners were to hold their meetings either within the manor or at some place not more than eight miles from 'Brooklands, the manor house of the manor'. This latter reference is interesting since it suggests that Brooklands was once the centre of the demesne lands formerly held by the lords as their home farm. In fact this was not so. The former demesne lands that lay near the foot of the Downs and in Hassocks had been sold about the end of the 16th century when Brooklands, together with Birchetts farm, containing in toto about 200 acres, was an important copyholding then held by Edmund Attree. The engrossed farm had been acquired in 1728 by Abraham Addams Esq. the then lord of the manor who was also living there at the time. Thereafter it seems to have been bought and sold each time the manor changed hands. Because of this it seems not unreasonable that a century later everyone concerned with the Enclosure Award should refer to Brooklands as the manor farm.

A rough minute book recording the business discussed at the meetings of the commissioners and interested parties has, remarkably, survived, along with the bank pass book detailing all receipts and payments; a printed account of the perambulation of the bounds of the manor and parish of Keymer; particulars of the first 20 parcels of land put up for auction and the clerk's note-book showing the response of the tenants to the proposal to enclose the commons. For the preservation of these important documents, now in the safe custody of E.S.R.O.,[6] we are indebted to the Sussex Archaeological Society and to Messrs. Howlett and Clarke of Brighton, the firm of solicitors of which Thomas Attree was senior partner in 1828. As Dr. Peter Brandon has pointed out in his article on the Keymer enclosures in S.N.Q. (vol. 15 November 1960, p.181 *et seq.*), the survival of these valuable working papers on an Enclosure Award is quite exceptional. Similarly, W.E. Tate refers to the existence of 4,200 separate awards in England and Wales but could trace only about 230 surviving minute books.[7] In this chapter the maximum use of these valuable primary sources will be made.

The first step, clearly, was to obtain the reactions of the tenants to the proposal to enclose, a task that nominally fell to the steward of the manor, Thomas Attree. About this time he had engaged the services of Somers Clarke, a young solicitor who had been articled to a London solicitor in 1819 when he was 17 years old. Admitted by the Master of the Rolls in January 1824 (there was no examination in those days) he came to Brighton nearly four years later to take up the post of managing clerk to Thomas Attree, at a salary of £100 p.a. with the further prospect of buying a partnership and acquiring the lordship of the manor of Atlingworth then held by Mr. Attree. To Somers Clarke fell much of the detailed work associated with the Enclosure although he is not mentioned in the extant working papers until May 1829, by which time he had acquired his partnership in the firm and had been appointed by the commissioners as joint clerk with Thomas Attree.

In 1887, when he was 85 years old and living at Torquay, his son suggested that he should set down his recollections connected with the family. This he did; and a remarkable manuscript, written on notepaper and divided into eight sections totalling some 260 pages and more, has been handed down through the family and is now preserved in E.S.R.O.[8]

Mr. Clarke takes us through the early part of his life in vivid prose. His father was a clergyman who moved to Plumpton in 1809 when the family stayed temporarily with the Turner family of Oldlands in Keymer (to whom they were related) whilst the parsonage was being refurbished. About this time there was a large encampment of soldiers at Lewes 'awaiting the arrival of Boney as the country people say'. The family seem to have been comfortably off but even so two cows were kept on the premises at Plumpton and when he was old enough it was one of the tasks of young Somers to feed them each morning before breakfast. On a never-to-be-forgotton visit to London in about 1811 his Uncle Theo, who lived at Putney, took him for a trip on the river where 'we went to London Bridge and saw water wheels in action and afterwards shot the bridge in a wherry'.

He gives a not very flattering description of one of the local residents, John Marten Cripps of Stantons, East Chiltington, who at that time owned property in the town, notably Burgess Hill farm and Lottmotts. He says: 'I remember him as a gouty old man with a big purple and pimply nose and he used to swear dreadfully'. He records that hay was still sold in the Haymarket in 1819 and that London at that time was poorly lit; 'no gas for lighting in London . . . all lighting was done with oil and very poor and dingy it was'.

Travel was by stagecoach and '. . . all coaches between London and the south of England stopped at the Elephant and Castle and I have seen as many as twenty there at once'. He once took a coach from the Elephant and Castle to *Friars Oak* in Clayton and from there walked through Keymer, Ditchling and Westmeston in the middle of a dark, wintry night to inform his parents of the illness of their son Samuel in London. How much easier it was to be a few decades later when he would have been able to telegraph his parents at Plumpton, then less than two hours away from London by train. He also records seeing the last man in the country ever to be set in the pillory where 'with both hands and head confined he was subjected to attack by rotten eggs, filth and garbage . . . his offence was perjury . . . I also saw the last man whipped in public . . . he was tied to a cart's tail and lashed round Covent Garden market making the blood flow. His offence had been stealing in the market'.

This then, in brief outline, was the London that Somers Clarke left in late 1827 when he returned to his beloved Sussex to take up his new post. He could have been in Brighton only a few weeks before he was given considerable responsibility in connection with the Inclosure Award, about which he says:

> One of the clients of the firm was the Rev. Henry Bayntun lord of the manor of Keymer who owned the manor farm, Brooklands, and a good deal more property in Keymer and Clayton. There were two commons in the manor: St. John's or St. Jones's as it was called by the country folk, and

Valebridge both in Keymer parish,[9] but a great proportion of the copyholds were in Balcombe and belonged to the Chatfields ... These copyholds were fineable at will and a part of the treaty with the Chatfields was enfranchisement in lieu of allotments on the waste.[10]

One thing was to get the consent in writing of all the copyhold tenants who lay far and wide. Mr. Attree lent me his pony for the work which lasted some days some [properties] lying as far off as Copthorne. It had to be done in person to prove the signatures and last of all the signature of the lord of the manor who lived at Devizes. I went there for the purpose and found him residing in a handsome house, a widower with three or four daughters grown up who were ready to devour me and were supposed to be Ladies of Fortune as Mr. Bayntun had married a lady from Spy Park near Devizes with a fortune as reported of £90,000,[11] but I did not bite. The private Act was passed ... George Smallpiece of Guildford a surveyor and land steward; Robert Clutton a cousin of the Chatfields of the same calling, and James Hodson of Birling near Eastbourne were the commissioners named in the Act to hear the claims of the copyhold tenants for shares, or allotments as they were called, of the wasteland. One thing was ascertaining the boundaries of the manor which was done on foot and great fun. The commissioners sat at the *King's Head* in Cuckfield for several days together and I with them and before the business was concluded I became Mr. Attree's partner and we were joint clerks to the Inclosure.

We are indebted to Mr. Clarke for this and other information about the lord of the manor at that time, the Rev. Henry Bayntun. The official records frequently give the names of lords (and ladies) of the various manors, sometimes their occupation and place of residence but as a general rule they appear as shadowy figures; always there but without any real substance. It is therefore worth continuing with another extract from Mr. Clarke's narrative:

Mr. Bayntun had several sons. The eldest, Captain Bayntun, contested Goole which cost his father more than £20,000 but he gained the election. Another was in the War Office who was the only decent one. They all pulled their father's pocket and at last to get rid of them he gave each £3,000 on the understanding that they were to have no more. He got into other hands than ours and bought a government annuity of £400 and mortgaged Brooklands and the manor through some London solicitors and I and Mr. McWhinnie [a colleague and later a partner] bought the manor of the mortgagers. After McWhinnie's death I bought his half of his widow as I did his half of Atlingworth manor. Two of the sons pestered me afterwards about the purchase alleging that we had bought the manor of our own client and given an inadequate sum for it which was altogether untrue and at last I told them if they pestered me any more I would proceed against them criminal [sic] for attempt at extortion. When I built my last lean-to conservatory at Valebridge Garden, Voller my then gardner told me that some of the materials were brought in a fly from Haywards Heath and the driver asked about me and the manor and said he was the grandson of old Henry Bayntun ... Major Bayntun, a brother of Henry, had an estate in Clayton [now Woodfield Lodge in Isaacs Lane] ... both families of the Bayntuns have, I believe, come utterly to grief.

On 22 October 1827 a second notice appeared in the local paper to the effect that application would be made to Parliament in the coming session for a Bill to enclose the Keymer commons and to have them exonerated from the payment of tithes. Interested parties were given the opportunity to learn of the contents of the draft Bill at a meeting to be held at the *King's Head*, St John's Common on 22 February 1828.

The next step was the presentation of a Petition to the House of Commons 'praying that leave may be granted to bring in a Bill' – in our case for the enclosing of the Keymer Commons. A full transcript of the presenting of the Petition as recorded in the House of Commons Journals is as follows:

11 February 1828.

A Petition of the Lord of the Manor of Keymer, in the County of Sussex, and other Proprietors of estates having rights of common in or over the wastes or commonable lands within the said manor was presented and read; setting forth, That there are within the said parish and manor divers Commons, Heaths and Wastelands or Grounds which might be improved, if enclosed, and praying, That leave may be given to bring in a Bill for the same.

Ordered That leave be given to bring in a Bill accordingly: And that Mr. Curteis and Mr. Burrell do prepare and bring it in.[12]

There is no further reference to Mr. Burrell and it took Mr. Curteis until 10 March to present the Bill, which was then given a formal first reading and ordered to be read for the second time. This was done on 14 March and on the afternoon of the same day the Committee met in the Speaker's chamber to consider the Bill in detail.

It should be noted that Bills of this nature did not pass through both Houses of Parliament 'on the nod'; they were subject to the same detailed scrutiny as other Bills. Two weeks later the report stage had been reached and on 27 March:

Mr. Curteis from the Committee on the Bill for inclosing lands in the Manor and Parish of Keymer . . . [reported] That Standing Orders relative to Bills of Inclosure had been complied with; and that they had examined the allegations of the Bill and found the same to be true; and that the parties concerned had given their consent to the Bill to the satisfaction of the Committee; and that they had gone through the Bill and made several Amendments thereunto; and the Amendments were read and agreed to by the House.
Ordered That the Bill with the Amendments be ingrossed.

The Bill was read a third time on 28 March when it was ordered 'that Mr. Curteis do carry the Bill to the Lords and desire their concurrence'.[13] The 3rd and 18th of April witnessed one of those delightful, ancient customs once so beloved of visitors to the House of Commons from countries abroad when the official records contained the following entries:

3 April 1828. A message from the Lords by Mr. Stratford and Mr. Harvey:-
'Mr. Speaker the Lords have agreed to the several Bills following without any Amendment viz:-
[here followed details of other Bills] . . . a Bill intituled An Act for inclosing Lands in the Manor and Parish of Keymer in the County of Sussex'. And then the Messengers withdrew.

The final action came on 18 April when the Commons were informed that the Royal Assent had been given to 'our' Bill along with that for five others. The entry in the official records reads:

A message by Mr. Quarme, Yeoman Usher of the Black Rod:
'Mr. Speaker
The Lords, authorized by virtue of His Majesty's Commission for declaring His Royal Assent to several Acts agreed upon by both Houses, do desire the immediate attention of this Honourable House in the House of Peers, to hear the Commission read'.
Accordingly Mr. Speaker with the House went up to the House of Peers: and being returned:-
Mr. Speaker reported that the House at the desire of the Lords, authorized by virtue of His Majesty's Commission, had been at the House of Peers where a Commission under the Great Seal was read, giving, declaring and notifying the Royal Assent to the several Public and Private Bills therein mentioned; and that the Lords thereby authorized, had declared the Royal Assent to the said Bills which Bills are as followeth:-
[details of other Acts]
An Act for inclosing Lands of the Manor and Parish of Keymer in the County of Sussex.

This was the very last stage in an operation that had taken only marginally more than two calendar months from the time the petition was presented.

As previously suggested, the initiative for presenting the petition seems to have come jointly from Clutton, Carter and Fearon, and Thomas Attree then steward of the manor, probably after some prompting by the three major copyholders – Bine, Whiteman and Miss Chatfield. The fact that Somers Clarke made a special journey to Devizes to see the lord of the manor suggests either that Rev. Henry Bayntun had given his blessing to the proposal by letter and only his formal signature was needed to be added to the petition, or that he had not been consulted earlier and that he was now presented with a list of tenants, the majority of whom were in favour of the proposal.

As Mr. Clarke has hinted in his 'Recollections', the task of obtaining the consent of the tenants was a formidable one. His note book shows that in fact he made two visits to each tenant; the first at the end of January 1828 to collect signatures for the petition; the second, about a month later to get signatures to the consent Bill. The list contained the names and addresses of all copyhold tenants, including cottagers, and a few freeholders whose former copyholdings had been enfranchised with common rights reserved. Among these latter were Sheddingdean farm and two or three holdings outside the town boundary. Many of the tenants lived outside the boundaries of both the parish and the manor which extended as far north as Copthorne. Whether Somers Clarke made arrangements to meet them on the site of their holdings or visited them at their homes is not stated; but since the tenants' home addresses were as far apart as London and Maidenhead, Tunbridge Wells and Sompting he must have met them, or their lessees acting for them, within the manor. Obtaining signatures for the petition was accomplished in only five working days, an impossible time-table if he had gone to London to interview three people and to Tunbridge Wells and Sompting to see two others. The journey to Maidenhead and back, too, would have taken more than one day and most of these visits would have involved him in an overnight stop.

In the event, 27 of the 59 tenants named on the list signed the petition: seven were described as neuter, which means that they did not much care one way or the other. Of the remainder, some were not at home and do not seem to have been re-visited. There were no observations against the names of: Miss Chatfield, a tenant with property in Worth, and of 'Mark Lane' who owned a former small encroachment on Haywards Heath. The Rev. Henry Halliwell, rector of Clayton-cum-Keymer, who then held Grove farm in Station Road with about 16 acres of land (on condition that he preached a sermon in Clayton church on Ascension Day each year), signed the petition, but Thomas Turner one of the trustees of these premises had died and Mr. Clarke did not apparently then know the name of his successor or indeed of Turner's fellow trustee. In any event the office staff were wrong to include both the rector and the trustees for the same property.

Mr. John Marten Cripps refused to sign the petition and a month later similarly declined to sign the consent bill. He was not alone: Thomas Broomfield of Bedelands, Mrs. Broomfield of Grovelands, John Hodson who had claimed for a small part of Ockley manor which he held in trust and was not entitled to an allocation anyway, all expressed themselves as being against enclosure. Thomas Welfare Ford who held Valebridge mill and other premises in Burgess Hill signed the petition but said next month that whilst he consented to the enclosure 'he does not like to sign the consent bill because of the expense' [connected with the fencing of any possible allotments]. Elizabeth Dann who owned a cottage and five acres of land in Freeks Lane was then living at Dunkirk and her affairs were being handled by a Mr. Willard of Lewes who, on her behalf, said that he would not oppose enclosure 'but does not like to sign'. Old William Newnham, owner of Whitehouse farm and other premises in Balcombe, but living at West Hill, Ardingly, was then aged 84 and in bed when Mr. Clarke called. He, it seems, was in favour of enclosure but 'wished his son to sign for him but did not like to sign himself'. William Taylor, the brickmaker (see page 53) gave his assent to the bill insofar as his own property was concerned 'but does not wish to sign but hopes to have first offer of the clay veins'. Interviewed on behalf of Sarah Taylor his wife, who held Blackhouse farm in her own right, he said 'he would not sign now but would wait and see what his neighbours did'. Henry Marten, who held Little Burgess Hill farm, wanted time to consider before he signed the petition, but later did sign the consent bill. John Gainsford, who held just over a quarter of an acre of land previously part of Grovelands, readily signed the petition (and later the consent bill) but boldly claimed an allotment for his windmill on St John's common, which had been conveyed to a former lord of the manor and had never been a copyholding – the Commissioners quite rightly later rejected his claim in respect of the mill. The name of Mrs. Elizabeth Bennett who held Woodwards also appeared in the list of tenants and, although her death had been recorded in the court records less than a year earlier,[14] Mr. Clarke recorded: 'no such person known or recollected in Keymer'. The most poignant observation was made as a result of Mr. Clarke's visit to the *King's Head Inn* then owned by William Pagden who had 'hanged himself since the last court – left a family – Mr. Tamplin manages the estate and Pagden's youngest son is customary heir – the property is on mortgage . . .'. Finally there was Richard Stringer of Brighton who owned Leylands farm; he agreed to the enclosure and gave his verbal assent to the bill but stubbornly refused to sign either.

Such was Somer Clarke's introduction to the firm that was later to include his name and to the initial task of getting the enclosure under way. In order to alert interested parties to the various stages in the Enclosure procedure a number of public announcements was made in the *Sussex Advertiser*. The first, which appeared in the issue dated 5 May 1828,[15] reads:

Keymer Inclosure

Notice is hereby given that the Commissioners nominated and appointed by the Act of Parliament passed in the ninth year of the reign of his present Majesty King George the Fourth, for inclosing lands in the manor and parish of Keymer in the county of Sussex will hold their first meeting at the *TALBOT INN* Cuckfield on Friday the 16th day of May instant at eleven of the clock in the forenoon. Dated the 3rd of May 1828.

The first meeting was in fact held at the *Talbot*, Cuckfield, barely a month after the Bill had been given the Royal Assent. Here the Commissioners took the oath, as prescribed in the Act, and immediately appointed as Clerk Thomas Attree the Brighton solicitor previously mentioned, and a surveyor, Henry Walter of Bray, Berks. who was ordered 'to produce such maps and plans as would be necessary'. A second advertisement was to be inserted in the *Sussex Advertiser* inviting interested parties to submit their claims before the next meeting arranged for 4 June.

The advertisement duly appeared and gave detailed instructions as to the form in which claims were to be submitted. All persons who had any claim or common or other rights to, or in the lands to be inclosed: '. . . are required to deliver to us [the Commissioners] an account or schedule in writing, signed by such persons, or their respective claims and therein describe the property in respect whereof they claim . . . with the names of the persons in actual possession thereof and the particular computed quantities of the same respectively, and of what nature and extent such right is, and . . . distinguishing the freehold from the copyhold or leasehold, And . . . to produce any maps or plans in their possession . . . And we [the Commissioners] do hereby give notice that at such meeting a Banker or other such person or persons as shall be approved by a majority, in value, of the Proprietors then present will be appointed to receive all monies to be raised under or by virtue of the powers contained in the said Act'.

In the event 34 people submitted claims ranging from Caroline Chatfield, with her several hundred acres in Balcombe, to John Gainsford with his quarter of an acre of land in Burgess Hill. Hall, West and Borrer of the Union Bank Brighton were appointed Bankers.

The *Talbot Inn* was apparently not suitable for this type of meeting, some of which, including the one held on 4 June, attracted large numbers of people. It was decided therefore that the June meeting and all meetings thereafter would be held at the *King's Head*, Cuckfield,[16] which was able to provide more adequate facilities.

A detailed study of the minutes of the 16 meetings, some of which extended over three days, shows that the proceedings were very business-like and that the Commissioners acted fairly without fear or favour. Indeed, one cannot escape the impression that one or more, perhaps all, had acted in a similar capacity before.

One of the first priorities was that of securing sufficient cash to meet the cost of the Enclosure. Initially, between 160 and 170 acres were offered for sale by auction by 'Mr. Creasy', a Brighton auctioneer, at the *King's Head*, Cuckfield, on 17 September 1828. To attract potential buyers the particulars included the following interesting description of the 20 lots to be sold on St John's and Valebridge commons:

> This property is situated in a central part of the county of Sussex; commanding rich and extensive views; surrounded by a finely wooded and highly cultivated country, abounding with game of all descriptions, and possessing every facility for the diversions of hunting, shooting and fishing; within a distance of four miles from Cuckfield, ten from Brighton, fourteen from Lewes and Horsham (to which market towns there are good turnpike roads) and 42 from London. Several of the lots on St. John's common have been chosen with a view to afford desirable scites [sic] for building and consist of various quantities of land most eligibly situated, fronting and adjoining the turnpike road from Brighton, through Cuckfield to London. The Clay Veins on this Common are very extensive and afford a plentiful supply of brick earth of a superior quality, which has for some time past been dug by Messrs. Taylor and Shaw, brickmakers, by permission of the Lord and Tenants of the Manor of Keymer, for which an annual compensation has been paid. This permission now no longer exists, and the purchaser will be entitled to the exclusive right of digging. Valebridge common is divided by an extensive piece of water,[17] covering several acres, down to which the land gradually declines, forming an agreeable slope, calculated in all respects for the erection of Villas.

Mr. Creasy then goes on to assure potential buyers that they would be put to no expense in investigating the title as the Act of Parliament formed a complete title in itself.

The auctioneer was to some extent hedging his bets in that he was claiming that the sites were eminently suitable both as prime building land *and* a source of raw materials for the local clay based industries. He (and the Commissioners) were probably hoping to attract well-to-do Brighton businessmen anxious to build new houses for themselves in new and attractive surroundings, and if this failed to concentrate on those interested in the clay.

Later, more lots were put up for sale and, although a few purchasers lived in Brighton, some of them were also local landowners and few, if any, built houses on the plots they acquired. Charles Bayntun of Brighthelmstone, for example, who bought five acres in Freeks Lane, held a copyhold cottage in Isaacs Lane adjoining his 75-acre farm called Diggons, now the site of Woodfield Lodge. Richard Stringer, also of Brighton, who bought six and a half acres in what was later to become Leylands Road, owned Leylands farm and for an outlay of £69 16s. 0d. wisely took the opportunity to increase the size of his former 30-acre holding. Thomas Packham, although described in the Award as 'of Brighton' was in fact the owner of Smeeds; the quarter acre plot (no. 76 on the Award) that he purchased for the sum of £5 5s. 0d. was later given by him as the site for the first church to be built in Burgess Hill.[18] William King and William Attree, both of Brighton, paid £630 for 33 acres in the vicinity of lower Church Road; and part of this site was later to become St John's park.

The land offered for sale on Valebridge common lay partly to the south of the old mill pond, extending to Jane's Lane, and partly either side of Rocky Lane near where the trains from London to the south coast now thunder over the road leading to Haywards Heath. The former was purchased by W.H. Bacchus then living at Theobalds farm; the latter by Stephen Bine to add to his extensive holding now called the Rookery. No part of Valebridge common became the site for the villas the auctioneer had in mind.

The price paid for the sites varied enormously. So anxious were the brickmaking Norman brothers to secure their new site adjoining the turnpike road that they were prepared to pay about £58 an acre for the eight-and-a-half acres on offer. The seven-and-three-quarter acres adjoining it to the north, and later forming part of the southern boundary of lower Church Road, were knocked down to a Brighton businessman for the comparatively ridiculous sum of £125 – roughly £16 an acre. John Gainsford, then the owner of the post mill in Mill Road, purchased initially over $14\frac{1}{2}$ acres of land bounded by Mill Road and Leylands Road for £260 – about £18 an acre. He later added to this by acquiring by private treaty more land adjoining at a cost of £16 an acre. Two plots almost opposite the *King's Head* – one slighly more, the other a little less than half an acre – fetched £29 and £26 respectively; whilst on the same (western) side of the London Road and south of West Street a rectangular roadside plot containing about seven-eighths of an acre was snapped up by Thomas Attree for £48 (i.e. about £55 an acre). The five-and-a-half-acre plot on the corner of London Road and Station Road was purchased by William Shaw who paid roughly £51 10s. 0d. an acre for the site which was to be known first as Shaw's brickworks and later as 'Gravetts'.[19]

Away from the turnpike road some 88 acres were eventually sold at prices ranging between £17 and £20 an acre. The sale allotments on St John's common covered most of an area bounded by London Road, Leylands Road, Mill Road and Station Road – a substantial proportion of St John's common as a whole. William Taylor negotiated the purchase of 13 acres of land he wanted for clay (bounded roughly by Station Road, and parts of Mill Road and the present Church Road) for £420 – about £32 10s. 0d. an acre; and later added to this by acquiring a further three-and-three-quarter acres (almost all adjoining his 13 acres) at a cost of about £20 an acre. By so doing he overstretched himself financially and was obliged to apply for extra time in which to find the purchase money, permission that was readily given by the Commissioners.

At the meeting held on 4 June 1828 it was decided that the Commissioners would perambulate the boundaries of the manor of Keymer. A date of 25 June was agreed and the party arranged to meet at the *King's Head* on St John's common. It was ordered: 'that the clerk do cause notice in writing to be given to the lords of the manors adjoining the said manor of Keymer of the intentions of the Commissioners to perambulate such boundaries'. As noted earlier the Commissioners, accompanied by Mr. Somers Clarke, did the whole exercise on foot and although it was described as 'great fun' it represented a very long walk indeed – little short of 40 miles. It would not have been great fun on a bleak February day when cold, blustery winds and heavy showers were sweeping over the Downs; or when a north wind was bringing snow showers down from the Weald. In the event, it is not surprising that the task took three days to complete. It was recorded that the 'boundaries adjacent to the house of Captain Bacchus [of Theobalds] where an encroachment had been made were trodden by (blank) Deering and Thomas Ford who were present when the boundaries were last trodden'. It was important to determine whether any illegal encroachments had been made and continued within the previous 20 years as specified in the Act. It so happened that the Commissioners were entirely satisfied that no unauthorised encroachment had been established on this or any other part of the commons.

Two weeks later, on 7 July, the surveyor, H. Walter, produced a printed report describing in great detail the route that had been taken. The walk began in Isaacs Lane a little to the north of Woodfield Lodge and covered the entire parish including Franklands, New Close and Hassocks farms, two farms in Hassocks called Newlands and Westbrooks, Lodge farm and Whitelands, all former demesne lands once owned by the lord. Ockley manor was also included as it was a sub-infeudation of the manor of Keymer paying an annual rent of three barbed arrows,[20] though it is doubtful whether these were ever demanded or paid, any more than a peppercorn is today.

It was said earlier that the boundary between Clayton and Keymer snaked across the present London Road and that with a 19th-century O.S. map and a little patience one could still trace it today. It is also clearly shown on the extract from the enclosure map (plate 18) which also illustrates some of the allocations in the London Road and St John's park area.

The following extract from the surveyor's report is also of interest to those attempting to trace the old boundaries. The party has just left: 'the old inclosures of Sheddendean and

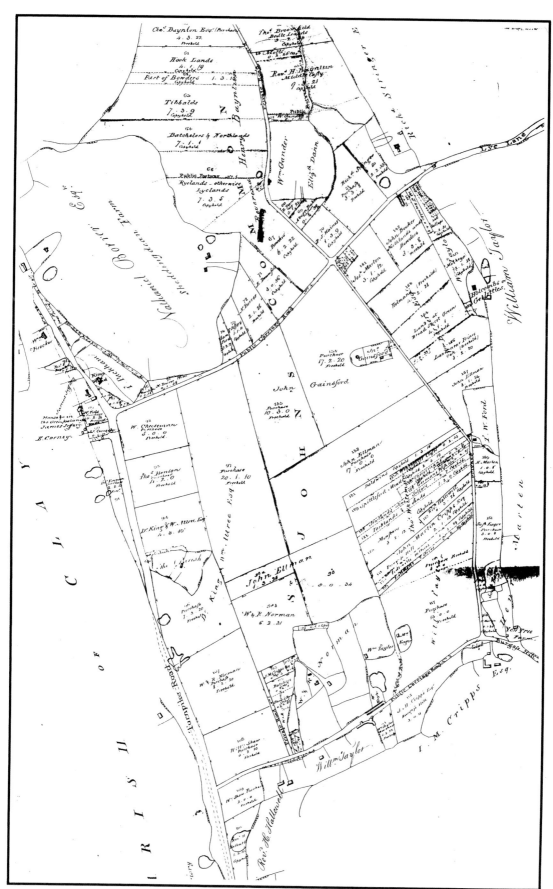

18. An extract from the Keymer Enclosure Map of 1828.

Chapel lands [Sheddingdean and Chapel farms] to the south eastern corner of a hovel belonging to Thomas Ford at the corner of St. John's Common'. They then go:

> obliquely across the turnpike road to a cross on the knoll by Fair Green;[21] then southwardly to and across the garden of William Brooker[22] leaving the house on the right and straight across the orchard and a pond called Fairplace pond,[23] to a boundary stone on the waste. From thence in the same direction into and over an orchard of James Jeffery,[24] and a garden of John Marten,[25] into the common close to a palisade fence in front of the cottage occupied by the said James Jeffery,[26] and following the fence and the edge of the ditch of the meadow adjoining and passing close to the front of the house of Mrs. Corney,[27] and including all the front court to a cross on the pales on the south side; and from thence in a straight line to a cross by Penny Royal pond, and by several other crosses following the course of an old bank obliquely across the said turnpike road to another boundary stone . . .

This small part of the perambulation extends only from Dunstall Avenue to the present Methodist church. The report continues in the same vein for the whole of the parish including Burnt House farm now in Cuckfield but then a detached part of Keymer. Manorial holdings in Balcombe and Worth were similarly described. Field names were sometimes given and the names of owners and occupiers are frequently mentioned e.g.: 'to the south-west corner of a meadow belonging to Eliz. Broomfield in the occupation of Edward Maris'.[28] There could have been no doubt in anyone's mind as to where the boundaries lay, and having been published and not subsequently challenged, they were thereafter quoted and accepted as officially established.

At the September meeting the attorney for Mrs. Philadelphia Farncombe, owner of Green farm in Keymer Road, questioned 'whether Broad Street Green was in fact waste of the manor at all and if it were it was waste of the manor of Ockley not Keymer, and furthermore the Green was part of the public highway'. He also claimed that tenants of the manor of Ockley invariably turned out their animals on Broad Street Green and that the proprietor of Green farm paid a quit rent to the lord of the manor of Keymer . . . and that litter and rushes had been cut by the owners of Green farm and Ockley and others . . . and that Green farm was sold on 28 June 1797 with rights of pasturage over the Green. It was recorded in the minutes that 'the Commissioners found the objections were not well founded; that the matter had been decided by the publication of the boundaries and highways *without appeal* and that Broad Street Green was to be considered as part of the land to be inclosed'. Not only that, but when the Award was finally made Mrs. Farncombe received no allocation of the waste in respect of her farm (variously called Backwick, Bakewick, Buckwick and then Green farm) despite her claim that the sale in June 1797 included common rights. To add to her existing holding she was obliged to purchase 10 acres for which she paid £200.

Not all those who claimed an allocation of common were successful. The following are a few typical examples of those rejected:

Samuel Brent for the Ashenground, now Catts Wood in Haywards Heath. This was a fair claim. The premises had once been a copyholding but had been enfranchised in 1676, and presumably were later found to be *without* common rights.

Francis Scawen Blunt, Esq. for Crabbetts in Worth. Crabbetts, or Crabbett Park, was an important freehold paying an annual rent of 3s. to the lord of the manor. It seems doubtful whether Mr. Blunt really expected to be given an allocation.

Stephen Marten for Inholmes, later Birchwood farm. He admitted from the outset that he was not sure whether, as a freeholder, he was entitled to an allocation and was probably neither surprised nor disappointed when his tentative application was turned down.

Richard Stringer for Cants farm. Mr. Stringer was also owner of Leylands farm for which he received an allocation of almost three-and-three-quarter acres. His claim for Cants, which also included Frankbarrow (both in Junction Road), must have been a 'try on'. Cants had once been a freeholding paying a manorial rent of 10s. p.a. and had never enjoyed rights of common.

On the other hand several people were given an allocation when they really had questionable rights. The Norman brothers, for example, submitted a claim in respect of 'nine acres of land called Butchers and four other acres' and in support thereof 'produced an abstract of title by which it appeared that part of these lands had been enclosed for more than 90 years and the other part for more than 70 years and stated that they had evidence of exercising rights of common in respect of these lands as far back as the memory of man could reach'. As previously noted,[29] the nine acres (originally described as 10 acres) had been taken in from the waste during the Commonwealth. A year after the site had been acquired in 1703 by Rev. Josiah Povey, rector of Telescombe, Mr. Povey 'acknowledged that he had no common pasture for his sheep on the waste of the manor as a right and disclaimed all right'.[30] Whether this disclaimer applied only to sheep and not to other animals is not clear but the clerk in his other role as steward of the manor should have been alerted to a possible dubious claim. There is no evidence that there were any similar restrictions on the use of common by the owner of the four acres adjoining and now (in 1828) held by William and Richard Norman.

Strictly speaking, these two small properties were 'cottage' holdings paying a fixed heriot and fine and as such, along with many others, were not entitled to an allocation. Time and again the Keymer court officials stressed that only copyholders *not being cottagers* had rights of common; yet this seems to have been ignored by the Commissioners when allocations were finally made, probably because of an oversight by the clerk/steward. As stated earlier, freeholders of former copyholdings that retained rights of pasture qualified for an allocation, yet one cannot feel entirely happy with the claim by the lord of the manor in respect of Brooklands farm. Here it is recorded that Mr. Attree, in support of the lord's claim, examined as witnesses: Mary Shepherd, John Geering and John Comber and the Commissioners 'on hearing the evidence were of the opinion that the exercise of rights of pasturage over the commons was clearly proved and decided in favour of the lord's claim accordingly'. Unfortunately the evidence, though taken down at the time, has not survived so a reappraisal of the conclusions cannot now be made even if, a century and a half later, there would be any point in so doing. It must be assumed that the former copyholding retained its rights of common when it was acquired in 1728 and became a freeholding.

At the meeting held on 22 and 23 July 1828 the Commissioners heard, in addition to the above, a few other objections tabled by Thomas Dominick Whiteman, Stephen Bine and Mr. Fearon on behalf of Miss Chatfield. Some of the premises concerned were cottages that had been erected illegally on the commons in the 17th century; among them was the site of the cottage and the potters kilns from which Sampson Bagnall and his family were so ignominiously ejected in 1769. Claims in respect of two cottages and a few acres of land in Freeks Lane were also challenged, as were claims for two of the cottages used as poor houses. But in the end all were given allocations of common.

By the end of July the proposed layout of the new roads had been advertised in the *Sussex Advertiser* and posted on the door of Keymer church. The surveyor was instructed to search the commons that were to be enclosed, and elsewhere in the neighbourhood, for suitable materials that would be of use in making roads. This he did, and later two acres on Valebridge common were set aside for the use of the surveyor of highways for the parish of Keymer with the right to dig sand and gravel for road repairs.

Objections to the new roads were heard by the Commissioners on 19 August after which, with the concurrence of two magistrates acting for the county of Sussex, they confirmed the public roads and ordered the stopping up of 'old and accustomed' roadways and paths over the commons. Notice was also given that all rights of pasturage and other common rights were to be extinguished from 1 December 1828.

William Taylor and William Shaw, the two brickmakers who had previously held licences from the manor court to dig clay, had already been ordered 'to desist from digging brick earth on St. John's common' but, on presenting a petition to the Commissioners seeking leave to continue, a licence was granted 'to 20 October next'. Extension of the licence was typical of the reasonable and understanding attitude taken by the Commissioners throughout the whole undertaking. When, in March 1829, a petition was presented by several people from Keymer and the nearby neighbourhood requesting that certain footpaths over the common (St John's) might be kept open, it was received very sympathetically by the Commissioners who by then could do very little about it. They found upon inspection that the footpaths the local people wanted to retain lay across lands sold by them at public auction but 'they allowed that the lack of footpaths was a public inconvenience'.

Tenders for the construction of the new roads were invited in August 1828 by way of the following advertisement in the *Sussex Advertiser*:[32]

Keymer Inclosure

To roadmakers and others.

Any persons desirous of contracting to form and make the NEW ROADS over Saint John's and Vale-bridge Commons and Broad Street Green are directed to send SEALED TENDERS for each road separately addressed to the Commissioners for the said Inclosure at the *King's Head Inn*, Cuckfield on or before eleven o'clock on Wednesday the 17th day of September next.

A specification may be seen and particulars known on application to Mr. Hillman at Mr. Mare's cottage on St. John's common.

Several tenders were received and considered by the Commissioners. John Soden was awarded the contract for making three roads on St John's common: from Burgess Hill Lane westwards to the turnpike road [later Station Road]; westwards from the turnpike road towards West Street [the short stretch of road in West Street as far as the Clayton boundary] and eastwards from the turnpike road towards Lye Lane [the present Leylands Road] where it ran across the common.

The second contract went to Stephen Putland for two roads: northwards from Lye Lane to Rocky Lane [the present Valebridge Road and the part of Rocky Lane which crossed Valebridge common] and eastwards from Valebridge common towards Oat Hall Lane [the present Janes Lane as far as the Ditchling boundary]. It seems reasonably certain that Soden's contract also included the making up of the former track across Broad Street Green, and that Putland was instructed to bring up to standard the short stretch of road at the top of Rocky Lane where it crossed part of Haywards Heath. According to the minute book and the Bank pass book these were the only two road contractors involved.

By the middle of May 1829 this work, which included bridges over watercourses as well as roads, had been completed, and after inspection by the Commissioners the clerk was ordered to procure the attendance of two Justices of the Peace on 23 June at Cuckfield to certify that the roads had been duly formed and completed.[33] As it happened the clerk could procure the attendance of only one J.P. in June. He inspected the roads on both commons and expressed himself satisfied, but said he could not *himself* issue the necessary certificate.

Six weeks later the roads had still not been passed by the magistrates and the Commissioners were getting worried, for this was the first real setback they had experienced. In an endeavour to speed up the process they engaged the services of Robert Wood, a road surveyor from Lindfield, to inspect the roads and to give evidence at a special session of the magistrates should they [the justices] decide not to inspect the roads in person. A day or two later, on 7 August, the special session was held at Cuckfield and the Commissioners accompanied Sir Henry Ryecroft, knight, and Francis Scawen Blunt Esq. (the two J.P.s) over the new public carriage roads and highways on both commons, and afterwards an order was made declaring that the said roads and highways were duly formed and completed.

At the same time John Soden applied to the Commissioners for payment of an account for work he had had to do since completing his contract; work that he claimed was necessary in consequence of the difficulty in obtaining the magistrates' certificate. There had been a delay of only about six weeks, yet the Commissioners after inspecting Soden's account *and reducing it*, allowed him an additional £45 4s. 2d. for the extra work that had been required. It does not say much for the condition of the new roads if they had deteriorated to that extent in so short a time!

Costs continued to mount and in March 1829 it was found that yet more land would have to be sold. The Award could not be finalised until it was known just how much land would remain after the sales had been completed. These plots were all situated well away from the turnpike road; all fetched about £16 or £17 an acre, and all were sold by private treaty.

Early in March 1829 several people made application in writing to the Commissioners, anxious to know where their allocations were to be, and once the additional money required had been raised by the sale of the extra land the way was clear for the Commissioners to complete the work of dividing up what remained. The final settlement of allotments was presented at a meeting held on 26-28 March when the surveyor was ordered to proceed with the preparation of detailed plans. At the same time the clerk was instructed to prepare 'with all despatch' a draft award. Both plans and draft were to be ready before the next meeting fixed for 11 May. This was done; the draft was read by the Commissioners and a meeting of the interested parties was arranged for 25 June at which the draft was read to them.

In the normal way one would reasonably expect that this was virtually the end of the matter. In fact, this was not so. In addition to the delay in obtaining the magistrates' agreement to the roads, as mentioned above, numerous minor problems remained to be settled. John Ellman, the well-known Sussex sheep breeder, for example, who purchased altogether about 30 acres about half of which was later to form part of the southern boundary of Park Road, complained to the Commissioners that John Gainsford, his neighbour to the north, had cut his ditch too narrow. Gainsford was ordered to make it four feet wide within the next three months. Similarly, the new owner of land on the north-eastern corner of London Road and Leylands Road, later to become the site of St John's house, had failed to form a proper ditch at all. He, too, was given until Michaelmas next (three months ahead) to put the matter right.

Then there was the task of getting in the money due on allotments sold. A Mr. Thomas Cooper, who originally bought for £290 nearly 12 acres that lay to the north of the old enclosure called Butchers, had not paid the balance or completed the purchase nearly a year later, though the Commissioners still held his deposit of £58. When pressed to do so he reported that he had contracted with William Norman (the brickmaker) to become the purchaser and that Mr. Norman would complete the purchase on or before 3 September. In due course Thomas Cooper's deposit was refunded. He was not alone in having difficulty in finding the purchase money. Mrs. Eager, who purchased about three acres lying between the present Grove Road and Mill Road; Stephen Bine and William Field were all overdue with their payments. It had been a simple matter to persuade buyers to take up some of the cheap allotments of the common that were offered for sale; quite another to get the money.

Finally, there was the question of fees due to the steward of the manor, which for some reason had not been agreed and recorded earlier. This was done at a meeting held between 21 and 24 September 1829, when it was decided that the steward's fees should be 10s. for allocations of less than an acre; £1 for an acre and less than two acres, and 5s. for every acre after the first. At the same meeting the Award was executed and the clerk was directed to proclaim the fact at Keymer church the following Sunday.

There remained only the settlement of outstanding accounts from the clerks and the surveyor, and a detailed examination of the 'General Accounts of the Inclosure'. This was done at the end of October 1829, yet the Commissioners and the clerk met just once more (on 5, 6 and 7 August 1830), presumably to tie up any loose ends; and to discuss the final outcome. The actual enclosure from the time that signatures were obtained for the petition to Parliament to its execution had taken just under 20 months.

Within a few months the face of the Keymer commons in present-day Burgess Hill had changed beyond all recognition. Gone were almost all the old tracks and paths, and the open spaces extending from Freeks Lane to Station Road and London Road to the east of Mill Road, and the large expanse of Valebridge common. The allotments were now neatly pegged out and ditched, if not actually planted with hawthorn or similar hedging (the Award stated that they were to be fenced within six months of the date of its execution). Mill Road and Freeks Lane had been laid out as private roads, the upkeep of which was to be undertaken by those awarded allotments which adjoined them.

The entire exercise had cost £4,501 13s. 7d. Of a total area of almost 455 acres about 210 had been sold for £4,739 13s. 0d. leaving the balance of £237 19s. 5d. to be distributed among the successful claimants. This was done by means of an advertisement in the *Sussex Advertiser* of 9 August 1830 when 'all Proprietors and Persons interested therein' were to apply for their shares to the joint clerks at their offices in Ship Street, Brighton. But where did the money go? The following statement of money spent is derived from the bank pass book and from minutes of the meetings:

Clerk(s) (Messrs. Attree and Clarke)	£1057 02s. 11d.
Commissioners:	
Mr. Smallpiece	£ 274 01s. 00d.
Mr. Clutton	£ 987 14s. 07d.
Mr. Hodson	£ 268 16s. 00d.
Auctioneer (Mr. Creasy)	£ 60 05s. 06d.
Surveyor (Mr. Walter)	£ 649 12s. 03d.
Road contractors:	
J. Soden	£ 531 06s. 01d.
S. Putland	£ 595 09s. 00d.
Notice Boards (Edwards & Davy)	£ 3 08s. 03d.
Lithographic plans (Lake)	£ 5 08s. 00d.
Allowance for land lost for road widening	
(W. Shaw)	£ 2 00s. 00d.
Faggots, drainpipes, etc. (W. Shaw)	£ 5 07s. 00d.
Inspection of roads (R. Wood)	£ 3 03s. 00d.
Refund of deposit (T. Cooper)	£ 58 00s. 00d.
	£4501 13s. 07d.
	========

It will readily be seen that the clerks' expenses accounted for almost a quarter of the total. There are no details of how this was made up but clearly it covered the journeys and the perambulation of the boundaries by Mr. Somers Clarke described earlier. It certainly covered part of the cost of obtaining the Act of Parliament, quoted in *Sussex Advertiser* of 18 May 1829 as £1,086 6s. 8d., and it must have included fees to Mr. Attree in his role as steward of the manor.

The claims of two of the three Commissioners appear to be very reasonable, but there is no obvious reason why Mr. Clutton's share was nearly twice as much as that of his two colleagues put together unless he, too, incurred heavy expenses in connection with getting the Act through Parliament.

The surveyor's expenses, too, appear to be reasonable since he must have been involved in surveying and mapping the original commons, the plots that were sold, and the final allotments. Moreover, he it was who wrote up the detailed account of the perambulation of the manor and parish. The cost of roads seems very reasonable indeed by today's standards; though it seems doubtful if 'making the roads' involved much more than dumping cart-load after cart-load of stones on an existing track and, after rough levelling, covering them with a thin layer of sand or gravel. The roads may have had a light horse-drawn, rolling but certainly they were in no way comparable with the roads of today.

Most of the remaining items are self-explanatory or have already been mentioned. William Shaw lost a small part of his site for road widening when it was found that Station Road, as originally planned, would be too narrow. He seems to have been content to accept £2 as compensation perhaps in the hope that future business would result. In the event he did get a small sub-contract for work on the roads but of so minor a nature as to be insignificant.

As Dr. Peter Brandon has pointed out in his article on the Keymer Enclosures,[34] the surveyor and the Commissioners, in making the Award, were unconsciously establishing the line of some of the future roads in Burgess Hill. When the town began to grow in the 1850s and 1860s and new roads were formed, it is evident that St John's Road, part of Upper St John's Road, almost the whole of Park Road, part of the lower end of Church Road where it runs west from the church to its junction with London Road, Grove Road, and the more recently created Middle Way, all follow property boundaries fixed by the Award.

But this was still in the future. There was no immediate scramble for building land on the newly enclosed commons. Sixteen years later, in 1845, when the whole parish was accurately surveyed for the first time following the Tithe Commutation Act, much of the former common had been ploughed and cropped. Nearly 29 of John Gainsford's 30 acres (almost all of which he acquired at the time of the enclosure) were described as 'arable' and let to William Brooker, a local farmer. Similarly, Charles Bayntun, who had acquired about 54 acres of former common in Freeks Lane mostly from his brother, Rev. Henry Bayntun, had ploughed about 42 acres which he was using to grow crops. The Rev. Mr. Powell, who by then owned about 27 acres in the present Mill Road/Crescent Road area, had let his land to Philip Jenner, a well-known local farmer who had nearly $25\frac{1}{2}$ acres of this under the plough. A 12-acre holding, near the site of Middle Way and then owned by William Shaw's widow, was also described as arable. Much of the land that had been purchased originally for its clay by William Taylor and the Norman brothers was now, by 1845, largely under cultivation, the clay veins presumably having been exhausted. There are other examples, but these were some of the more important ones associated with the present town centre.

A detailed study of the Award shows that, as a general rule, when allocations are compared on an acre-for-acre basis, cottagers tended to benefit rather more than tenants with larger holdings. Nathaniel Borrer who held Sheddingdean, for example, was awarded just over $3\frac{1}{4}$ acres for his 57 acres (about 10 poles for each acre); Elizabeth Broomfield who held 24 acres, part of Grovelands in London Road, also received $3\frac{1}{4}$ acres but this represented 21 poles per acre; whilst at the bottom of the scale Susanna Eager, who held the half-acre site where Sampson Bagnall once set up his potters kilns, was awarded 38 poles thus increasing her smallholding by nearly 50 per cent. Similarly, the old house in Keymer Road now called Farthings, then owned by John Wood of Bart's Hospital, London, was awarded 37 poles for the half-acre site. John Marten Cripps' allocation of $7\frac{1}{4}$ acres for Burgess Hill farm and Lottmotts looks reasonably generous, but when divided into 120 acres works out at marginally under 10 poles an acre – about the same as for Sheddingdean. There is no suggestion whatever that the Commissioners tended to favour the larger and more influential tenants, rather the reverse.

The person who benefited most from the enclosure was the lord of the manor, the Rev. Henry Bayntun. Apart from his manorial allotment of about $16\frac{3}{4}$ acres and the 21 acres he was allocated for Brooklands and Burchetts farm, he acquired nearly $90\frac{1}{2}$ acres representing the allocations made to Caroline Chatfield, William Clutton and William Newnham, all of whom had copyholdings in Balcombe. These tenants surrendered their allotments in return for enfranchisement,[35] which released them from manorial dues: rents, heriots and fines for ever. As previously suggested, probably none of these people (or their sub-tenants) would have had any use for the former common land as a source of grazing, though at the then current rate of about £20 per acre Clutton's four acres would have been worth £80; Newnham's 17 acres £340, and Miss Chatfield's 73 acres no less than £1,460. Enfranchisement of copyhold premises was not cheap.

With completion of the enclosures to the west of London Road in the 1850s the area stood on the brink of great changes as will be seen in the next chapter.

Chapter Seven

The Coming of the Railway and Enclosure of the Clayton Common

The second great event that helped to lay the foundations of the new town was the completion of the London to Brighton railway in 1841, with its provision for a small station at Burgess Hill.

Proposals for a rail link between London and Brighton were first mooted as early as 1823 when a William James suggested that a rail-road, operated by steam locomotives, should be built to run from Waterloo Bridge via Croydon and the Adur valley to Shoreham and thence along the coast to Brighton.[1] Two years later, John (later Sir John) Rennie, acting for the Surrey, Sussex, Hants, Wilts and Somerset Railway Company, came up with two alternative schemes: (1) a direct line running more or less due south from Croydon to Brighton and (2) an alternative route from Nine Elms through Wandsworth, Dorking and Horsham to Brighton via Shoreham. None of these schemes came to anything and a later one of 1829, via Bolney and the Newtimber gap through the Downs, similarly failed to attract the interest of investors, mainly because of national economic problems at the time. A further attempt was made in 1833 for a direct route surveyed by Francis Giles under Rennie's control; this got as far as being deposited in Parliament before it, too, was abandoned.

Sir John Rennie had been the engineer for the then new London Bridge, planned by his father, and was knighted in 1831 when the bridge was opened. In addition to the schemes already mentioned, he produced in 1834 yet another variation to the proposed railway, this time involving tunnels which, because of their high cost, had previously been avoided wherever possible. He now proposed a more direct route with tunnels at Merstham, Balcombe, Cuckfield and Clayton Hill. South of Cuckfield there was to be a cutting 96 feet deep followed by an embankment and a viaduct up to 69 feet high near St John's common.

By 1835 no fewer than six schemes were under active consideration. Four showed routes that avoided the Downs, reaching Brighton by way of Shoreham; a fifth via Keymer and Patcham left the then proposed South-Eastern line to Dover at Oxted. Rennie stuck to his direct line. A year later only four contenders were left and serious consideration was being given to Rennie's direct line and the three alternatives via the Adur valley. The respective schemes proposed by Rennie and Stephenson (the latter one of the main contenders advocating the Adur valley route) became the subject of intensive enquiries by a House of Commons Committee headed by Lord George Lennox in the spring of 1836. Discussions on the merits of the four alternatives continued for over a year, including the time taken by the House of Lords. Finally, the Commons Committee agreed to appoint an ordnance engineer, Capt. Robert Alderson, R.E., to survey the four 'active' routes and report back to the house. An entirely new 'joint plan', prepared by the four contenders, was also sent to Capt. Alderson for his report.

Appointed on 2 June 1837, Alderson with commendable speed reported on 27 June recommending Rennie's scheme, which by then had been slightly modified to include a longer tunnel at Balcombe, the building of a longer viaduct over the Ouse valley, and abolishing the Cuckfield tunnel and replacing it with a shorter one at Haywards Heath. Clayton tunnel was to be lengthened by over 500 yards and a new tunnel at Patcham was needed as a result of realignment of the proposed line. The 'joint plan' drawn up by Rennie, Stephenson, Gibbs and Palmer for a line to Brighton via Shoreham would have entailed construction of nearly 70 miles of new track in addition to having the use of some 14 miles of other companies' lines to reach the proposed London termini of Nine Elms and London Bridge and was not therefore recommended.

The final plan, signed by Rennie and Rastrick, who had been appointed resident engineer,[2] included nine new stations south of Croydon of which Burgess Hill was one. Among others in our area were Haywards Heath and Hassocks Gate, as it was first called.

The Bill was given the Royal Assent on 15 July 1837 and work commenced just over a year later. It is interesting to note that as late as May 1838 Rastrick was instructed 'to prepare plans for obtaining such lands as might be required for the main line between St. John's common and Brighton'.

On John Urpeth Rastrick fell much of the burden of the detailed planning and supervision of the work. The impressive Balcombe viaduct with its four pavilions in classical style, familiar to hundreds of commuters from Burgess Hill, stands as a lasting monument to his skill. It seems appropriate to mention here, too, that he was also the inventor of the semaphore system of railway signalling which continued to operate on the London to Brighton line until electrification in 1932-3.

Once started, work was pushed ahead with the utmost speed. In all 18 contracts were let. One of the first, awarded in September 1838 and valued at £57,647 for the stretch of line between Burgess Hill and the northern end of Clayton tunnel, went to James and George Thornton of Walton who, in January 1839, secured the contract worth £55,000 from Haywards Heath to Burgess Hill. By October 1838 it was reported at a committee meeting that work on the Balcombe and Clayton tunnels was proceeding 'very fast and most satisfactorily', and that work at Hassocks Gate was 'proceeding well'. The first permanent track was laid on 4 February 1839 at Hassocks Gate. By July 1839, 4,769 men and 570 horses were being employed and a year later these numbers had been increased to 6,206 and 960 respectively, by which time five locomotives were also in use.

The winter of 1840-1 brought bad weather which delayed progress between Burgess Hill and Clayton tunnel and in April 1841 it was reported that 'Keymer parish embankment [immediately to the north of Wivelsfield station] was tending to slip' – a problem that was to recur in 1957 as some of the older residents and commuters to London will recall. But despite these delays the line from London to Haywards Heath was opened on 12 July 1841 and the remaining section of line to Brighton on 21 September 1841. Thus the complete line from Norwood Junction, where the London-Brighton line joined the rails of the London-Croydon railway, took just three years after the first contract had been let. It should be noted that Stephenson, in his evidence to the House of Commons in March 1836, had said that he had estimated that Rennie's plan for a direct route would take a minimum of five years to complete – a time scale he later amended to six to seven years because of the size and complexity of some of the embankments.

Variations of Rennie's direct line insofar as they would have affected Burgess Hill are illustrated on map 3.[3] One shows the proposed line crossing the old mill pond at Valebridge, passing over Leylands Road at the house called Peppers, and over Station Road near its junction with Mill Road. The second shows the line much further west, crossing Leylands Road near Petworth Drive, continuing west of Mill Road, crossing Crescent Road to the east of St John's church and the playing fields of Oakmeeds school before reaching Hassocks at or very near the site of the present station.

It seems incredible that this major feat of building and civil engineering with its tunnels, viaducts, bridges, embankments, cuttings, station buildings, level crossings and the like could possibly have been completed in so short a time by gangs of men using little more

_19. The first railway station at Burgess Hill, built in the early 1840s.

than picks and shovels. Whilst long stretches of the track passed through open, agricultural countryside one cannot escape the feeling that it was only with the maximum co-operation of the various landowners that the scheme got off the ground at all.

The early years of the 1840s marked the beginning of the 'railway fever' that was to sweep through the country with ever increasing momentum. A new line was constructed south of the present Wivelsfield station and opened for through traffic to Lewes and Hastings in October 1847. The extension to Newhaven was opened two months later, and by May 1849 a branch had been provided to serve Eastbourne.

Following representations in 1857 from a number of people from Lewes, Ditchling and other villages in the area for a station at the junction of the Brighton line and what was termed the Keymer Branch, and after a delay of nearly five years, a small halt called Keymer Junction was eventually established near the level crossing in Junction Road. This operated for just over 20 years – between 1862 and 1883.[4] Wivelsfield station, sited in a much more suitable place and built to replace it, was opened in 1886. Initially also called Keymer Junction, it received its present name in 1896. The station has changed very little since it was built a century ago. On the other hand Burgess Hill's 1840s station building (now demolished) was replaced by the present buildings on the road bridge over the tracks in 1877.

This major, revolutionary undertaking completely changed the visual scene in our area. It included the building of the viaduct at Valebridge, affectionately known locally as the Eight Arches; the steep embankment north of Wivelsfield station, and the cutting leading to Burgess Hill and beyond. Local people no longer enjoyed an uninterrupted view west from Valebridge Road and the new cutting must have created a sense of wonder, even awe, in the minds of the local populace. Franklands and Burgess Hill farms, which lost strips

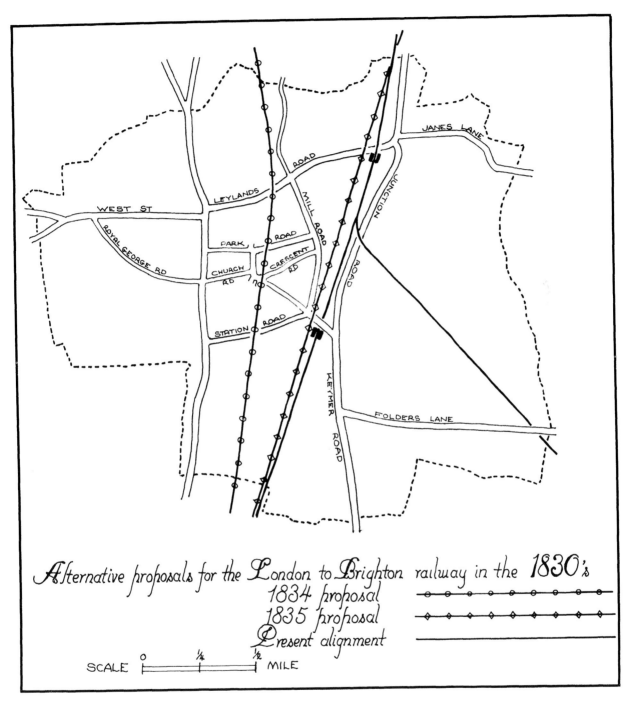

WEST ST · LEYLANDS · ROYAL GEORGE RD · PARK ROAD · ROAD · CHURCH RD · CRESCENT RD · MILL ROAD · STATION ROAD · KEYMER ROAD · JUNCTION ROAD · JANES LANE · FOLDERS LANE

Alternative proposals for the London to Brighton railway in the 1830's

1834 proposal ⊙⊙⊙⊙⊙⊙⊙⊙⊙⊙
1835 proposal ◇◇◇◇◇◇◇◇◇◇
Present alignment ─────────

SCALE 0 ¼ ½ MILE

Map 3

20. Old signal box at the junction near Wivelsfield Station in 1905, looking south. It was later replaced by a signal box in Junction Road, now demolished.

of land, were bisected; and little Burgess Hill, also called Yew Tree farm, virtually disappeared when Henry Marten sold it for £1,000 to the London and Brighton Railway Company in 1840. With this sale went about an acre and a half of former common land on part of which now stand Bank Buildings in Station Road. Similarly, part of the ancient holding called North Inholmes disappeared when John Attree sold nearly six of its original 11 acres to the Railway Company. For this 'privilege' he paid to the lord of the manor as a heriot 'one bullock valued at £15 15s. 0d.', a transaction that took over two years to finalise.

In the part of the town that was formerly in Ditchling, One o'clock farm, the land called Inholmes belonging to the house now known as Freckborough manor, and Pollards

Inholmes farm adjoining Folders Lane, all lost strips of land to the Railway Company when the branch line to Lewes and beyond was constructed, creating problems of access for the farmers whose fields had been separated from the main holdings. A small plot of about quarter of an acre, part of Blackhouse farm, was sold for £10 to the Railway Company and strips of land were also acquired from the owners of Frankbarrow and Cants farms, leaving certain fields isolated from the main holdings.

Roads were not affected to any great extent though Valebridge Road near the Eight Arches viaduct needed some realignment, near where it crossed the stream to the west of the old mill pond. The distinctive bend in the road at that point, clearly visible today, dates from the time the railway was constructed. Lye Lane, now called Leylands Road, acquired a new bridge (part of Wivelsfield station) looking today much as it did in 1841.

The area around Wivelsfield station must have appeared to the 'navvies' as a bleak and forbidding spot, for they called it Worlds End, a term that despite attempts to rename it North End, still persists today.

The immense task of railway construction resulted in a substantial increase in the local population. The 1841 Census, which recorded a total of 2,111 souls in the parishes of Clayton and Keymer, included no fewer than 587 labourers and other railway workers and their families only some five months before the line to Brighton was opened.[5] Many of these people were accommodated in Burgess Hill, and the problems of finding living quarters must have been enormous as were those of catering for such large numbers of extra people. Most of the newcomers seem to have been crammed into already overcrowded houses; others

21.   The house adjoining Ditchling Common, now called Freckburgh Manor, was once a copyholding held in the manor of Ditchling. The rear, illustrated above, is almost certainly of Tudor date.

were housed in railway huts specially erected for the purpose. At least one man lived in a temporary hut about five or six feet square and only four feet six inches high *containing a fireplace*, a luxury that was to cost him his life. The following poignant entry in the *Sussex Advertiser* of 21 December 1840 tells the story:

> Inquest held on the body of Richard Thornby Hemston aged 40, a plate-layer on the London to Brighton railway. Deceased lodged in a temporary hut . . . [described above]. A bed of loose straw covered the floor reaching within a short distance of the fireplace and being separated by a wooden slab. He went to his hut from work between seven and eight o'clock on Wednesday last, but not being at his post as usual the next morning he was sent for when he was discovered in the hut . . . very much burnt and quite dead. There was a small fire in the fireplace and a slab of wood was burning. His clothes and nearly all the straw were consumed. Everything in the hut appeared to be burnt.
>
> Verdict: that he had died from burning and suffocation but by what means the fire took place no sufficient evidence appeared to the jurors.

Although a formal inquest was held and the usual evidence heard, one is left with the impression that both the coroner and the jury looked upon the mishap as 'just one of those things'.

Several householders converted their cottages into temporary inns. The *Brickmaker's Arms* put up seven excavators and navvies, whilst the *Navigators Arms*, the *Queen's Head* and the *Blacksmith's Arms* between them accommodated 16 labourers, all of whom were employed on the railway. None of these inns survived after the railway became operational. It is difficult to say precisely where they were situated. The *Brickmaker's Arms* was certainly in the vicinity of the present Burgess Hill railway station and could indeed have been a predecessor of the *Burgess Hill Inn* now called *Burgess Hill Tavern*. The *Blacksmith's Arms* stood on the site of no. 170 Leylands Road. The other two mentioned above were also in or near Leylands Road, though their exact location has yet to be established. Thus the locals cashed in on a short-lived boom when money was plentiful and beer could be sold at almost any time during the day and well into the night.

At the end of the 19th century, before the beginning of the decline of the railways, wide strips of land were acquired near Wivelsfield station with a view to improving the lines to Brighton and, via Lewes, to Eastbourne and Hastings. Nothing came of the proposals because of the age-old problem – lack of capital. But the land is still (in 1987) undeveloped and the pleasant meadows provide a welcome rural oasis in the northern part of the town.

Perhaps not surprisingly in an age when scant regard was paid to what today would be considered elementary safety precautions, the construction of the railway took its toll in terms of human life. The following extract from the *Sussex Advertiser* of 14 September 1840 is typical of the kind of mishap that occurred from time to time:

> An inquest was taken on . . . the body of Joseph Cooper a labourer of 16 years employed on the London and Brighton Railroad. . . The deceased was driving a waggon drawn by one horse which had just been filled with earth and had been emptied at the top along the metal of the road to be refilled. He was walking on the metal and on coming to the place where the waggons stopped he took hold of the trace for the purpose of unhooking the horse from the waggon when his foot slipped from the metal and he fell upon his stomach across it and the wheels of the waggon then passed over his back. Deceased then stood up for a short time when he appeared to faint and sat down. He did not speak afterwards and died in about an hour.
>
> Verdict: Accidental Death.

This was by no means an isolated case. Labour was cheap and plentiful a century and a half ago. There were no unions to provide a welfare service or secure reasonable housing facilities and working conditions for the navvies. Men slept and ate where they could in this age of *laissez faire*. Welfare services in 1840 were not provided by managements; neither were they expected by the work force. In the case mentioned the workmates of the unfortunate Joseph Cooper did not, apparently, even summon medical assistance. So cheaply was human life rated.

The opening of the railway gave a new impetus to the local brick, tile and pottery works whose finished products could now be despatched quickly and relatively cheaply much further afield. It also provided a fast and safe passenger service to Brighton and the south coast towns on the one hand, and to London on the other. Those who for business reasons or for pleasure needed to travel eagerly seized the opportunity to patronise the new and unusual mode of transport. No longer was it necessary on a relatively short journey to endure the discomfort of several tedious hours perched on the top of a swaying stage coach, half frozen to death in winter, choked with dust in summer. Travel facilities inside those coaches were little better though at least the occupants were kept dry.

Yet the new mode of transport was still far and away beyond the means of most ordinary working people, for even at a penny a mile the fare to Brighton and back would have cost about 1s.6d. per person – a large slice out of the wages of a working man struggling to support a wife and family on anything between 12s. 6d. and £1 a week. Cheap travel for the working population was still a couple of generations or more away, and it was only after the First World War that popular travel for all finally came into its own.

Enclosure of St John's Common in Clayton
Nearly 30 years were to elapse, following the enclosure of the Keymer commons before the hundred or so acres of land to the west of the London Road were enclosed and the scene was finally set for the rapid growth that, gaining momentum particularly during the period 1850-80, resulted in the establishment of the bones of the town as we know it today. The period of social and economic change that began in the 1820s continued unabated; there was no lessening of the great wave of self-confidence, nationally, that swept the country and saw a giant leap forward in the growth of steam power, the development of the canals, and later of the railway network. Here in the Burgess Hill area the clay-based industries were enjoying an unprecedented boom, partly because of the relative ease with which their finished products could be distributed. By about 1850 the entire area was ripe for development; all that was needed was the enclosure of the remainder of the common.

By 1847, in and near the present Keymer Road, within easy reach of the railway station, one or two well-to-do Brighton businessmen had bought large plots of land on which to erect new houses of the type envisaged in 1828 when part of the Keymer commons was offered for sale. Thomas Crunden of Brighton, for example, bought for £796 nearly six-and-a-half acres of Burgess Hill farm lying between the railway and Keymer Road. On this he built his handsome villa, Oak Hall, now demolished but remembered in the residential road called Oak Hall Park. A little to the north three-and-three-quarter acres, also formerly part of Burgess Hill farm, had been acquired by Lewis Slight, the former Brighton town clerk, who built for himself the villa called Tudor House. Demolished many years ago it lay slightly to the east of the railway station. Greenlands in Keymer Road also dates back to about this time and other large houses in Keymer Road were soon to follow, to establish that particular locality as the middle class residential area of the future town.

Situated as it is on the elevated plateau that continues south-east to Ditchling, with the ground falling away to the west to provide attractive views, the area is pleasant enough and one can easily see why Messrs. Crunden and Slight and others were attracted to it. Nevertheless, had the Clayton side of the common been enclosed 20 years earlier it seems highly likely that the western part of the present town would have proved to be a much more attractive site for the type of mid-Victorian housing that can still be seen in Keymer Road. Set on open ground with magnificent views of the South Downs; with pleasant agricultural land adjoining and to windward of the brick and pottery kilns, the location was infinitely superior to the Keymer Road area, even if it was less convenient for the station. When, in November 1854, about 12¼ acres of the Clayton side of the common were sold to pay for the cost of Enclosure, the auctioneer waxed lyrical in his description of the land on offer.[6] Much the same view as he described can still be seen today from Fairfield recreation ground and the adjoining houses.

As with the Keymer commons in the 1820s, St John's common in Clayton had long ceased to provide the grazing and other facilities so prized and safeguarded by manorial tenants a century or two earlier. By the early 1850s the population was increasing and the need for working-class housing was becoming a matter of urgency. The new villas near the railway were creating new demands for labour: gardeners, coachmen and indoor domestic staff. The brick, tile and pottery industries, too, were absorbing more and more workers who needed to be adequately housed. It seemed reasonable that employers, casting around for suitable housing sites, and men with money to invest, should look to the Clayton side of the common as a possible solution to their problems.

The Enclosure Act and Preliminary Stages

Between 1828 and 1852 changes had taken place in the procedure for Enclosure. A General Act of 1836 permitted enclosure by consent of two-thirds of the interests affected without the necessity of any special application to Parliament. Owners could appoint their own Commissioners as though the enclosure had been specifically authorised by the Act. This, however, covered only open arable fields; though it was sometimes alleged to have been improperly applied to common pastures.[7]

The last great General Inclosure Act was passed in 1845 and provided for the appointment of a Standing Inclosure Commission. This was to work through Assistant Commissioners who were to carry out local enquiries in each case of proposed enclosure and, if the enclosure was sanctioned by Parliament on the Commissioners' recommendation, they (the assistant Commissioners) were to be responsible for the actual work of enclosure and allotment. Under the terms of the Tithe Act of 1839 waste lands had been freed from liability for increased tithe upon enclosure, a factor that may have further encouraged to proceed those interested in this proposal. The Act also allowed interested persons, if they thought fit, to authorise the Commissioners to make allotments for public purposes: roads, drains, charities, etc., and to allocate land for the benefit of the labouring poor, making special reference to recreation grounds. Every enclosure of waste had to be submitted to Parliament for approval and the Act for enclosing St John's common in Clayton was passed in 1852.

There is very little detailed information about the Clayton Enclosure, nothing like the wealth of primary sources associated with that for Keymer. Nevertheless, thanks to the generous help given by the Clerk of the Records, House of Lords Records Office, copies have been obtained of the report to the Home Secretary by the Enclosure Commissioners, and the Act of 1852.

The Commissioners' report of November 1852 drew the attention of the Home Secretary to the need to proceed with enclosure with as little delay as possible and

> Since the presentation of our last report the necessary consents have been received to the following proposed inclosures to which we have severally appended the grounds on which we are of the opinion that they are expedient . . .

There followed comments on 26 commons and areas of open arable fields up and down the country ranging in size from Hareshaw common in Northumberland (9,000 acres) to Ditton common in Kent (24 acres). Item 18 shows:

Clayton, County Sussex.

The waste lands of the manor of Clayton containing about 103 acres.

An allotment for the labouring poor has not been required, as the quantity of land to be enclosed is not large. All the cottages are provided with good gardens, with the opportunity of garden allotments should they desire them.

The land is most suitable for building purposes and is required for such purposes.

A printed schedule attached to the report provides the following background information not available from any other extant source:

CLAYTON

Date of Application – 1 April 1852.

Extent – 103 acres.

Assistant Commissioner's Inquiry Meeting – 26 April 1852.

Report of Assistant Commissioner Received – 4 May 1852.

Date of Provisional Order – 7 May 1852.

Allotment for Exercise and Recreation – 3 acres.

Allotment for the Labouring Poor – Nil.

Allotment to the Lord of the Manor – a perpetual rent charge of 2s. an acre, 1s. for half an acre and 6d. for quarter of an acre or less quantity.

The last item is a little unusual since most of the allotments of common land to lords of manors at this time were one-fourteenth or one-sixteenth of the total exclusive of mines, etc.

It has not yet been established who initiated action to have the common enclosed. One early writer,[8] says:

The tenants (or copyholders of the manor of Clayton) made application to the late William Campion Esq., of Danny (the lord of the manor) to enclose the common which was granted; the consent of the Enclosure Commissioners of England and Wales was also obtained, and the late Mr. John Wood, Valuer of Hurstpierpoint, chosen to plan and allot it, to make tenantry roads where required, and to sell the sites that would be likely to realise most money for building, to pay the whole cost of making the roads and the expenses of the enclosure.

But that is all. Many of the major tenants of the manor at this time were absentee landlords. Locks farm, Hurst, part of which lay within the town boundary, was owned by Sir Peregrine Acland of Fairfield, Somerset; Clayton Wickham farm by Nathaniel Borrer of Pakyns manor, Hurst; and West End farm by Sir John Dodson, H.M. Advocate General who resided in London. John Gainsford, owner of Scotches farm and a cottage in Fairfield Road, once the alehouse run by William and Elizabeth Brooker, had retired from business at this time and was living at Brighton; whilst the address of John Shelley, owner of Shelley's farm, was given as Avington, Hants. It is difficult to see how they could have got together to initiate enclosure action unless prompted to do so by, say, the steward of the manor or by some other influential local man.

The reference to an allotment of land for the labouring poor suggests that this had been considered by the tenants of the manor and the Assistant Commissioner but that a future need for such land, to grow vegetables and keep a pig or a few hens, had not been established. The allotment of three acres for 'exercise and recreation' was of course the initial area set aside for what is now called Fairfield Recreation Ground. Not mentioned in the Commissioners' schedule, but later provided, were one-and-a-half acres of land on the Clayton side of the common for the express purpose of building a parish church.

The Act (16 and 17 VIC CAP III) [16 December 1852] was surprisingly brief and reads as follows:

An Act to authorise the Inclosure of Certain Lands in pursuance of a Special Report of the Inclosure Commissioners for England and Wales.

Whereas the Inclosure Commissioners for England and Wales have, in pursuance of 'The Acts for the Inclosure, Exchange and Improvement of Land', issued their Provisional Orders for and concerning the proposed Inclosures mentioned in the Schedule to this Act, and the requisite Consents thereto have been given since the Date of their Seventh Annual General Report; And whereas the said Commissioners have by a Special Report certified their opinion that such proposed Inclosures would be expedient; but the same cannot be proceeded with without the previous Authority of Parliament; Be it enacted by the Queen's Most Excellent Majesty, by and with the Advice and Consent of the Lords Spiritual and Temporal, and Commons, in this present Parliament assembled, and by the Authority of the same, That the said several proposed Inclosures mentioned in the Schedule to this Act be proceeded with.

II. And be it enacted, That in citing this Act and other Acts of Parliament, and in legal Instruments, it shall be sufficient to use either the Expression 'The Second Annual Inclosure Act, 1852' or 'The Acts for the Inclosure, Exchange and Improvement of Land'.

Schedule to which this Act refers . . . [this listed 26 Inclosures in various places in England and Wales including Clayton, the only one in Sussex].

It had been ordered on 16 February 1852 that 'leave be given' to bring in a Bill to authorise the enclosure of the lands specified in the seventh annual report of the Commissioners. The Bill was in fact presented the same day and had completed all its stages through both Houses of Parliament by 20 April.[9] By this time the passing of what had become an annual Act was fairly routine though amendments to the original Bill, presented in February, were made by both Lords and Commons.

Even before the Bill completed all its stages through Parliament an Assistant Commissioner had been appointed. His first task was to hold a meeting to hear objections to the proposed enclosure. Consequently the following advertisement appeared in the *Sussex Express* on 10 April 1852:

CLAYTON INCLOSURE

Whereas an application for the Inclosure of St. John's common and Clayton common in the parish of Clayton . . . has been duly made . . .

And whereas the said application has been referred by the said Commissioners to me, an Assistant Commissioner duly appointed under the said Act.

I hereby give notice that I shall hold a meeting on the 24th day of April instant at the hour of eleven in the forenoon at the *Royal Oak Inn* in the said parish for the purpose of hearing any objections which may be made to the proposed Inclosure and any Information or Evidence which may be offered in relation thereto.

Witness my hand this 8th day of April 1852

STEPN MARTIN.

Assistant Inclosure Commissioner.

It was not an auspicious start. The *Royal Oak Inn* was not, and never had been, in Clayton but stood, as it stands today, on the Wivelsfield/Ditchling boundary to the north of Ditchling Common. Presumably because the error was discovered a fresh announcement was made a week later changing the venue of the meeting to the *Friars Oak Inn*, Clayton and the date to 26 April.

After this meeting nothing much seems to have happened until 1853, when Stephen Martin had been replaced as Assistant Commissioner by John Wood, an auctioneer and valuer from Hurstpierpoint. An official advertisement in the *Sussex Express* on 13 and 20 August announced that a meeting would be held at the *Friars Oak Inn* on 29 August 'for the purpose of receiving claims in writing from all persons claiming any common or other right in the said lands . . . '. Whether some of the tenants asked for further time to prepare their claims or whether there were other unforeseen difficulties is not known, but a similar notice appeared again early in September stating that another meeting for the purpose of receiving claims would be held on 19 September 1853.

On 15 April 1854 John Wood gave notice that[10] a statement of all claims received by him had been deposited at *Friars Oak Inn* and were open to inspection. Anyone objecting to a claim was required to do so in writing before 10 May.

Sale of Allotments

Much of the preliminary work had now been done and so far John Wood and his predecessor, Stephen Martin, had not been paid. To raise money to cover the cost of the enclosure it was necessary to sell some of the common land as building sites, and initially six plots adjoining the Brighton to Cuckfield turnpike road [the present London Road] were advertised for sale in August 1854.

With frontages ranging between 530 feet to as little as 60 feet, these long, shallow plots of roadside waste lay either side of London Road south of the present Royal George Road. The advertisement appeared in the *Sussex Advertiser* on 8 and 15 August and the auction was to be held at *Friars Oak Inn*, Clayton on 25 August. It seems reasonable to assume that either the sale was cancelled, or that the lots were withdrawn because of lack of interest by potential buyers, since the same land was put up for sale again as part of 25 lots later auctioned on 6 November 1854, also at *Friars Oak*.

On both occasions the Auctioneer laid great stress on the attractiveness of the locality as the following transcript of the advertisement shows.[11] It reads:

> Building sites in the rapidly improving locality of St. John's common, Clayton, Sussex in the immediate vicinity of Burgess Hill Station on the London and Brighton railway nine miles from Brighton, and adjacent to the London, Cuckfield and Brighton turnpike road. Delightful sites for the erection of detached or semi-detached VILLA RESIDENCES with appropriate grounds.

Mr. JOHN WOOD

> **WILL SELL BY AUCTION** with the approbation of the Inclosure Commissioners for England and Wales at the *Friars Oak Inn*, Clayton, on Monday November 6th 1854 at one for two o'clock precisely in 25 lots eighteen of which comprise half an acre in each lot, situate on high ground, commanding very extensive and magnificent views of the most picturesque scenery imaginable, embracing the great beauties of a fertile valley and innumerable groups of ornamental and majestic Sussex oaks with a long crescent sweep of the far-famed Sussex Downs forming the outline of the admired landscape.
>
> The attention of Freehold Land and Building Societies is earnestly invited to an inspection of these Eligible Sites.
>
> The first six lots average a frontage of upwards of 100 feet; the next ten lots a frontage of 86 feet 6 inches, with a depth of 264 feet each; and the remainder of the lots have long and important frontages abutting on the Brighton and Cuckfield turnpike road.
>
> The lots will be staked out for view and full particulars and conditions may be had 10 days prior to the sale at the *Old Ship Hotel*, Brighton; *Red Lion*, Lindfield; *Friars Oak*, Clayton, and of the Auctioneer, Hurstpierpoint, at whose offices a plan of the several plots may be inspected.

The first six lots mentioned in the advertisement were on the north side of West Street and some of these can still be identified today. On the opposite side of the road are the 10 slightly narrower plots and these, too, can be identified if one takes a little time and trouble. The remaining nine plots adjoined London Road and, in addition to the long stretches of roadside verges previously mentioned, included the site of the *Royal George Inn* (now *Georgie's*) and other land to the south thereof.

The sale seems to have been an unqualified success and a total of £1,182 was raised to defray the cost of the Enclosure. When the final accounts were settled it was found that this was more than enough to cover expenses and consequently each tenant of the manor received a small refund proportional to his holding.

The prices realised varied considerably. The six half-acre sites in West Street with a 100-foot frontage, for example, (going east to west) were sold for £70, £54, £50, £46, £47, and

£36 respectively though admittedly the £70 plot had an area of two roods 14 poles and was nearest the turnpike road end of West Street. Two of these sites were purchased by Thomas Allfrey and Henry Woolven, local builders, and three by Henry Beney, a Clayton hawker, who seems to have done well enough financially to be able to afford to invest a total of £228 altogether in four plots. Half-acre sites with a narrower frontage on the south side of West Street, too, showed wide differences in price, varying between £50 and £78. Land adjoining the London Road, surprisingly, fetched rather less on average. George Godley, then landlord of *Friars Oak*, bought just over half an acre for £56 on which he built his *Royal George Inn*; but a little to the south Richard and Nathan Norman, the local potters, were able to pick up half an acre for only £15, and William Norman paid only £32 for over half an acre which was later to become part of the site of Norman and Burts. Among other well-known local men who bought land at this sale were Thomas Avery and John Gravett, the local potter. Other purchasers included a Lindfield accountant, a Brighton timber merchant, a couple of auctioneers and a Hurstpierpoint innkeeper. The lord of the manor, Mr. W.J. Campion, also joined in the bidding and found himself at the end of the day owner of nearly one-and-a-quarter acres of land in London Road which cost him £104 – about £84 an acre.

About a year was to elapse before John Wood announced that 'a schedule of all claims and objections which have been made . . . and of my determinations thereon' had been deposited at the *Friars Oak Inn* and was available for inspection.[12] Another year elapsed before the Enclosure Commissioners gave notice that the Valuers Report and an estimate of expenses had been deposited (as usual) at *Friars Oak*. This gave objectors a final opportunity to complain about allocations or any other matter relating to the enclosure.[13]

The Award

The Award was finally signed by the Commissioners, William Blamire and H.C. Mules, in London on 30 April 1857.

In the absence of working papers there is no way of establishing why, after the passing of the Act in 1852, the allocation of about 100 acres of open common land should have taken five years to finalise. John Wood seems to have worked entirely on his own and may well have fitted in his Enclosure work with the running of his own practice. Certainly by May 1859 he was acting in a similar capacity for the enclosure of the waste lands of the manor of Great Ote Hall in Wivelsfield.

The Award differed substantially from that of Keymer in that all tenants, both copy-holders and freeholders, benefited. Certain freehold land in Clayton village, for example, had been acquired by the lord of the manor in 1847 from the successors of Thomas Dominick Whiteman (see page 93), and since these premises apparently still retained rights of common Mr. Campion was allocated a small parcel of waste containing about three-quarters of an acre called Clayton common, also situated in Clayton village. Similarly, six small freeholdings, once housing workers on the Hammonds estate containing a combined area of some 25 acres, each qualified for an allocation of the common, although some of these premises had, for the past 40 years, been merged into the grounds of Clayton Priory, which was built and landscaped just after the end of the Napoleonic Wars as a mansion house for the estate. All the other freeholders owing suit of court and paying a manorial quit rent received an allocation in just the same way as the copyholders.

As with the enclosure of the Keymer commons, the small freeholder and copyholder, with perhaps a quarter or half an acre of garden attached to his house, tended to benefit rather more, acre for acre, than the larger tenants. The old freehold cottage in Fairplace Hill, for example, where Elizabeth Ford once kept her shop, with its $3\frac{3}{4}$ acres of land, attracted an allocation of just over half an acre, thus increasing the size of the holding by almost 14 per cent. Thomas Avery, who held a cottage and about a quarter of an acre, now the site of the *Weald Inn*, was allocated 11 poles – about 28 per cent of the original area; whilst Charlotte Jeffery, who now owned the site of the cottage granted to Henry Peckham in 1655 and who was shortly to marry C.D. Meads, was awarded 32 poles to increase her holding by 16 per cent. On the other hand, Charles Bayntun, who held Freeks farm of about 77 acres, was awarded little more than five acres or 6.7 per cent of the area of his holding. His other farm in Isaacs Lane, containing about 72 acres, was allocated only about three acres – 4.2 per cent of the total area. Shelley's farm with its 33 acres was given an allocation of 2½ acres (7.6 per cent of the total). Many more examples could be given but enough has been said to illustrate the point.

Every effort seems to have been made to ensure that allocations of common were located as conveniently as possible to the premises entitled to them. Thomas Avery's nine acres, for example, actually adjoined his existing farmland called Fowles and Barbers, as did the allocations in respect of West End farm, Shelley's, and one or two other premises that abutted the common. Those landowners whose holdings were situated some distance away had to be content with what they were given.

The task of ditching and fencing the newly enclosed land must have been costly in terms of both labour and money. Ditches were dug by hand (this was about a century before the invention of the mechanical excavator) and the earth thrown up provided a low bank on which quick-growing hedging could be planted. The hedge on the north side of West Street near West End farm house, that still existed at the time this chapter was drafted, can be dated to about 1856, when the nearby strips of common were enclosed, as can the tall, thick hedge on the west side of London Road near Hammonds Place. Other remnants can be traced with the help of a copy of the enclosure map by anyone prepared to devote a little time to such an exercise.

It will not have escaped the reader's notice that in their report to Parliament the Enclosure Commissioners said that the land was required for building purposes (see page 119). Yet apart from the sale allotments previously mentioned there was no immediate scramble for building plots. Three small plots to the north of Cromwell Road, containing in all about one-and-a-half acres, had been acquired by William Whiteman in September 1857, and these were sold 18 months later for £100 to John Gainsford of Brighton, who had been investing in land here since 1828. Gainsford was not a builder and, since the land was enfranchised in 1860 and from that time disappeared from the records, there is no simple way of determining when it was first used for housing. In July 1859 about five acres lying to the south of West Street were sold by Charles Bayntun for £150 to Charles Tulley,[14] then farming at West End. This was almost certainly used at the time as arable or pasture farm land.

Thomas Avery seems to have been among the first to start selling off his allotments of common as building sites. One plot of about 2½ acres lay to the south of Royal George Road, opposite the turning into Fairfield Road. In December 1862 he sold, as the first of several future plots, a parcel of this land measuring 100 feet x 44 feet to Thomas Allfrey, a local speculative builder. The price paid for this attractive site on a newly-made road was £13! Nearly two years later Thomas Allfrey had built two houses on the site but, like many men in similar circumstances, had run short of money; he was obliged to borrow £300 at 5 per cent interest from two ladies from Brighton. About the same time Avery sold for £10 a plot of similar area, adjoining the *Royal George Inn* to the south, to his kinsman Charles Tulley who by now had probably extended his business interests to include the erection of houses for renting.

Within the next 20 years land values in the town were to increase enormously and building plots were fetching much higher prices. An advertisement in the *Mid Sussex Times* of 10 January 1882, for example, shows that a plot suitable for a villa near St John's church, measuring 56 feet x 204 feet, 'well stocked with trees, fenced and drained', was on offer for £180. £150 was asked for a similar plot with a 100-foot frontage near Burgess Hill station suitable for a £450 house; whilst £100 was the asking price for 'a plot of land suitable for cottages measuring 72 feet x 85 feet'.

By 1865 building operations on the former common in Clayton to the west of London Road were in full swing. They were to continue with little appreciable break until about 1880. Nevertheless, it took about 40 years to lay out the present network of roads bounded by Royal George Road, West Street and London Road, which were to establish the lineaments of that part of the town for all time.

New Roads

The principal roads set out under the terms of the Award were Royal George and Fairfield, though part of the latter (from London Road to West Street) had already been in existence for many years. Now it was extended towards the south to run parallel to London Road and join Royal George Road as it is seen today. Both were planned purely as tenantry roads; that is, they were intended simply to provide access for animals, carts and horses to the newly enclosed land. Both had an overall width of only 20 feet. Whilst this was adequate at the time, within a few years, as the town began to develop and more traffic was generated, it became necessary to widen them to cater not only for the increase in the number of vehicles but also to provide footpaths for pedestrians. West Street already existed as a highway over the common and, apart from now being fenced as allocations of the common were ditched and hedges were planted, it remained virtually unaffected by the enclosure.

According to one earlier writer,[15] the Assistant Commissioner consulted some, at least, of the manorial tenants and sought their advice on whether the new roads should be 20 or 30 feet in width. At this meeting, minutes of which unfortunately have not been preserved, it was decided that since they were to be only tenantry roads, maintained and repaired by the tenants, it seemed sensible to keep the roads as narrow as possible to avoid excessive repair bills, whilst at the same time leaving more land available for distribution among the interested parties. No one apparently foresaw the rapid development of the town over the next few years. When, in the early 1860s, Church Road was laid out and adopted by Keymer parish as a parish road, both Royal George Road and Fairfield Road were taken over by Clayton parish with the result that, shortly afterwards, additional land had to be acquired for widening them.

It is easy with hindsight to criticise our predecessors for being so short-sighted, but decisions can only be taken on the basis of known facts at the time. The Assistant Commissioner and the local landowners might perhaps have been somewhat lacking in vision in not anticipating a building boom and planning the new road layout accordingly. What they could not possibly have foreseen was the rise of the motor car, then only a few decades away.

These two principal roads were not the only ones laid out on the Clayton part of the common at this time. A 20 ft.-wide road led north from West Street to provide access to premises which then lay between Fairfield Road and London Road. It disappeared as a road long ago, but still exists as a narrow footpath to the west of the Fairlea estate. The small Gattons estate was connected with a 16 ft.-wide road leading from West Street but this, too, has long since disappeared, and can no longer be traced even as a footpath. Povey's farm in the present Povey's Close area would have been entirely isolated if the Assistant Commissioner had not made provision for a short stretch of new road. This has now been completely realigned and superseded by Weald Road and Poveys Close. The narrow track called Colmer Place dates from this time and now provides a short cut for pedestrians from Royal George Road to Western Road and the recreation ground. Finally, there was a small stretch of new road near Fowles farm to give access to a two-acre plot allocated to the then owners of part of Clayton Wickham farm. No trace of this now remains.

The Effect of the Enclosure

The immediate consequence of the enclosure was the abolition of almost all the old paths and tracks across the common, access to which had hitherto been enjoyed by all whether they had common rights or not. After 1857 it became private property which owners could use in any way they wished and from which the general populace was barred. It is likely that on some allotments trial holes were dug to determine what precisely lay below. The demand for top quality clay was probably greater than it had ever been and the local industry was here on the fringe of the common. Marle, which had been so highly valued two-and-a-half centuries earlier was a good natural fertiliser and soil conditioner and could be sold locally; and there was always a demand for stones, sand and gravel – still the main basis of road maintenance. Working farmers whose holdings adjoined the common, such as Thomas Avery and Charles Tulley, doubtless quickly incorporated the new enclosures into the curtilege of their existing property. As previously noted, the value of land for building was very low even by the standards of the day, so there would have been little point in selling – at least not until demand for sites had increased considerably. Nevertheless the way was opened for the wave of building development which in the next 20 years would see the end of a long gestation period and the birth of a new Sussex town. The great changes that occurred during the remainder of the 19th century form the subject of the next chapter.

Chapter Eight

The Birth of the Town

Enclosure of the Clayton side of the common set the scene for further development of the new community, which had been growing slowly over the previous ten years. It is this phase in the town's history that has been the subject of so much research, the results of the most recent of which, covering the period 1840-1914, are contained in *A Very Improving Neighbourhood*, edited by Dr. Brian Short. This is based mainly on the census returns 1841-81 inclusive, but also includes valuable sections on education, religious activity, local government, transport, trades, health and welfare, the work of Dr. Short's team of researchers over the three-year period 1981-84. Readers who are interested in a detailed account of the development of the town in this period are recommended to consult this excellent work.

Similarly, in 1979, F.M. Avery published privately a well researched pamphlet, *Development of Burgess Hill and its Potteries (1828-1978)*,[1] which describes in some detail the history not only of the local potteries, but also the brick and tile industries which played such a major role in the town's history. Nevertheless, many readers will not have access to these authoritive sources, who will wish to know something of the development of the town during the second half of the 19th and the early years of the 20th century. For their benefit included here is a brief resumé of the early beginnings of just a few of our permanent institutions: public utilities, churches, schools, and so on.

For part of this chapter which covers the period from about 1850 to the present century the author has drawn upon the work of the two earlier writers mentioned in the Foreword; Historicus (C.D. Meads) who compiled his *Historical Notes of Burgess Hill* in 1891 and A.H. Gregory who in his *Story of Burgess Hill* continued the theme of growth of the town during the 19th and early 20th centuries up to 1933.

Neither author gives any hint of his sources. Mr. Meads was almost certainly writing mainly from his own recollections, supplemented perhaps by newspaper cuttings and discussion with some of his older contemporaries when he was stuck for a date or some point of detail. Mr. Gregory was for many years on the staff of the *Mid Sussex Times* and it seems likely that most of his information, from 1881 at least, was culled from this, our popular local newspaper.

A few of the facts and dates given by both authors have now been superseded as a result of more recent research: Gregory's date of 1672 on the door of Theobalds farm house, for example, which, as anyone passing today can see for themselves, should have read 1627; and his date of 1769 on the windmill on St John's common in Mill Road, which we are now sure had been similarly transposed from 1796. Nor is there evidence of anyone buying, as C.D. Meads claims, an acre of former common land in Station Road where Bank Buildings now stand for a £5 note. This land was allocated to Henry Marten, owner of Little Burgess Hill farm, who in 1840 sold it together with the rest of his farm land to the London and Brighton Railway Company.

But despite the occasional inaccuracies and their slightly rambling style we must be grateful to these two writers for making some attempt to record the enormous changes that occurred from the enclosure of the commons through to 1934, when Burgess Hill first

22.   An Edwardian wedding party of 1908. The bride in this picture was a great aunt of Mr. F.M. Avery who has kindly co-operated with the author in providing some of the illustrations for this book.

became a civil parish and a town in its own right. It is easy when we live through a period of great changes to accept them as part of every day life with no thought of recording them. Not everything of local importance gets a frequent mention in the local press. A new development involving the loss of scores of acres of former farm land, for example, will certainly be mentioned in the Planning Applications Received column of the local newspaper; there may even be a short article about it and a further report stating that 'approval is given'. Then quite often nothing more is heard until advertisements appear extolling the merits of the latest housing scheme many months, perhaps years, later. The visual scene before a major development started is seldom recorded. Why should it be? It has always been like that, familiar to many residents from childhood – no point in taking photographs or making a drawing or painting of green fields, hedges, and small pockets of woodland. Yet within a few years, when a new housing estate begins slowly to mature, with its neat roads, well kept gardens and established shrubs or trees, it is difficult to imagine how it had looked a few years before – indeed, had looked for centuries.

   Although C.D. Meads made no use of illustrations and A.H. Gregory's were mainly of people, in their own way they did their best to leave a picture of what the town was once like. With them we may trudge through the muddy, ill-lit lanes so familiar today as: Park and Church Roads, Keymer and Mill Roads, and so on. With them we can follow the growth of the town during the hundred years that they spanned. The mention of a soup kitchen from time to time, and especially during the bitterly cold winter of 1881,[2] evokes a shudder: of horror that honest, hard-working people should have had to resort to such a measure however kindly it was intended; of chill at the thought of our predecessors struggling to keep warm at a time when wages were abysmally low, fuel was costly and central heating was virtually unknown – quite unknown in the house of the ordinary working man. Through them can be seen the beginnings of local government as it is known today and much can be learned about the dedication to public service of many of the locals, some of whom were quite humble trades people struggling to earn a decent living yet willing to give up precious spare time to serve their fellow citizens.

But two qualities that shine through unmistakably are those of optimism and self-confidence. To the energetic Victorian the world was his oyster; his county was the best in the kingdom, his town, despite its faint suggestion of a frontier town, was the best in the county; his house was as good as the next man's, and, given the opportunity, there were no heights to which he could not aspire. The fact that many of these men could barely read or write seemed to make little difference. They had 'drive' and the will to succeed in the calling of their choice. These qualities, when linked with a strong personality, frequently more than compensated for the lack of a formal education.

The years following the turn of the mid 19th century were years of continuing change. Both locally and in the country as a whole the population was increasing and there was a switch in emphasis from a rural to an industrial based economy. It was the day of the small businessman who at this time, with an initial capital often of just a few pounds, either laboriously saved or perhaps inherited, and with a minimum of tools or equipment, set up in business on his own account and then by dint of hard work, frugal living and a fair measure of good luck made a success of it. Many still thriving businesses today can trace their origins to enterprising businessmen who, operating on a shoestring budget, started them in the early and mid-Victorian period. All too often however, a successful business can come to grief in two or three generations.

Before touching on this aspect of life in Burgess Hill, however, let us consider a few of the factors that led to the final breakup of our local manors.

The Demise of the Manor

The enclosure of the commons coincided with the great wave of reform that swept the country from the 1820s as the industrial revolution gained momentum. There was reform of the voting system with its extension of the franchise and abolition of the rotten boroughs; reform of the Poor Laws; reform of the tithe system, and the beginnings of reform in the system of land tenure.

The latter had been in operation with no significant change since the Middle Ages, and was in need of overhaul. One of the most cumbersome procedures the early Victorians had inherited from their medieval predecessors was concerned with the difficulty of transferring land previously entailed by a former owner. If, for example, a man inherited premises which had been left to him and his heirs, but not to his assigns, he could not legally sell them. To do so he was obliged to go through a laborious and time-consuming procedure called in the case of a freeholding a 'fine', and in the case of a copyholding a 'common recovery'. This could often result in a man having to give up a whole day to attend the manor court, play an active part in the long, drawn-out proceedings and sometimes to pay the necessary heriots and fines before finally obtaining the requisite document that would allow him to dispose of his property as he wished.[3] All this was to change from the early 1830s in accordance with the provisions of: 'an Act of Parliament, 3 and 4 William IV for the abolition of fines and recoveries and for the substitution of more simple modes of conveyance'. A few years later 'an Act for the Commutation of certain manorial rights in respect of lands of copyhold and customary tenure and in respect of other land subject to such rights and for facilitating the Enfranchisement of such lands and for the Improvement of such Tenure' was passed.[4]

Enfranchisement was the term used to describe the process whereby a tenant of the manor could escape the endless succession of heriots and fines when a property changed hands either by sale/purchase or by inheritance, and of course the regular payment of an annual quit rent. To purchase his freedom a tenant could negotiate an agreed capital sum with the steward of the manor and convert his holding, whether copyhold or customary freehold, to a true freeholding as we understand the term today. Here are just two examples:

Some time between 1857 and 1864 C.D. Meads, now married to Charlotte Jeffery who owned an ancient cottage in Fairfield Road, acquired about quarter of an acre of the former common also in Fairfield Road, allocated originally under the Enclosure Award to William Packham of Bolney, then the owner of Dunstalls. In accordance with the terms of the award the site, being slightly in excess of a quarter of an acre, attracted a manorial rent of 1s.0d. p.a. In addition, a fine and heriot of 6d. respectively became due to the lord of the manor on death or alienation. To free himself of 'all payments, rents, quit rents, fines, heriots, fealty, suit of court and other services, customs, claims and demands', Mr. Meads was obliged to pay the lord the capital sum of £6 which, on the face of it, seems an excessive amount to pay to be free of such small outgoings. Nevertheless, this is what was agreed between the deputy steward and himself, and this is what is recorded in the court records.[5]

The second example concerns John Attree, who owned Inholmes farm then in Ditchling, to be acquired by Sampson Copestake for the purpose of establishing what is now the site of the Keymer Tile Works. This ancient copyholding, together with a cottage and quarter of an acre called Gurrs Inholmes, paid quit rents totalling 5s.11d. (5s. 8d. and 3d. respectively). Other periodical outgoings included a heriot of the best animal and a fine at the will of the lord for the farm; and a fine and heriot of 6d. respectively for the cottage. In 1868 a deed of enfranchisement was drawn up and agreed under the terms of which John Attree paid £331 10s. 0d. to be free of these tiresome manorial outgoings.[6] It should be noted that in 1802 when John Attree, then aged nine years, was admitted to the premises his guardian paid £36 as a 'fine at the will of the lord' – a continuing liability that had probably doubled in the intervening years.

Although legally the way had been open for some years for these two individuals and, indeed, all other manorial tenants to buy their freedom from the manor there was little response, locally, in the short term. The reason for this was probably due to shortage of ready cash; though excessive demands by lords, or stewards acting on their behalf, may also have contributed. In fact, it was not until quite late in the 19th century that, following the passing of the Copyhold Act of 1894, the trickle such as we have described above became a flood and hastened the final break up of the manor.

Throughout the 17th and 18th centuries courts (presided over by the steward and attended by the reeve or beadle and a few copyholders serving as jurors – the homage as it was called), were normally held once, sometimes twice, a year though occasionally the interval might extend to two years. From the second quarter of the 19th century, however, formal courts were being held less and less frequently until by the 1850s almost all manorial business was transacted directly between tenants and the steward of the manor who was, of course, a qualified solicitor. In common with the general movement towards modernising the economy, the manor got caught up in the main stream of change at this time and within a matter of only a few years it had become irrelevant: it had outlived its usefulness. Its long-winded procedures, of the kind described above, and the still extant theory of fealty and service to the lord now had no place in the fast changing society of the early Victorians.

The tempo of life had quickened; and with it went gradually many of the old ways and traditions redolent of a more leisurely way of life, a process that, hastened by two world wars in the present century, has continued ever since.

In the case of Keymer manor some of the tenants were more substantial men, financially, than the lord. The Rev. Henry Bayntun, who held the manor until 1853 and who died a relatively poor man almost ruined by his large and greedy family, could, for example, name among his tenants Sir John Dodson, H.M. Advocate General, who acquired Bedelands farm in 1846 and who held other manorial land once part of Valebridge common then merged with Theobalds, Antye and Dartfords farms, which he had purchased about a decade earlier.[7] John Marten Cripps, owner of Burgess Hill farm and Lottmotts, too, was a very wealthy man with large holdings to the south of the town boundary and in East Chiltington. By about 1850, both could probably have bought out their lord twice over. In 1853 the manor was acquired jointly by Somers Clarke and J.S. McWhinnie, then partners in the firm of Brighton solicitors that had long been associated with the manor. Neither possessed great wealth and social standing; but both were typical of the then rising middle class who were eventually to supplant the aristocracy and landed gentry as the future governing caste in the country. Nearly a century was to elapse before that process, which had its genesis about the middle of the 19th century, would be completed.

The gradual decline of the manor was spread over the next three-quarters of a century. The Copyhold Act of 1894 with its provision enabling a lord to enfranchise premises, or alternatively allowing a tenant himself to apply for enfranchisement, further accelerated the process. The last Court Baron for the manor of Keymer, attended by the steward, the reeve and a homage of two members (James Meeds and Richard Norman, the well-known Burgess Hill potters and brickmakers) was held on 28 April 1876; that for Clayton, the first for many years, in May 1907. There had been no court held for the manor of Wickham since September 1826. Ditchling held its last court on 15 September 1842; a few land transactions were recorded later that year after which the court books, which go back in unbroken sequence to 1598, are completely silent.

The curtain finally fell with the passing of the Law of Property Act of 1922 which provided that, as from 1 January 1926, every parcel of copyhold land was to be enfranchised and cease to be of copyhold tenure,[8] a provision that also applied to customary freeholds. Under the terms of this Act the custom of Borough English which had been in force in our area from time immemorial was also abolished, together with other manorial customs which need not be discussed here. The extinguishment of 'manorial incidents' – rents, heriots, fines, licences etc. – was subject to payment by the tenant to the lord of compensation within ten years from 1 January 1926, and the amount payable could in certain circumstances be decided by a valuer appointed by the Minister of Agriculture and Fisheries for the time being. On the other hand, certain rights were preserved to the lord. Enfranchisement did not affect lords' or tenants' rights to mines, minerals, limestone, clay, stone, gravel, pits or quarries; nor the franchises and privileges of the lords in respect of fairs, markets, rights of chase or warren, piscaries, or other rights of hunting, shooting, fishing or fowling. These were not manorial incidents as such, but the lord or tenant might include them in a compensation agreement if so desired and so extinguish them.[9]

Thus ended, with more of a whimper than a bang, a system of land tenure dating back a thousand years. Devised in Saxon times or earlier when men looked to a local chief for a measure of protection, and paid their heriots and fines perhaps not always unwillingly in return, the system had for many centuries had little to offer its tenants except servitude. Now, some 60 years after its demise, one may look back with some astonishment that it survived so long, for even before the First World War the cost of collecting petty manorial rents, often of only a few coppers, must have been prohibitive. Many went uncollected for years and in some instances arrears were probably only paid when a property came before the steward for transfer of title.

Even as far back as 1844, when the then reeve for Keymer, Jesse Kensett, submitted the only known reeve's account since 1600 to survive,[10] many rents had been outstanding for long periods of up to six, eight, even 12 years. Of the 55 proprietors he visited, 29 did not pay, seven promised to pay later, four were not seen at all, and in four cases he was unable to find either the person listed or the property. The total of rent due for the year was £11 5s. 7d. although with some of the arrears he managed to collect £28 12s. 10½d. altogether. But what this actually cost in terms of time and money must have been staggering even for 1844.

A few years later, in May 1848, the then reeve submitted a statement of the expenses he had incurred when he seized a cow due to the lord as a heriot on the death of John Broomfield, owner of Holmbush farm. The cow, which had to be collected from Nutley, some miles away, was sold for £6; but William Kensett's expenses for the journey to Nutley and two journeys to Brighton (presumably to see the steward) came to no less than £2 5s. 0d. – nearly 40 per cent of the total value of the heriot!

Now all that was in the past. There would have been few who regretted the passing of the manor for, immediately after the First World War, the new breed of farmers, who had been able to sell their produce at a handsome profit for the first time since about 1880, had little time for demands made on behalf of the lord of the manor, whose title now they often held in something akin to contempt. To the lords the title was little more than a status symbol, for manorial profits were minimal and hardly worth bothering about. To the redundant steward it was immaterial if property transactions were done through the manor or privately, so long as he continued to receive an adequate fee for his services.

The final break up of the manor was a severing of one of the last remaining links with medieval England which now seemed strangely more remote than ever.

Public Utilities

As early as 1854, when John Wood was advertising for sale plots of St John's common, he described the area as 'a rapidly improving locality'. At this time the infant town was beginning to develop as two separate entities: St John's common to the north, centred in the area near the *King's Head*, and the post office and shop on the opposite side of the road; and Burgess Hill centred around the railway station and the inn called *Burgess Hill* which had been established about 1845. An early directory of 1855, for example, says of Keymer: 'the village consists of a few houses the principal parts being St. John's common where there are two potteries and Burgess Hill which is a very improving neighbourhood. At St. John's Common there is a chapel of ease and a National school for boys and girls'. Similarly Harper, in his *Brighton Road*,[11] written as late as 1892, refers to 'the twin towns of St. John's Common and Burgess Hill', though local affairs had by then been in the hands of the Burgess Hill Local Board for some 13 years.

The rapid development of the town in the second half of the 19th century brought in its wake many problems. Public utilities were, in effect, non-existent; there was no proper drainage nor piped water, no gas, and it was still much too early for electricity. The new houses depended for their water supplies upon wells, and rain water caught in tanks or butts,[12] and in common with older residents the newcomers found that, when these sources failed, the only alternative supply was to be found in the nearby streams: at the foot of Fairplace Hill, near New Close farm and in what is now Manor Road, all tributaries of the river Adur which empties into the sea at Shoreham. The labour involved in carrying heavy pails of water over long distances on hot days during a dry summer was bad enough, but its quality left much to be desired. As 'Historicus' points out,[13] no provisions were made for adequate drainage 'the overflow of every person's drains and soil tanks flowed upon his own or his neighbour's land and found its way into the natural water courses'. The problem had become acute as early as 1850 when the then Sanitary Inspector to the Cuckfield Board of Guardians ordered several property owners to obviate the nuisance by making cesspools and installing pipe drains. Yet even so the overflow continued to run into the local streams.

With the passing of the Public Health Act of 1873 every 'Union' was obliged to appoint a Medical Officer of Health in addition to the Sanitary Inspector who had already been appointed in accordance with earlier legislation. When the new M.O.H. inspected conditions in Burgess Hill a year or two later he was appalled at what he found; they were so bad that some local owners were found to be liable to prosecution under the provisions of the Rivers Pollution Act. Pollution of the river Adur as far away as Mockbridge near Henfield could be traced in part to the awful state of drainage here in Burgess Hill where, in the vicinity of Royal George Road, the sub-committee appointed to investigate and report on the alleged nuisances found 'one open ditch blocked with black sewage two feet deep and three feet wide'. Upon discovery this was removed at once and pipes were laid over some considerable distance at a cost of £50 which was borne by local owners using the drains.

Thus in the short term some alleviation of the terrible sanitary conditions was effected, though it turned out to be only a temporary measure. In other parts of the growing town, in Freeks Lane and at Worlds End for example, nothing had been done and complaints to the Board of Guardians became so numerous that those responsible were told in no uncertain terms that if they did not take steps to improve the sanitary facilities the Board would do so and send them the bill. The upshot was that, following a public meeting in 1879, the townspeople decided to form a Local Board in accordance with a provision in the Public Health Act of 1873.

One of the first tasks of the newly elected Local Board was that of improving the almost non-existent drainage facilities. With the drive and enthusiasm so typical of our Victorian predecessors the preparation of plans was given top priority. It soon became clear that this would involve engaging the services of an expert in this field, and advice was sought from a Mr. Bailey Denton, then known nationally to be particularly well qualified in this type of work. His plans showed two sewage works, one in Freeks Lane, the other to the south of Royal George Road; but eventually, after the Local Board had ordered a second survey, it was found that one sewage farm would suffice.

It was a far reaching decision, since the ultimate site to the north of the town, where it remains to this day, concentrated an unattractive civic necessity well removed from what was to be very near the town centre. Had the 'two farm' proposal been adopted, the future layout of the town in the vicinity of Orchard Road and Condor Way would have been quite different. Its presence would almost certainly have blocked any proposal for the subsequent establishment of the Victoria Pleasure Gardens in 1898, which gave such delight to children of all ages for the next 40 years. It is doubtful, too, whether the present prosperous Industrial Estate could have been sited where it now is, and certainly the pleasant residential roads mentioned above would have been non-starters.

So it was that over 23 acres of land were purchased from the then owners of Freeks farm and South Bridge farm and the sewage farm sited where it continues to function today. Initially, the Local Board borrowed £15.000, nearly £6,000 of which was spent in laying five miles of sewers; the sewage farm itself cost a little over £3,000 and the remaining £6,000 was swallowed up in compensation to owners and occupiers of land through which the sewers passed. Later, the system was extended to include parts of the town not then catered for, and for this a further £10,000 was borrowed, repayable over a period of 30 years. It had taken 30 years since the first complaints were made to provide this vital service that we now take for granted. Yet not all houses were connected with the new 'flush' system. Many continued until modern times to rely upon an outside lavatory situated at the bottom of the garden where a noisome bucket that needed to be emptied from time to time served for many years to come.

But now there was control over the disposal of sewage unconnected to the mains. No longer was it allowed to flow into open drains and ditches ultimately to contaminate the streams and rivers. How many people in the meantime suffered agonising illnesses through drinking water unfit for human consumption; how many died from the same cause, will never be known. We can only give thanks that such times have gone for ever.

The provision of a permanent water supply had to wait until 1870, a few years after the growing town had been well and truly established. The new parish church of St John the Evangelist had been built; the Clayton side of the common had been enclosed and a few houses had been, or were being, built thereon. Elsewhere other roads had been laid out and were also in the process of being developed for housing and shops. About this time the local consensus of opinion seems to have been that, given a good piped water system, more potential house buyers might be attracted to the area. Whilst the provision of wells (some of which survive to this day) ensured a steady supply of good quality drinking water for most of the year in a normal season, during a prolonged period of drought there was always the danger that they would dry up as, indeed, seems to have occurred from time to time.

As a result of a meeting held at the *Railway Hotel* in July 1870 the Burgess Hill and St John's Common Water Company Ltd., with a capital of £10,000 in £10 shares, was formed. It was a truly local undertaking, promoted by locals (some of whom were newcomers) and managed by locals. The original water works was established at Combe Down, Ditchling near the northern escarpment of the Downs upon land leased from the Earl (later Marquess) of Abergavenny, the lord of the manor of Ditchling. Its purpose was to supply water to (the twin towns of) Burgess Hill and St John's common, taking in parts of Clayton and Keymer on the way. So great was the demand for piped water that the works quickly became inadequate and it was found necessary to form a dam at Whitelands – near the foot of the Downs in Keymer, once the site of a water mill mentioned in Domesday Book – and to pump extra water into the main in order to keep up supplies during the summer.

Within 15 years this, too, had become inadequate and in 1886 the old company was dissolved and a new one formed under the title Burgess Hill Water Company. The new company was given powers to establish additional permanent works at Whitelands. Capital invested was increased from £10,000 to £30,000. The area supplied once more outgrew capacity within a matter of 15 years and in 1901 six acres of glebe land in Clayton village, also near the northern escarpment of the Downs, were purchased and a new well was sunk to provide an excellent water supply for many years to come. By 1925 share and loan capital stood at £85,000 and the company was supplying water to the beautiful downland and wealden villages of Streat, Westmeston, Ditchling, Wivelsfield, Hurstpierpoint, Albourne and part of Pyecombe in addition to Clayton, Keymer and Burgess Hill. Thus in little more than half a century the company had developed from a small, almost insignificant undertaking to one of major local importance. It was to grow even more rapidly in the half century that followed; but that is another story outside the scope of this present work.

Prior to 1866 the only form of lighting in the developing town was by candles or oil lamps and, according to Mr. Somers Clarke, 'very dingy it was'. As with the Water Company, the Gas Company was formed following a public meeting, also held at the *Railway Hotel* in November 1866. It, too, was promoted by local people anxious to provide a modern facility for the benefit of the townspeople, though the fact that there might be profits to be made may also have influenced the instigators of the scheme.

23. Simeon Norman, founder of the building firm of Norman and Burt which specialised in ecclesiastical and other high grade building and restoration work from 1862 to 1974.

24. Henry Burt, brother-in-law and partner of Simeon Norman from 1894. The Catholic and St Andrew's churches in the town were both built by the firm after he became a partner.

The initial capital of £5,000 in £5 shares was not taken up so quickly as had been hoped but eventually, mainly due to the efforts of the company's secretary, a sufficient number of shares had been sold to justify making a start with the buildings and plant on land in Leylands Road which had been bought for the purpose. The contract for the buildings was awarded to Simeon Norman, already becoming well established locally as a successful builder. The contract for the plant and mains went to a Huddersfield firm, Holmes & Co., who clearly specialised in this type of work.

About 12 miles of mains were laid in the principal roads in the town, but nearly 30 years later only 230 consumers were using the gas – a figure that had risen in 1920 to only about 700, though gas was also supplied to the then street lamps.

The original plant which extracted gas from coal has long since been demolished. On the same site in Leylands Road now stands the massive natural gas holder and, on a plot of land adjoining, is the house once occupied by the resident manager.

Many years were to elapse before the town could enjoy the benefits of electricity.

According to Gregory the Urban District Council obtained a Provisional Order (the Burgess Hill Electric Lighting Order) from the Board of Trade in 1901 giving them powers to establish a small power station in the town. Yet it was not until February 1906 that a local electricity supply was first inaugurated and the generator of a small power station in Cyprus Road (the premises of the Burgess Hill and District Electric Supply Company) was switched on. The installation was very small, just enough to light about 1,000 bulbs; but at least it was a start. In 1931 local supplies became available through the national grid. By then the original power station had been greatly extended to cope with the growing demand for electricity over the previous 25 years.

For the present generation life today without electricity would be unthinkable. Yet until relatively modern times the week's wash was often done entirely by hand; vacuum cleaners and electric irons were almost unknown as were deep freeze units and refrigerators. Radio only came into popular use in the 1920s and 1930s; television from the 1950s. Today we switch them on with barely a second thought. Yet this major revolution occurred during the lifetime of elderly people still living.

So much, then, for the beginning of public utilities. If they were inaugurated by people with more enthusiasm than professional know-how, at least the schemes got off the ground reasonably quickly and with a minimum of red tape and officialdom. Our Victorian predecessors knew what was required; they set about finding means of meeting those requirements and then, often by trial and error, fulfilling them. It should never be forgotten that much of what we use, and see around us today – the layout of some of the main roads and many of the older houses and gardens with their mature trees and shrubs – can be traced back directly to the mid-Victorians.

The Church

Among the many Acts that were passed through Parliament in the 19th century was the Tithe Commutation Act of 1836 and, before going on to discuss the development of the churches in the town, a few words about this important Act seem appropriate.

The Act gave facilities for the voluntary commutation of payment of tithe – such commutation being confirmed by a body of Commissioners – or if necessary for compulsory commutation whether the parties concerned wanted it or not.[14] The tithe surveys are worthy of mention here since they provide a very detailed picture of what existed at the time. In addition they can in some instances provide a vital primary source and starting point for anyone tracing the history of their house.

The Act of 1836 finally put a stop to the system of compulsory contributions by house and landowners, or occupiers, of one tenth their annual income to support the local Anglican clergy. Up to this time an incumbent of the Church of England could, in theory at least, demand an annual payment in kind of one tenth of a person's corn, hay, eggs, honey, and so on, though in practice money payments by mutual agreement had been going on for many years. The only local exception we have noted during the century from 1733 to 1834 refers to Clayton Court farm where, in 1772, the local tenant farmer (Mr. Kemp) paid £34 and 'a load of hay and the running of a horse for the winter season'. This was not a permanent arrangement, for the following year Mr. Kemp's successor, Mr. Bull, paid £40 and 'a load of meadow hay out of the rick at any time demanded'.

During this same period tithes of Clayton cum Keymer rose from £193 6s. 0d. to £694 1s. 6d. p.a.[15] an increase in real terms of 40 per cent after allowing for inflation. The tithe payable for Burgess Hill farm in 1733 was £4 10s. 0d. p.a., but had risen to £32 0s. 0d. a century later. That for Lyeland (later called Leylands Farm) rose from £1 6s. 0d. p.a. to £8 16s. 0d. for the same period, whilst Hammonds increased from £9 9s. 0d. to £80 0s. 0d. p.a.

The tithe awards (of 1838 for Clayton and 1845 for Keymer) give, in addition to the monetary assessment of tithe due to the rector, a detailed description of every property in the parishes with the names of owners and occupiers; the area, sub-divided between arable land, pasture and woodland or underwood, together with all roads, ponds, houses and gardens. The map for Keymer, on a scale of 26.6 inches to a mile, shows that a few new houses had been built on the former St John's common, enclosed about 17 years earlier, although as we have previously noted new development was still but a trickle, even though the railway had now been operating for almost four years. Some of the houses erected about this time have now been demolished to make way for the new housing estates built after 1952. The forerunners of Wyberlye in Leylands Road, and St John's house on the corner of Leylands and London Roads, both fall into this category. Others recorded in 1845 were rebuilt later in the 19th century, and many of these have now gone.

As the infant town grew the need for permanent places of worship became a matter of urgency. First in the field were the Congregationalists with their church in Leylands Road, built in 1829 on a small plot of former common land given by Thomas Packham, of nearby Smeeds. The original building, constructed of local bricks and materials donated by public spirited local people, has been altered over the years; and in more recent times a Memorial Hall was built at a cost of £1720 and dedicated in 1924 to the memory of members of the church who gave their lives during the First World War.

As previously noted, when the Clayton part of St John's common was enclosed, one-and-a-half acres of land were set aside as the site for a new Anglican church. The plot lay on the north-eastern corner of Royal George Road and London Road; but later, when serious consideration was being given to planning the new building, it was found to be too far west of what was envisaged would become the new town centre.

A new church to replace temporary accommodation in the school room in London Road, that had served as a make-shift church since the 1840s, had been mooted as early as October 1854, when the following news item appeared in the *Sussex Express*:

> Within the last few years a great deal of building has taken place on and in the neighbourhood of St. John's common in consequence of which the two old Sussex churches of Clayton and Keymer have now become too small to meet the wants of the rapidly increasing population independently of which they are both situated in the south of these parishes and are three or four miles distant from the newly erected houses. We understand that it is therefore in contemplation to erect a church on St. John's common for the accommodation of the more northern parts of the said parishes. The two old churches were perhaps sufficiently large for the original inhabitants but now that another church has become imperatively necessary and as the funds for the erection thereof must be almost entirely raised by voluntary subscriptions it is hoped that this desirable object will be promoted by the immediate neighbourhood, the county at large and by all those who take an interest in the spiritual welfare of the members of the established church.

Little appears to have been done until 1861, though the proposals had been kept alive at occasional meetings held in the intervening years.[16] In that year a block of some 32 acres of farm land called Warners farm,[17] on what had once been part of the Keymer side of the common, which lay to the east of the church and extended as far as Mill Road, came on to the market and was bought by a Mr. John Archer, a property developer who had settled in the town. Learning of the problem that had arisen over the siting of the new church, he at once offered to exchange part of his newly acquired land for the plot in London Road, but finding that there were certain legal obstacles he generously agreed to donate two acres free of charge. He also donated strips of land for what later became Church Road, to link

25. Church Road in the days of the horse and cart. The building on the left was constructed in 1892 and was for many years the offices of the Burgess Hill U.D.C.

26. An architect's drawing of the elevation of St John's church completed in 1863.

the then Pottery Lane (later Station Road) and Mill Lane (later Mill Road) with the church and Park Road, the various sites being valued at the time at £300.[18] These were generous gifts for the times though it was probably in Mr. Archer's own interest to make them since then, as now, the Anglican church was usually situated in or near the centre of a village or town. It followed therefore that, if the new church was built on and adjoining his land, and subsequently the growing community clustered around it, his remaining land would inevitably appreciate in value.

Meanwhile, the proposed change of site brought a howl of protest from several substantial landowners and parishioners in Clayton. Twelve people, including Mrs. Elwood of Clayton Priory, George Godley, Thomas Avery, William Kinchin – the local road surveyor – John Gravett and James Pronger, among others inserted an advertisement in the *Sussex Express* on 23 July 1861 registering a strong protest at giving up a site that had been 'expressly set out by the Inclosure Award for the purpose of a District church'. They went on to 'express our desire that the allotment should be used only for the purposes for which it was set out in the Award'. They probably had a point, and Mr. Archer had almost certainly met it when he wanted to exchange sites, for the authority for the original allotment was an Act of Parliament. But in the end they lost the day.

Events moved rapidly in 1861, as they so often did in Victorian times. Between June and the middle of September an architect, a Mr. Talbot Berry of London, had been appointed, plans had been prepared and tenders received from six firms of builders – three from Brighton, whose prices varied between £5,095 and £5,448, one from London (£4,645), one from Burgess Hill (Norman and Woolven, £4,797) and Ellis of Chichester (£4,173), who submitted the lowest and who was awarded the contract.

By October 1861 the foundations were complete and by 4 November the foundation stone had been laid by the Bishop of Chichester. The *Sussex Express* reported this ceremony in considerable detail, giving among other things the dimensions of the building, a list of the prominent local people who attended, and a précis of a sermon by Archdeacon Otter of Lewes at a service held in the old school room conducted by the then rector of Clayton cum Keymer, Venerable Archdeacon Garbett. This was followed by another address by the Bishop which was again reported in great detail. The dominant theme of both preachers was a plea for adequate seating for the poorer members of the local Anglican community at a time when more than half the seating capacity of 700 was allocated to those who could afford to pay an annual subscription which, it should be said, produced £260 p.a. – a substantial proportion of the vicar's stipend.

When the final accounts were received after the church was consecrated in June 1863, it was found that the total cost was £6,045 3s. 3d.[19] The consecration service warranted a detailed report in the *Surrey Standard* of 16 June, for St John's must have been one of a very few new Anglican churches built in mid-Sussex at this time. The report includes a reference to the weather 'which unfortunately was very wet, indeed so heavy was the rain that the new roads in the neighbourhood were miniature quagmires. Consequently the attendance was not so large as might otherwise have been the case'.

The following year, on Tuesday 6 December 1864, the Bishop of Oxford preached an anniversary sermon in the church 'in behalf of the Building Fund' at which a collection raised £40 – little enough when it was stated that there was still £1,700 owing to the builders, the interest alone on which amounted to £75 p.a. In the event, according to Historicus, the debt was finally cleared by Christmas 1865 and the emerging town had a magnificent new parish church, complete with tower and spire much as we see it today, a century and a quarter later.

Originally a 'chapel' of the parent parishes of Clayton and Keymer, it became an ecclesiastical parish in its own right in June 1865 when it was dedicated to St John the

27. The former Mission Hall at World's End, built in 1887 by Mr. Somers Clarke, is now two shops.

Evangelist. The first and subsequent generations of parishioners have all devoted time to, and spent money on, beautifying the interior of the building, which any visitor with half and hour to spare can see for himself. A few minutes spent in silent meditation in the quiet of this splendid church in the heart of our bustling town can be a rewarding experience.

St John's church struggled bravely to cope with the spiritual needs of the expanding town until about the turn of the century. In 1902 the parochial district of St Andrew was formed. A mission room,[20] to serve the eastern part of the town had been built in 1887 near the junction of Valebridge and Leylands Roads at the expense of Mr. Somers Clarke, then lord of the manor of Keymer. Here for a time was a Sunday school for children, whilst church services were held on Sunday afternoons for older people. Each evening during the week the building served as a reading room.

By 1898 services were being held in a school room in Cants Lane (later part of the garage next to the stream and now demolished), but about a year later were moved to a recently acquired corrugated iron building which had been erected in Junction Road immediately to the south of the present churchyard. Whilst this temporarily eased the problem of lack of space, the need for a permanent new building became ever more pressing. One of the prime movers in its founding was Sampson Copestake, a well-to-do businessman, who generously donated the land for the church and churchyard, together with the several acres of glebe,[21] and the site for the present vicarage. In addition, he made generous donations of cash towards the cost of both the temporary corrugated iron church and the permanent building.

The nave and two transepts were completed and consecrated on St Andrew's day (30

28. Wynnstay at Hoadley's Corner in Keymer Road was built and occupied by Sampson Copestake in the last quarter of the 19th century. It is now demolished and has been replaced by a block of residential flats.

November) 1908 when the district was given full parochial status. The new parish was not wealthy. It will therefore come as no surprise to learn that the eastern end of the church that now forms the sanctuary was not completed until 1924. The tower, that was to have been added when finance became available, remains unbuilt today.

On the Clayton side of the former common a mission room known as St Alban's was built in Fairfield Road in 1885 and here for many years regular church services were held. The building, originally erected at a cost of £324, stands today and is used by Age Concern.

Of the non-conformist churches, the Congregationalists (now United Reformed Church), in addition to their original church in Leylands Road, established another in 1858 in Grove Road,[22] to serve the more central and eastern parts of the developing town. It served its purpose for only about 15 years before it, too, became inadequate. In 1872, as St Andrew's was to do later, the Congregational church moved into a temporary galvanised building in Junction Road. A permanent building on the same site was dedicated in June 1882, having been completed in less than a year at a cost of £2,000. The land, given by the Doubleday family, was once part of Anchor farm which William Doubleday had purchased in 1835 and which then extended from the present Oakwood Road to Birchwood Grove Road.

A Baptist church was established in the town in 1870 when Ephraim Standing, formerly of Albourne, began preaching here, first in the open air and shortly afterwards in what had once been a commercial school room in Church Road. A new purpose-built church, or chapel, or tabernacle, was also erected in Church Road, in 1895. The site was sold and the building demolished in the 1960s, when the Martlets shopping precinct was planned, and with the proceeds an attractive new church was built on its present site in Station Road in 1965.

Among the other non-conformist churches[23] built in the town during the 19th and early 20th centuries was the Strict Baptist Church in Park Road (1875) which, looking south over the park, is still in regular use.

The Salvation Army began in a small way by opening a hall in Mill Road in 1898. By 1906 the present permanent hall was built in Cyprus Road and was free of debt two years later. The 'Army' was not very popular at the time. An officer from Guildford, for example, served a six weeks' sentence in Lewes gaol in 1911 for preaching on the beach at Hastings. In the same year, the Burgess Hill U.D.C. tried to stop evening open air services in the town, though the matter was dropped after about a couple of months.

The Methodist church began with 16 members holding services in a hired room in 1880, but by 1885 these had ceased. A second attempt was made in 1898, and a year later services were being held in a tent pitched on land on the corner of Gloucester and Fairfield Roads. The foundation stone for the new building, now used as a meeting hall, was laid in July 1900.

Christian Brethren meetings were first held in a house in Mill Road in 1870 when two local men broke away from the Anglican church. This small community attracted more

29. The Salvation Army Citadel, built in 1906.

members over the next 30 years or so, and by 1903 a new meeting house had been established in lower Church Road. The building, no longer used as a religious meeting house, is now the Red Cross Hall, available to other local organisations for secular meetings, exhibitions, and so on.

The local Catholic community for many years attended services in St George's Retreat on Ditchling Common, founded in 1866 with six nuns from Belgium. The handsome modern building in Station Road was built about 1940.

Thus the spiritual needs of the growing community were reasonably well catered for before the end of the 19th century when the population of the town had reached about 4,800, representing a five-fold increase since 1851 when it stood at 908. Now, nearly 90 years later, with the population standing at about 25,000, almost all those places of worship described very briefly above still manage to accommodate the present congregations. It is true that the Methodists built a new church on their site in London Road in 1958 to provide additional seating capacity; St John's established the daughter church of St Edward in Royal George Road shortly after; but otherwise the original buildings remain substantially the same as when they were built.

Yet, despite relatively low attendances, the churches still exert considerable influence in the modern town and appeals for money usually meet with a ready response. When, for example, a few years ago St Andrew's needed to replace the temporary hut that had served for many years as a youth centre with a safer, modern and permanent building, many people blanched at the thought of raising the £45,000 required to pay for it. Yet, an appeal was launched; donations flooded in not only from regular attendants but also from people who very rarely go to church; enthusiastic groups organised coffee mornings, sales of work and entertainment; several people generously lent money free of interest; and enormous efforts were made by the youth organisations themselves. Here was something worth working for. The agony of a sponsored walk or some similar strenuous fund-raising activity seemed worthwhile at the end of the day when the money raised was counted up and proudly handed over as a contribution to the new building. The present building has been in use since 1980 and is now free of debt.

Among the various denominations there is now a new spirit of collaboration. No longer are the Baptists violently against the Methodists, or the Anglicans bitterly at odds with the Catholics and non-conformists generally. The old bigotry of even half a century ago has gone, it is hoped, for ever. Today the church-goer looks upon himself as a Christian – a member of a wider community than of just his local church.

Education

At the same time as the spiritual and civic needs of the growing town were being satisfied, education was not neglected. As early as 1811 the 'National Society for promoting the Education of the Poor' had been founded with the aim that the national religion should be the foundation of national education.[24] In practice, the National Society offered financial help in establishing such schools when help was desperately needed.

It is not known precisely when the first National school was established here; but certainly one was well established by 1837 and Henry Breeds, a teacher, was living at School Cottage in 1841.[25] The school which, as previously noted, also served as a church on Sundays, was situated in London Road opposite the turning into Station Road where now stands a terrace of cottages. It continued to provide 'instruction for the poor children and other inhabitants of St. John's common in accordance with the principles of the Church of England' until 1850 when a new school was built at a cost of £674 on the site almost opposite, and with Henry Breeds and his wife as the first teachers. Additions to the original building (now replaced by a new building within the Oakmeeds complex) costing £450 were made in 1858.

30. The old school in London Road, built in 1850, replaced an earlier school on the opposite side of the road. It has now been replaced by new buildings in the Oakmeeds complex.

All the money required for these new buildings was met from voluntary subscriptions led by the rector, the Ven. James Garbett, Lt. Col. Elwood of Clayton Priory, who played a very active part in local affairs at this time, and Philip Jenner of New Close, a well-known public spirited farmer.

The great Education Act of 1870 was financed by a compulsory rate, thus reducing if not entirely superseding the previous method of voluntary subscriptions. The school in London Road was the only permanent state school in the town until 1890, when new buildings were erected in Junction Road to cater for children living in the east of the town. They replaced those previously rented as a temporary measure in Cants Lane. There was to be little change in these facilities for elementary education until the late 1940s, when the school leaving age was raised from 14 to 15, although both schools had been extended in the interim.

The introduction of a compulsory rate resulted in the formation, in 1873, of the Clayton and Keymer School Board, with five elected members and a permanent clerk. The clerk and his staff were later to be accommodated in a handsome brick building in Mill Road,[26] now occupied by Messrs. Bodle, erected in 1893. The School Board continued to function until 1902 when its responsibilities were transferred to the County Council.

In addition to the facilities for elementary (state) education, there were a number of private schools in the town from at least as early as 1851 when the Misses Crunden of 'Burgess Hill Lodge (near the station)' announced that the spring term for their establishment for Young Ladies would commence on 13 January and that they had vacancies for two or three more pupils. By 1858 this private school seems to have been taken over by a Miss Sowton who had renamed the house Keymer Lodge. Also established as early as 1857 was Newton Hall School, originally started 10 years earlier in Brighton by a Mrs. Thompson and now removed to 'spacious and commodious premises [formerly?] occupied by Lewis Slight Esq. . . . having extensive pleasure grounds attached to the house in a locality well known for the salubrity of its air'. Typical of this sort of school was the following from the *Sussex Advertiser* of 3 July 1866:

CHESTER HOUSE BOARDING SCHOOL
Mill Road, Burgess Hill

For the education of young gentlemen, conducted by Mr. W. Bennett.
The subjects taught are the usual branches of English and in addition Latin, French, Book-keeping and Mathematics. The house is pleasantly situated within 15 minutes walk of two railway stations, Burgess Hill and Keymer Junction.
References and prospectuses on application.

Later, others sprang up in or near the town centre to cater for the children of the better-off middle-class residents of the area and from farther afield. Some provided boarding facilities with one in 1900 charging fees of 100 guineas (£105) p.a. Fees for day boys at the same school, in Inholmes Park Road, were 15 guineas (£15 15s. 0d.) p.a. Some were described as Ladies' Boarding School or Young Gentlemen's School; others simply as Private School. One, run by a Mr. Leonard Myddleton Wellich, M.A. (Cantab.) at Inholmes Mansion about the turn of the century, was described as a 'Preparatory School for Public Schools and Royal Navy'.

Throughout the Victorian era and indeed in some quarters up to the present day parents went to great expense to ensure the best possible education for their children. Great emphasis was laid upon their having the 'right' accent – something they would not perhaps have acquired at a National or Council school. Etiquette and deportment, too, featured large in the curricula of private schools. Boys were taught from a very tender age to be brave and courageous in the face of adversity; and boarders in particular led a spartan existence with plain fare, lots of sport and strenuous games, and not infrequently compulsory cold baths throughout the year. Girls would almost certainly have come away with more than just a smattering of a foreign language, usually French, and a certain proficiency in music. In short, both sexes would have had a grounding in all the qualities then considered essential by the rising middle classes.

Whilst the Victorian concept that a basic elementary education for the poorer classes was desirable insofar as it was an appropriate vehicle with which to teach the doctrine of the established church, the authorities were not encouraged to take the principle too far. Throughout the period there was great emphasis on keeping people in their proper places, socially, and schools were expected to communicate to the poor only 'such knowledge and habits as are sufficient to guide them through life in *their proper stations* . . .'.[27] It can be argued that this in itself may not have been a bad thing. So long as an unorganised working class had great difficulty in rising above the class into which it had been born, acceptance of its lowly status may well have discouraged revolt against it.

The first stirrings of change in this attitude came at the end of the 19th century when an Evening Continuation School was started at the London Road premises. Here, the more ambitious young man or woman, whose education was limited to what they had picked up before they left school, often as early as 12, had an opportunity to study, in addition to the basic three Rs, book-keeping, history and geography. By the early part of this century shorthand and typing were added to the curriculum.

Proposals to establish a Day Secondary and Technical School in the 1890s seem to have split the town from top to bottom. Several prominent members of the Town Council were in favour of purchasing for this purpose the Constitutional Club building, later to become the offices of the Burgess Hill U.D.C. and now partially occupied by the Town Council; others wanted to defer a decision until the matter had been put to the rate-payers. Some, whilst not wishing to oppose secondary and technical education, seemed more concerned with the effect the ensuing expense would have upon the rates. In the end, because of the lack of consensus within the town, the scheme failed to attract the support of the County Council, who refused to make a grant towards the cost of equipment and maintenance of the proposed school. This was not an attempt by those opposing the scheme to discourage further education and 'keep people in their place'; it came back to the age-old problem – cost, and who was to find the money.

How different it is today when the highest educational opportunities are open to all. No longer need a particularly bright and gifted child be denied a higher education because of lack of money or, as then, because he was required to leave school at the earliest possible age in order to find work and help with the family budget. The modern system of comprehensive education, too, ensures that the late developer is no longer denied the opportunity to apply for a university or technical college place. Until a few years ago, those who failed the examination set at the age of 11-plus could only do so by obtaining the necessary entrance qualification by studying at night at adult evening classes or even by correspondence course. These facilities, of course, still exist and continue to attract large numbers of mature students at the present time. Today there is no reason why anyone should be denied the opportunities of a full education either during childhood or in later years.

The Late 19th-Century Scene

Agriculture continued to be practised within the town boundaries whilst the centre was being developed. By the mid-1870s many of the roads within the rectangle bounded by London, Leylands, Station and Mill Roads had been laid out and all of these, except Crescent Road, had been fenced. Little had changed in the area west of London Road, which had recently been enclosed, though much of the land in the eastern half of West Street had been developed with new houses. Cromwell Road had been set out; but of the other roads that now lead from London, Royal George and Fairfield Roads there was no sign.

Sheddingdean, Leylands and Bedelands farms to the north of Leylands Road; and Blackhouse and North Blackhouse to the south remained virtually unaffected by the new development. To the east of Junction Road parts of Frankbarrow and Cants still functioned as working farms, but the 80 acres that was once known as Anchor farm, or Doubledays, had all but disappeared as Birchwood Grove Road and the newly laid out Ferndale and Silverdale Roads were filling up. The 40-acre holding, bounded by Folders Lane, Birchwood Grove Road and the ancient Keymer/Ditchling boundary and later called Birchwood farm; the two farms lying to the south of Folders Lane called Woodwards and Purtons; and Batchelors in Keymer Road on the opposite side of the road to Purtons, were still mainly unaffected by the wave of new building now in progress.

Nearer the town centre, Burgess Hill farm, bisected by the railway since 1840, continued to function only to the west of the railway; whilst a large area of the ancient holdings called Lottmotts had become the grounds of the handsome new villa called Woodside, occupied by a retired army general. Grovelands farm was beginning to lose land to the encroaching town; the imposing Victorian houses – Holmesdale Villa and Groveland Villa, both with large gardens – had been built.

To the west of London Road, in what was still part of the civil parish of Clayton, Hammonds farm, which had long since lost about half its original area to provide an

31. The Burgess Hill Coachworks in Station Road was established by William Meeds, son of the well-known potter, in about 1880. The building on the right was demolished in the early 1970s.

32. The Burgess Hill and Mid-Sussex Volunteer Fire Brigade was formed in 1881 at their station in Church Road. The building has long been replaced by modern facilities at the Brow.

Leylands Farm

33. Leylands Farm as it was shortly before its demolition c.1970.

34. Burgess Hill farmhouse was probably built by John Rowe in the early 17th century. By the present century, it had been divided into three tenements and was demolished in 1958.

35. West End Farm in 1985 before the modern housing estate was commenced.

ornamental park for Clayton Priory; Tibballs alias Peppers, then renamed St John's lodge and later to be called Clayton Manor; Thomas Avery's combined farms called Fowles and Barbers; Poveys; Shelleys; and West End farms – all continued to operate as they had for centuries, and as most of them were to do for some years to come. The only holding really affected was Barbers, which had lost some land for modern development in the vicinity of the *Royal George Inn* and Portland Road.

Twenty years after the enclosure of St John's common in Clayton very little had been done within the area bounded by West Street, and London and Royal George Roads, except for the development in West Street previously mentioned. The cottage, once occupied by the 18th-century butchers, Nathaniel Turner and Arthur Gatton, had been improved and was now called Gattons farm, though only about five acres of land went with the house. Near Colmer Place (the narrow lane which still leads from Royal George Road to give pedestrian access to Western Road), St John's Laundry had been built to provide an essential service to the growing numbers of middle-class newcomers settling in the town. The laundry would continue to operate for another three-quarters of a century and more, for it was closed and demolished as recently as c.1960.

Despite the extreme difficulties involved in cultivating our heavy Wealden clay, particularly during periods of prolonged rain, much of the farmland in our area was under the plough. A few decades earlier, when the tithe surveys were prepared, Cants farm, for example, with a total area of over 104 acres had nearly 60 acres under crops. Similarly, Burgess Hill farm of about 120 acres, owned by John Marten Cripps who kept about 20 acres of woodland for himself but let the rest to Philip Jenner, had over 57 acres described as arable. The total areas of our parent parishes of Clayton and Keymer including downland, woodland, houses and gardens, roads, water, etc., were given as 2,353 acres and 3,538 acres respectively in *c.*1840, of which 968 (41 per cent) and 1,673 (44 per cent) were shown as arable.

The *Mid-Sussex Times*[28] gives an interesting example of what could be produced when a man broke up the virgin common and planted wheat. Some time in the second half of the 19th century Richard and Frederick Berry had established a brickworks to the south of the *Royal George Inn* on land which formerly belonged to the potteries run by the Norman brothers.[29] By 1887, when part of the site became redundant, Richard Berry decided to plough up two-and-a-half acres on which he planted wheat. The straw grew to an above average height of between five and six feet, and the small field produced 27¾ sacks, or just over 11 sacks an acre. This represented a yield of over 25 cwt. per acre, nearly 40 per cent above the national average at that time.

Sheep and cattle continued to be bred for their meat, wool and hides. Cattle housed in closed yards for much of the winter provided a valuable source of manure at a time when artificial fertilisers were expensive. Until about the middle of the 20th century the main source of power on the farms was provided by horses or oxen, though on most holdings corn was separated by means of threshing drums driven by steam engines – not, as early in the 19th century, laboriously by farm workers deftly wielding flails.

As the town grew, and especially during the last quarter of the 19th century, some farmers turned to dairying. Thomas Avery, for example, was described in the local directory of 1878 as 'farmer', but in 1890 his son was called 'dairy farmer', having decided that it was more profitable to produce milk and butter, and perhaps cheese, instead of struggling in the old ways with mixed farming. By this time cheap imported grain was flooding into the country from the prairies of Canada and the United States, and in any case growing of cereals had always been a risky undertaking even at the best of times.

Edward Garnett who farmed the 10 acres called Frankbarrow – all that remained after the Railway Company had taken what it needed and more, lying to the west of Junction Road – had by 1890 concentrated his efforts on poultry breeding. There had long been a local demand for good quality fresh eggs. And the more affluent middle-class townspeople would have created a demand for dressed poultry for the table. Such intensive use of the land would have provided Edward with a standard of living that was quite impossible from mixed farming on only 10 acres.

There was to be little change in farming practice up to 1938, the eve of the outbreak of the Second World War. By then Sheddingdean, too, with its 50 acres and more had gone over to dairying and so also had the small holding called Peppers in Leylands Road. Small areas of agricultural land were lost as more houses and bungalows were built, almost entirely along existing roads, in the early part of the present century and in the inter-war years. The great changes came after the Second World War, and particularly from the 1950s, which signalled the end of an era in the town's history: from that time the town can be said to have come of age.

Chapter Nine

The Fair and the Beginnings of the Modern Town

If Burgess Hill was 'a very improving neighbourhood' in the 1850s, and if by 'improving' is meant further industrial, commercial and housing development with its consequential increase in population, then it can be said that the town has continued to 'improve' throughout the whole of the 20th century to the present day, except for breaks during most of the two world wars.

In this concluding chapter the reader will be taken briefly up to c.1939. To the consequences of the Second World War upon the town; to the establishment of a thriving industrial estate, recently extended in Marchants Way and providing work for hundreds of families locally; to the effect on the town of the building of Gatwick Airport some 12 miles to the north in the late 1950s; to the enormous increase in house building since 1952; to the changes in life-style of ordinary working people over the past 40 years or so; to the great changes in education and building of new schools; to the changes in shopping habits and shopping facilities with the coming of the supermarket and the decline of the departmental store: to these and many more aspects of changes in the town and its people since 1939 we shall make no more than a passing reference.

We live in times of rapid change, so rapid that a former resident, familiar with the topography of the town for many years who returned today after an absence of a few years, would be completely lost if he were set down in the newly developed areas north of Folders Lane or those to the north of Leylands Road. Until the 1970s both these areas were what might, for want of a better word, be termed 'countryside' in its truest sense; for here he would have seen sheep and cattle grazing as they had done for centuries; and even now it is not an uncommon sight during the summer months to see lorry loads of hay and straw thundering along Leylands Road; occasionally even a combine harvester trundling its way to some uncut field of corn outside the town boundaries. Many people must have been very conscious of the great changes they have lived through since 1952; but how many made notes or kept newspaper cuttings or gathered sufficient research material to write an account of these recent, major developments? Probably very few. Yet it is a period in the town's history that cries out for attention and one that sooner or later must be written. As suggested in Chapter Eight, most important of all is the current task of recording those undeveloped areas of open land still awaiting the arrival of the bulldozer, and capturing for posterity on film or transparency the fields, and streams, and hedges, and remnants of woodland that were so familiar to our medieval predecessors; for much of that now being developed and the land still awaiting development is ancient farmland taken in from the manorial waste or commons during the Middle Ages – in some cases even earlier. Fortunately, there is now a thriving local history society whose active members are enthusiastically undertaking this important work and thus recording for the benefit of their successors scenes that are about to disappear forever.

St John's Fair

One of the oldest local activities that helped to establish Burgess Hill as an important centre from early times and which continued until well into the present century was the fair that was originally held on the feast of St John the Baptist (24 June), but was moved to 5 July after 1752 when the Gregorian calendar was introduced. The fair had been established at least as early as 1342,[1] though the original charter, which does not appear to have survived, may well have been granted a century or more before that.

The link between a sheep and lamb fair and St John the Baptist is one of great antiquity. The present Anglican church liturgy, and in former times that of the Catholic church, includes special collects, epistles and gospels for many of the saints. The epistle for St John the Baptist's day, taken from Isaiah, ends with the familiar words, 'He shall feed his flock like a shepherd; He shall gather the lambs with his arm and carry them in his bosom and shall gently lead those that are with young'. It is felt that the connection cannot be entirely coincidental.

An early attempt had been made to hold a second fair in September, for in October 1696 the inhabitants of Clayton and Keymer were indicted for 'keping of a faire without a charter on the 15th September every year att St. John's common'.[2] There are gaps in the Quarter Sessions records at this time so we cannot be sure of the outcome. It is probable that a small fine was imposed on both parishes and that they were ordered to refrain from holding unauthorised fairs thereafter. This seems to have been the only occasion on which the holding of a September fair reached the courts, yet certainly by the middle of the 19th century an autumn fair was being held regularly on St John's common as the following extract from the *Sussex Advertiser* of 1858 shows. It reads:

St. John's Common.

Our Autumn fair was held in the Fairfield on Monday last the usual day having fallen on Sunday 26th [September]. Although we do not expect a large attendance at the Autumn fair it was better attended than last year. About 700 sheep and lambs were penned, but there appeared no disposition on the part of buyers to give the prices asked. The sellers did not seem inclined to give way consequently trade was heavy. There were a few good young beasts shown some of which sold readily. The horses we cannot say much for, but there were a few good nags.

This brief report is illuminating since it shows that the autumn fair was then a regular, annual event, though the date had been moved to 26 September. It has not yet been established precisely how long it continued to function but certainly it had been dropped by about 1880. As will be seen later, the numbers of animals offered for sale were small in comparison with those at the July sale, yet the fact that 700 sheep and lambs were penned at all suggests that every autumn there were some farmers who were willing to face the cost in terms of time and money of getting animals to St John's common in the hope of raising a few pounds at a time when money was short.

The autumn fair seems to have been very similar to the one held in July but on a much smaller scale. The expression 'young beasts' refers to cattle – bullocks and heifers of a quality required by local butchers. The reference to 'nags' is interesting. Nowadays the expression is often used to describe horses that have seen better days; but another definition of nag is 'small riding horse or pony', and this is almost certainly what is meant in the above report.

By September 1863 it seemed that the autumn fair was on the verge of collapse. The report in the *Sussex Express* of 3 October is scathing in its comments. It reads:

The September sheep and cattle fair was held on Saturday 26th ult. but a more miserable display of stock we never saw. Scarcely 300 sheep were penned, nearly all lambs and mostly of an inferior quality . . . A few young stock were shown but nothing superior and three or four milch cows and old barrens only one of the former worth looking at. There was one pig or rather an old sow, in very low condition and a lot of coper's horses. Anyone would imagine to hear the noise and halloing that an immense amount of business was done in this line, but they would be terribly deceived if they did think so, for there were very few buyers and all the shouting related to sham deals among themselves [the sellers]. This fair seems to be in a state of consumption and recedes year by year as the July fair improves and we calculate will soon be reckoned among the things that are past. There was not a ginger beer stall, or even a tart and cake vendor to be seen and the booths on the ground received very slender patronage although ample provision was made for dinner as there were but few business men present.

The fair was better attended the following year and managed to survive another 20 years or so mainly because of the efforts of Mr. C.D. Meads, who in December 1869 changed the date to 5 October to avoid holding it so near the Lewes 'old fair', traditionally held on 28 September.

For most of the 19th century the fairs were held on the Fairfield that lay to the south and east of Fairfield Road on the site (later much extended) that was originally granted to Henry Peckham in the 17th century. The summer fair had once been held on the open common a little to the north but, according to Historicus,[3] about 1815 or thereabouts some misunderstanding about the supply of pens for the sheep led to its being removed from the common to the site on which it was held at the time he was writing (1891).

Much earlier, in the first quarter of the 18th century, entries in the manor court records suggest that the fair may have been held on the broad strips of roadside waste in what is now London Road. When, for example, in 1720 a small plot of land adjoining the present *King's Head* was surrendered by James Stone and William Smith to James Eager it was described as: 'quarter of an acre of land called Unicorns *next* the place where the Fairs are held'. Adjoining this site to the north was the house and smithy that once stood in London Road opposite the turning into Fairfield Road. This was described in 1710 as: 'cottage, smith's shop, stables and one acre of land called Smeeds lying *at* St. John's Fairplace'.

Quite frequently the description of premises in the manor court books continued without alteration for many years, sometimes for centuries. Yet these two properties contain references to 'at' or 'next' the Fairplace only between about 1710 and 1730, which suggests that, if the fairs were in fact held on the waste adjoining the main road, the arrangement may have been relatively short-lived.

The July fair was particularly well publicised from the middle of the 19th century until its demise in 1912. Between 1855 and 1903 management of the fair rested with C.D. Meads, who became a very familiar figure to flockmasters and buyers until his death. The following is typical of regular advertisements that appeared in the *Sussex Advertiser* in the mid-19th century:

24 June 1856.

St. John's Common Lamb and Cattle Fair.

Flockmasters and Buyers are respectfully informed [that] the above mentioned Fair will be held as usual on Saturday July the 5th. All persons requiring wattles are requested to make early application to Wm. Miles on the premises as heretofor or to Mr. Meads, Post Office, Lindfield.

N.B. an early application either by letter or otherwise will greatly oblige.

William Miles was then living at the cottage in Fairfield Road and, in addition to plying his trade as a blacksmith, seems to have acted as agent for Mr. Meads who had recently acquired the site in the right of Charlotte, his new wife. The animals were contained in pens separated by 'wattles' – hurdles made of interwoven hazel twigs – and fixed to posts firmly driven into the ground. Since lots on offer varied considerably in size it seems entirely reasonable that Messrs. Meads and Miles should have wanted some advance warning of the numbers they could expect to accommodate in order to have the pens ready to receive them on the day of the sale.

The proceedings were not conducted then, as later, by a qualified or experienced auctioneer. Buyers went the rounds of the various pens and were quoted prices by the farmer or flockmaster concerned. There was almost certainly some haggling over prices, but sellers had a firm idea of what their stock was worth and in many instances were known to have driven their animals back home rather than sell them at a knock-down price. From about the middle of the 19th century the local papers usually gave a reasonably full report of St John's fair. The following is just one example taken from the *Sussex Advertiser* of 14 July 1857.

Clayton.

Lamb Fair. On Monday last the annual lamb fair took place at St. John's common. The largest number of lambs known for many years was exhibited, about 6,000 including 750 tegs.[4] The fair was well attended and the pens of the most saleable lambs were cleared previous to the dinner hour (two o'clock) realising prices from 7s.6d. to 24s.0d. per head; one superior lot was sold at 26s. The tegs generally were not in the best condition and nearly one third were returned unsold; prices ranging from 26s. to 30s. There was a good sprinkle of neat cattle,[5] of various mixed breeds numbering between three and four hundred and those in good condition met with a brisk sale at advanced prices. There was an unusual supply of working horses the superior ones quickly changing hands at good prices whilst the remainder were left unsold. Altogether, taking stock of every description, the total amount exceeded any previous fair and holds out a promising hope of annual improvement.

The first thing to impress the reader must be the incredibly low prices paid for lambs when compared with those of today. The very best fetched only 30s. (say £34 at today's prices) but lambs sold by Messrs. T. Bannister and Co. at Haywards Heath market in February 1986 fetched between £39 and £48, depending upon size and weight, an increase in real terms of nearly 50 per cent over those of 1857. Whilst it is interesting to learn that horses were also offered for sale, the above report gives us no idea of the numbers involved nor the prices they fetched. Later local press reports show that about this time draught horses fetched between 33 and 40 guineas; yearling cattle £5 5s. 0d. to £5 10s. 0d., two-year-olds £7 0s. 0d. to £9 0s. 0d., and three-year-olds £9 0s. 0d. to £9 10s. 0d.

Generally, animals of all descriptions came only from Sussex; but from time to time small herds of steers were driven from Devonshire and from Surrey, and reports of dealers coming from as far afield as Worcestershire were recorded in the mid-19th century.[6] Nevertheless, as a general rule, both buyers and sellers of animals at the summer and autumn fairs tended to be men of Sussex, sellers in the main coming from villages in mid-Sussex and from the east of the county.

A charming 'olde worlde' custom was established in the 1860s when the shepherd employed by the farmer who made top prices for his lambs was awarded 'the blue ribbons' to wear in his hat or upon his clothing. Reports do not elaborate on this custom which persisted until the turn of the century (the last we have noted came in 1899); nor is it known what procedure was adopted in the event of a tie. Perhaps the issue was decided on the toss of a coin.

Refreshments were generally available on the Fairfield, and from the early 1860s were provided by two well-known local innkeepers: '. . . Mr. Pronger of the *King's Head* and Mr. Godley of the *Royal George* had booths on the ground that were pretty extensively patronised and the dinner at the *King's Head* very nicely got up was well attended'.

The summer fair seems to have reached its peak in the late 1860s when over 10,000 sheep and lambs were reported as penned on the site; but normally in the mid-19th century the figure averaged between 7,000 and 8,000.[7] By 1892 there was competition for, in addition to the 8,000 on the Fairfield, Mr. T. Bannister, the Haywards Heath auctioneer, held a sale in an adjoining field at which he disposed of some 275 lambs at prices very similar to those on offer at the fair itself. Thus the writing was on the wall and it was only a matter of time before the fair would cease altogether. From the 1890s, if not earlier, a visiting pleasure fair was set up on the Fairfield on 5 July with its roundabouts, swings, coconut shies and other side shows so typical of the age. The successors of these early travelling pleasure fairs continue to visit the town today though the 'amusements' they provide are now somewhat more sophisticated.[8]

The last fair to be held on the old Fairfield was in 1898, the same year that the site was sold. From 1899 to 1911 it was held 'on a spacious meadow near the Victoria Pleasure Gardens belonging to Mr. E. Street'. For a time Mr. C.D. Meads continued to make the penning arrangements, although he had reached his three score years and ten by 1899. By 1905, however, the *Mid-Sussex Times* correspondent says rather wistfully of the fair:

> This time honoured institution has lost several of its old fashioned characteristics. Gone are its swings and roundabout and missing is the quaint old gentleman with the tall white hat [Mr. Meads] and the smock frock of the homely old farmer, and the whole scene is changed from that of the tight little Fairfield to that of a large meadow near the Victoria Pleasure Gardens.

The numbers of lambs and sheep on offer, too, had dropped dramatically, from the previous average of about 7,000-8,000 to 2,000-2,500 by the early years of the present century.

The success of the fair for nearly half a century from about 1855 was almost entirely due to the efforts of Mr. C.D. Meads. His regular advertisements in the local paper; the excellent way the pens and other facilities were arranged, frequently commented upon by the local press correspondents; his constant presence on the Fairfield and his readiness to deal with any difficulties that arose – all endeared him to sellers and buyers alike. When, in March 1865, the parish officers of Clayton passed a resolution that a more suitable venue for the fair would be the recreation ground a little to the south, Mr. Meads was quick to remind them, through the local press, that it would be quite wrong to change the use of land that had been allocated by the Enclosure Commissioners (who of course had the backing of an Act of Parliament), even for a day or two whilst the fair was held. Furthermore he wrote to flockmasters asking for their continued support (to use the old Fairfield) and asked buyers to do the same. He had a vested interest, of course, since he derived income from the rent of his land. Nevertheless, he was right in protecting the recreation ground from unauthorised use and he was right, too, to keep the fair in the 'tight little Fairfield'. With his death in 1903 it was as if the mainspring of the fair had broken, for things were never to be quite the same again.

From as early as 1858 the Railway Company was making arrangements to transport animals from Hastings via Brighton to Burgess Hill and to pick up lambs en route for delivery to the Fairfield the same day. Up to that time the lambs and sheep had been driven on foot. As previously noted, Bob Copper's uncle usually took three days to drive his sheep from Rottingdean. If a journey of some 12 miles took so long how much longer would one have taken from the villages as far afield as those near Hastings, Bexhill and Eastbourne? The journey by rail would have been more costly in hard cash, but there must have been a substantial saving in labour if animals were to arrive in prime condition.

By 1912 the roads had been greatly improved and the increasing volume of traffic, including the motor car, made it difficult for those who continued to drive their animals on foot. It had to stop sooner or later and, when more and more dealers were attracted to Haywards Heath and Lewes markets, both having sites better served by rail, it was only a matter of time before St John's was forced to close. In 1912 the fair was moved again; this time to 'a field belonging to Mr. E. Street off Station Road not far from the ancient Burgess Hill farm house'.[9] No horses or cattle were sent and only about 1,400 lambs and 60 tegs were penned – a far cry from those halcyon days of two or three decades earlier.

This was the last sheep and lamb fair ever held. A year later on 8 July 1913 the *Mid-Sussex Times* reported that the fair had died: 'died', as the correspondent put it, 'from natural causes – senile decay'. Its closure came as a complete surprise to several farmers who arrived at Burgess Hill on the morning of Saturday 5 July and could not find the fair. No-one had troubled to notify regulars that no arrangements had been made, though Mr. Street had previously informed the flockmasters that although he was willing to place the necessary land at their disposal he could not continue to defray the cost of arranging the fair. It seems that only the local newspaper realised the historical significance of the occasion which marked the end of an era.

Roads and Housing

The period from the late 1840s to about 1875 witnessed the most rapid changes in our history, for then it was that the modern town was born. The last quarter of the 19th century saw no dramatic developments in the layout of the road system, and despite the general economic depression there was a reasonable amount of activity in the field of house building. A comparison of the 6 in. Ordnance Survey Maps of 1873/4 and the second edition of 1899 shows the main differences. By the latter date, houses had been built in the recently created St Mary's Road, then called Fairfield Place; Newport Road had been completed, and Livingstone Road laid out and built up along its eastern side. Cyprus Road, too, had been set out, but only the eastern part near where it joins Mill Road had been properly fenced. Slimbridge and Gloucester Roads and the western end of Western Road had all been pegged out, but none had been made up or even fenced. Commercial Road facing Fairfield Recreation Ground was then, as it is today, served only by a footpath. Many more houses had been built in Park Road but Crescent Road, although now made up and fenced, was, in 1899, almost entirely devoid of houses. There was to be little change in the road system in the next 13 years by which time Dunstall Avenue and Victoria Road had been established, as had Nye Road east of the railway.

Between 1912 and 1938 the only new roads to be created were Weald Road, Norman Road and part of St Wilfrids. Nevertheless there had been steady building activity in the 65 years between 1875 and 1938, almost all of it in roads already laid out where plots were slowly being purchased and filled. Prior to the First World War almost all new detached and semi-detached houses were individually designed, often to a client's specific requirements. The late 1920s and the 1930s saw the beginnings of the small new housing estates, where a speculative builder acquired a modest site of an acre or two of land and with little help, financial or otherwise, erected perhaps a dozen or so houses or bungalows for renting or sale. The small development forming Lowlands Road, and other small uniform groups of houses and bungalows in Leylands Road, forerunners of the modern housing estate, all date from the inter-war years.

Early planning arrangements left much to be desired. In one or two roads, rows of humble terraced cottages lay cheek by jowl with handsome, detached villas standing in large, well-kept gardens, and sandwiched among them were light industrial premises e.g. a smithy, a carpenter's shop, perhaps a pub or two and a petrol filling station. Junction Road, although now considerably improved, fell into this category in the 1930s. It remained virtually unchanged until modern times and even today it remains something of a hotch-potch of mixed development. Speculative builders tended to favour the main roads, most of which were on or near a bus route. Consequently, as the town grew, it suffered from the effects of what was popularly called ribbon development. A traveller from Haywards Heath approaching Burgess Hill via Rocky Lane and Valebridge Road in the late 1930s would have been in a built-up or mainly built-up area from the Eight Arches, through the town centre, along London Road almost to Hammonds Place before reaching open countryside again, a distance little short of three miles. No wonder that post-war governments took urgent steps to legislate for more rigorous planning controls when the great rebuilding programme commenced after the Second World War. By the 1970s, after several years of

36. Packham's Mill once stood in Church Road a few yards south-east of the church, an example of the haphazard town planning of the late 19th century. It was demolished c.1965.

building operations involving the erection of small housing estates on the many acres of waste land lying behind and between the main road (a process known as in-filling), new roads were again laid out as the town began to expand towards its outer boundaries.

Population

So far little has been said about the growth of the town in terms of numbers of inhabitants. The period 1841-81 has been fully covered in *A Very Improving Neighbourhood*, a result of much hard and detailed work by Dr. Short's team in analysing the census returns and in establishing the numbers of people listed under Clayton and Keymer who lived within what later became the Burgess Hill town boundary. This shows that in 1841 the population (much inflated by the influx of people working on the railway) was 1,187. By 1851 it had become more stabilised at 908, and during the next three decades had risen to 1,632, 2,461 and 3,140 in the years 1861, 1871, and 1881 respectively. New building and improvements in public health during the 1880s saw the population increase to about 4,410 in 1891, to rise steadily to about 4,800 in 1901 and to 5,124 in 1911. By 1931 it had reached 5,974.

These figures cover the area of the old Burgess Hill Urban District that had been carved out of its parent parishes of Clayton and Keymer in 1894 when the Burgess Hill U.D.C.

was formed. Later, in 1934, when the town became a civil parish in its own right, the boundaries were redrawn to include that part of Ditchling bounded roughly by the eastern half of Folders Lane, Ditchling Common and Janes Lane from the recreation ground to Little Ote Hall; and a small part of Wivelsfield parish that lay to the north of Janes Lane.[10] At the time it was estimated that this would have the effect of increasing the overall population by 425,[11] a figure which had probably changed very little since 1841 and which, if added to those previously quoted, would provide a fairer comparison with those of modern times (i.e. since 1951). A full analysis of the changes since 1951 is outside the scope of this work. Suffice it to say that at the time of writing the present population is roughly 25,000 and is likely to increase in the foreseeable future. A large new housing scheme on land that was recently part of West End farm is now under way and the possibility of future development to the south of the town near Hammonds Place cannot be ruled out.[12]

Occupations

This subject, like most of those above, deserves a chapter to itself. For the present purposes, it will be dealt with in fairly general terms, from about 1900.

There were three main employers about the turn of the century. One was the clay-based (brick, tile and pottery) industries which, according to Gregory, had by 1897 expanded to provide work for 340 people. This was a considerable increase over the 214 employed in 1881,[13] when the country was in the throes of an economic depression. Ten years earlier the numbers had totalled only 94. The 'people' employed in these industries supported almost as many households for few, if any, single women would have been employed, and single men would have been expected to make a contribution to the family budget. Again, using Gregory's figures, we find that 227 people were employed in the building industry in 1897, against 154 shown on the census return of 1881, reflecting the mini-building boom in the town about this time.

On the other hand, no fewer than 286 people, almost a quarter of the working population in 1881, were engaged in domestic service of one kind or another, ranging from indoor servants, maids, cooks, etc., to outdoor staff, gardeners, coachmen and so on. These were the days when middle-class households could secure the services of a maid or cook or footman for only a few pounds a year plus their accommodation and board, both of which were pretty spartan even by the standards of the day. And frequently these unfortunate people would be 'on call', if not physically at work, for up to 16 hours a day, with perhaps just one half-day free each week.

Yet many of those from poorer families welcomed the terms their employers offered. Some of these young men and women, perhaps for the first time in their lives, would have been assured of three square meals a day; a bed, perhaps even a room, of their own; and a few shillings a week to spend either on themselves or to send home to support younger members of the family. The system also gave young people a certain status in life and if, as we have previously indicated, the emphasis was on keeping them 'in their proper places', there *were* opportunities for advancement within their particular hierarchy. A bright young country girl taken on as a general maid in a large household, for example, could expect to work her way up to become a parlour maid or cook, or eventually perhaps a lady's maid or housekeeper, provided she remained single in her earlier years. Similarly, many venerable country house butlers could look back upon their youthful experiences as junior footmen, perhaps even house boys; whilst the gardening lad once set to work scrubbing out flower pots, and carting manure, could expect by hard work and dedication in due course to become a head gardener.

Daughters of the small farmer and shop keeper often 'went into service' if there was no paid employment for them in the family home. In, say, the employment of a clergyman or doctor or indeed of any professional man here in Burgess Hill, a girl would have learned good manners and how their masters and mistresses behaved in company and, in due course, these genteel qualities were transported into her own domestic life and subsequently handed down to her children. If the pay was low and the hours long, conditions were typical of the age. Many, perhaps the majority, were only too thankful to have a roof over their heads and regular, generally clean, employment.

By the turn of the century the number and varieties of trades and occupations were as large and diverse as those to be found in any small, thriving country town of about 5,000 inhabitants. In addition to the old established brick, tile and pottery kilns: the Norman Brothers in London Road; Meeds in Station Road; and Gravetts on the corner of Station Road and London Road, originally started by William Shaw when the Keymer commons were enclosed, there were the Keymer Brick and Tile Company in Nye Road founded about 1875; Berrys adjoining the *Royal George Inn* and William Bryant at Dunstalls who, although mainly operating as a builder and contractor and supplier of builders' materials, had reactivated part of the once thriving brick-making industry there. There was a firm making rakes and trugs in Station Road. Thomas Stroud of Twickenham had moved to the town in the 1870s, purchased a plot of land from Thomas Avery (for which he paid only £8 10s. 0d.) and had established a brewery alongside the one built a few years earlier by Thomas Charman near the present *Brewers Arms* in London Road. By c.1880 Mrs. A.E. James had established a mineral water factory at Cromwell Lodge, whilst 'The Pure Aerated Water Manufactury' of Harrington, Scrase in Church Road was then turning out quantities of a non-alcoholic concoction called Viresone together with 'aerated lime juice, champagne cider and all kinds of aerated beverages'. About this time Alfred Hyde was producing home brewed stout at the Bridge Brewery in Fairplace Hill. All had gone by 1900 except Thomas Stroud who was by then manufacturing only mineral water and selling wines and spirits from a shop in Bank Buildings.

Charles Wigg had taken over the premises once called Smeeds so frequently mentioned in earlier chapters. There in London Road he continued the business that had been in the hands of the Stone family since 1863, producing farm carts and wagons, bicycles, wrought iron work and farm implements – the nearest that late 19th-century Burgess Hill came to having a factory.

Frederick Hoadley with his large and thriving department store on the corner of Junction Road and Keymer Road, and other retailers, could supply all the requirements of all classes of customers by the late 1890s, though perhaps some of those in the upper echelons of local society may have had the occasional hamper sent from Fortnum and Mason if only for its snob value.

Leisure Activities

At a time long before the coming of the cinema, radio and television; when billiards and snooker were mainly pastimes of the well-to-do; when electronic fruit machines were still nearly three quarters of a century away, people, and young people in particular, had to create their own amusements.

By the middle of the 19th century an annual pigeon shooting match was being held at the *King's Head*. One, in March 1851,[14] attracted 14 competitors including at least one from Lewes and 28 spectators. Each competitor was given the opportunity to bring down five birds. Although William Stepney downed only one of the unfortunate birds, he challenged Henry Marten of Lewes, who had shot five, to a man-to-man contest a week or two later when again Marten proved to be the better shot. The contest was for a prize of £10 and of the 21 birds each was offered, Marten killed 17 and Stepney 13. It has not yet been established how long this primitive 'sport' persisted before finally being abandoned. It was certainly still going in 1864.

Football and cricket clubs had been formed in the second half of the 19th century; indeed cricket was being played by a Burgess Hill team at least as early as 1863.[15] An early athletics club was formed in 1897, and a sports meeting held that year in a field off Junction Road attracted competitors from clubs as far away as Watford, Reading and London Hospital.[16] A swimming club was formed in 1895 when, in the absence of a purpose-built pool, members used a large pond called the Big Hole, on the premises of the Keymer Brick

37. The World's End Fair Committee at World's End Park (now Jane's Lane Recreation Ground) in 1904. The 'fair', originated in 1895 to provide sports meetings, cricket matches etc., survived until c.1930.

and Tile Works. Tennis was once played in Clifton Road and later, in 1931, on courts on Janes Lane recreation ground. The Southdown Ladies' Golf Club with 120 members acquired new golf links in 1891 on land off Junction Road; whilst the Bowls Club, which once played on greens alongside the tennis courts in Clifton Road, subsequently had facilities first at the rear of the *Burgess Hill Inn*, later in Silverdale Road, and finally in 1929 in Royal George Road where it continues to function today. For those who simply wished to relax in the company of those of their own class there was always the 'pub'.

Public Houses
Almost all the 'pubs' in Burgess Hill today can be dated to the 19th century. Many had a stable and a shed which can still be seen today, to accommodate a trap or dog cart for travellers who wished to spend the night in the town. As noted earlier, the *King's Head* had been established as early as c.1780 and for many years thereafter was the only permanent Inn in the town. In 1847 John Agate was established at the *Burgess Hill Inn* whilst continuing to ply his trade as a wheelwright. By about 1855 the *Railway Hotel* and the *Royal George Inn* had also been built. Between 1855 and 1866, at a time when the town was rapidly being developed, the *Potters Arms* in Station Road, the *Cricketers* in Fairfield Road, and the *Watermill* at Worlds End had also been built. Some time before 1880 the *Junction* and *Windmill* inns, and the *Brewers Arms* were added to complete the complement of local pubs as they are today with the exception of the *Weald*, built in c.1960. In addition to these *bona fide* inns there were also one or two people described simply as 'beer retailers' but they had ceased trading by the late 1860s.

The pub served a useful purpose as a focal point for the local residents; for here they could just chat or let off steam, sometimes quarrel and fight to their hearts' content. If some drank too much and became a nuisance there was always the local lock-up where they could spend the rest of an uncomfortable night cooling off.

So much, then, for an outline of some of the activities of our turn of the century predecessors. There was to be no great change in the 40 years that followed, though August 1914 marked the end of the golden age of Victorian and Edwardian Britain, for after four years of bloody struggle, during which time the country was brought almost to its knees, life could never be quite the same again.

The Great War, 1914-18
The declaration of war in August 1914 evoked a wave of intense patriotism through all sections of society. There was an immediate rush to join the army or navy, many naive young men fearing that it would all be over before Christmas, before they could demonstrate to themselves and their fellows what stuff they were made of. They could not possibly have foreseen the long drawn-out agony of stalemate on the Western Front with its appalling combination of cold, mud, shell-fire, harsh discipline, indifferent food, and all the other hardships and discomforts associated with trench warfare; when a man saw his comrades killed or wounded alongside him and wondered when *his* turn would come; when he was even tempted to inflict wounds upon himself as a means of escaping the intolerable conditions.

Yet many, indeed most, coped adequately with the new way of life they faced after 'joining up'; and for those who managed to escape the terrible plight of their comrades in the trenches it was sometimes an educational experience, for many had never been out of their village or town before, even for an occasional night. In the services they met men from Scotland and Wales; Geordies from Tyneside; Brummies from the Midlands. They heard accents they could barely understand and soon their horizons were broadened as never before. Many learnt new skills and developed latent talents.

For those whose special training and skills kept them out of the services there was an opportunity to don a uniform and receive some basic military training by joining the Volunteers, an organisation not dissimilar to the Home Guard of the Second World War. The Burgess Hill force was at first a company of the Hove Battalion of the Home Protection

Brigade. Later called the Volunteer Training Corps and subsequently embodied in the Royal Sussex Regiment, the men from the town became ultimately D Company (Hassocks and District) of the 5th (Lewes) Volunteer Battalion of the Royal Sussex Regiment. Training was carried out first in a waterlogged field off Mill Road, though soon recruits to the new force were given the use of a cow shed in the same area, and later a rifle range was created near R. and N. Norman's pottery works just off the London Road. Finally, after making use for a time of the playground of London Road School as a parade ground, Company H.Q. became permanently established at The Oaks in Keymer Road, where officers and other ranks also had the use of a small meadow.

It is tempting to dismiss these enthusiastic part-timers as amateurs just playing at being soldiers and on a par with the characters in the amusing T.V. programmes 'Dad's Army' that were so popular in the 1960s and early 1970s. Yet they did stirling work usually at night, without pay, often after a long and tiring day at their particular trade or profession; they performed guard duties at night at a large storage depot at the brickyard in Nye Road as well as providing a similar duty at Ford Junction station where trains carrying munitions and provisions for the British Expeditionary Force were assembled. By so doing they were able to release full-time trained soldiers for service at the front. The presence of this volunteer force was also a great morale booster both for the women, children and elderly at home, and for the volunteers themselves, who now felt that they were as fully committed to the war effort as it was possible to be.

Up and down the country in every town and village stands a memorial of some kind or another to those who lost their lives in this ghastly conflict. Here in Burgess Hill, a splendid memorial in the form of a garden of remembrance, in which stands a handsome cenotaph surmounted by a bronze figure of St George, stands at the western end of Crescent Road opposite St John's church. On the panels at the base of the plinth are the names of 145 men of the town who failed to return. Among them are those of three young officers called Meautys, all sons of Major T.A. Meautys, of Hammonds Place. The War Memorial was dedicated on Armistice Day 1923 and is still the site for an annual armistice service to remember the dead of both world wars.

The Troubled Years

The inter-war years were overshadowed by grave stirrings of unease. Although on the surface everyone was trying to get back to normal, the old stability had gone. Middle class residents could still live in much the same style that they had enjoyed before 1914 for, despite a fall in the purchasing power of the pound, labour, including domestic help, was still relatively cheap and in plentiful supply. During the war when most active men were called for military service, women had to step in to keep the wheels of commerce and industry turning. In some cases they were kept on after the war and occasionally a demobilised ex-serviceman would find himself without a job – a situation that was the cause of much bitterness.

With the return to normal trading from c.1920 cheap food again flooded into the country, undercutting home producers. It seems incredible that a lamb could be reared in New Zealand, transported in a refrigerated ship some 12,000 miles, a journey taking several weeks, processed through the docks and one of the main meat markets and still be sold more cheaply by our local butchers than one born and bred on West End farm. The same can be said of beef from Argentina; and grain from the prairies of North America – both these commodities, too, could be obtained more cheaply from abroad. At the same time the Germans were paying the reparations imposed upon them by the Treaty of Versailles in the form of manufactured goods – a factor that did nothing to encourage our own indigenous industries. The result was that farmers who had been wooed by a government desperate to keep the country fed during the war years were suddenly abandoned as having served their

38. The staff of Meeds Potteries in the 1930s.

39. An example of the high quality terra cotta work produced in the Meeds potteries. These plaques were made to commemorate Queen Victoria's Diamond Jubilee.

purpose. Similarly, factories formerly engaged in producing munitions and weapons of war found little financial assistance forthcoming from what should have been a grateful country when they needed to re-tool and switch to peace time production.

Labour relations reached an all time low in the 1920s, culminating in the General Strike of 1926 when even some of the police withdrew their labour. Work was resumed within a few days in an atmosphere akin to that of armed neutrality, but what trust there had been between employer and employee was in many areas fast disappearing. The bitterness engendered during this period was to last for several decades. With the rise of the Fascist and Nazi parties in Italy and Germany the sense of unease was heightened until by the late 1930s almost everyone realised that it was only a matter of time before the country would again be at war.

Throughout the period money was in short supply. The old penny was not despised; neither were its fractions the halfpenny and the farthing. Competition between rival trades in the same or similar lines of business became intense, especially during the 1930s and to some of them the outbreak of the Second World War must have come almost as a relief, since bankruptcy was staring them in the face. Yet despite the economic depression of the late 1920s and 1930s, for the fortunate people who had jobs the era was not entirely one of gloom. Indeed for many it was a time when their standards of living rose considerably and when a man earning four or five pounds a week could afford to buy his own house through a building society and perhaps run a small car. The greatest worry was lack of security.

Thus the town, and the nation stood on the brink of a war which was to last for six years, the effects of which were to change the social and economic face of the country for ever. The last of the potteries, Meeds in Station Road, was forced to close in 1940 when the glow from the kilns contravened the black-out regulations. They were never again re-opened. Two of the other active brickworks and potteries – Normans and Gravetts – had already closed;

40. Norman's Potteries in London Road showing the drying sheds with St John's church in the distance. The potteries were closed in 1930.

Normans in 1930 and Gravetts as long ago as 1909, though even today one or two of the old buildings can still be seen on the Gravetts site, now used as a builders' yard by the local authority.

Conclusion

The town today has come a long way since the enclosure of the commons and the coming of the railway nearly one and a half centuries ago. Yet if we look around reminders of those far off days can still be found. Walk along Fairfield Road to the recreation ground and look towards the west and you will see several acres of open former common land now preserved by the local authority as open space in perpetuity. On the western portion it is still possible to see traces of the brick-making industry that thrived for a while in the second half of the 19th century. Adjoining this land, with access from Royal George Road, is a footpath along which one can still walk round the site that was enclosed in the 17th century and later occupied by Arthur Gatton, whose name is remembered in Gattons Close and The Gattons Infants School.

St John's Park, too, is a permanent reminder of the Keymer side of the common. Small pockets of the former common can still be found near Civic Way and Queen Elizabeth Avenue, whilst in Freeks Lane there are several acres waiting to be developed.

London Road and those roads leading from Keymer village towards Haywards Heath (Keymer, Junction and Valebridge) remain our most ancient highways. With a little imagination one can picture our Saxon predecessors setting out along them in early April

41. Junction Road, one of the two main north-south thoroughfares in the town. In Saxon times, this road linked Keymer village with the wealden grazing grounds in Balcombe and Worth.

with their flocks and herds to graze their animals on new grass in some of the wealden forest clearings, whilst their own pastures recovered from the ravages of winter. Much later, London Road would resound to the clatter of horses' hooves and the rumble of wheels as coaches and all manner of horse-drawn vehicles made their way from London towards Brighton and the south coast.

Lye Lane, that led from Valebridge common to St John's common, was called Leylands Road at least as early as 1851,[17] having for a short time after 1830 been called Chapel Lane after the Congregational Chapel at its western end. This, too, is a very ancient way linking the two main highways; it is in fact the *only* link in the north of the town before you reach Haywards Heath. Freeks Lane, ancient at the very beginning of our period, remains very much today as it was in 1600. Several houses were erected there during the middle of the 19th century and it is now crossed by Maple Drive, thus almost sealing off the southern section; but in essence it remains little more than the rough track it always was, although some efforts have recently been made to fill in some of the worst potholes.

Elsewhere the layout of the town conforms generally with that which evolved during the period of main development over a century ago. The 'in-filling' referred to earlier resulted in the creation, since the 1950s, of many new roads and closes as did the major modern housing estates which pushed back the frontiers of the early 20th-century town – Chanctonbury, Folders, Maple Drive, Sheddingdean, etc., all built on former agricultural land.

Important as these developments were, the changes that had the greatest visual impact were those that followed the building of the Martlets shopping and office complex, and the closing of part of Church Road to create in the early 1970s a pedestrian precinct. These, together with the formation of new car parks, the provision of a site for an open market and the development of The Brow, once the site of brickworks since the time of Samuel Marten, completely changed the face of the town centre. They gave the town the heart that had somehow been strangely lacking in former times. Today people come into the town from far and wide; to browse round the stalls in the open market on Wednesdays and Saturdays; to visit the popular public library; to shop in the supermarkets and privately owned establishments all of which provide excellent facilities and service; and to attend the exhibitions, meetings, craft fairs, etc., so often held at the Martlets Hall and other halls in the town centre.

Until recently Burgess Hill in one area was bursting at the seams. The thriving industrial estate in the south west of the town had expanded to such an extent that some buildings were in the parish of Clayton. Recently the boundaries have been adjusted to keep these new buildings within the town where they properly belong. A mile-and-a-half to the north east a similar situation arose with new houses. The road called Charlwood Gardens, Burgess Hill, is in fact in Wivelsfield. It lies not only outside the town boundary but also outside the county boundary, Burgess Hill having been transferred to West Sussex in the great local government reorganisation of 1974. Whilst this pleasant new housing estate is reasonably near good public transport services and shops, children living there have to attend either Wivelsfield Primary, or Chailey Comprehensive Schools, both some miles distant.

Despite the immense problems of unemployment today, created for the most part by the introduction of modern computerised office and production techniques, the town continues to thrive and by and large its people enjoy a standard of living undreamed of only half a century ago. Much of the 'labour' has gone out of most manual work, for there are few areas that have not been capable of *some* element of mechanisation. Yet there is still something eminently satisfying in a man exercising his muscles and working by the sweat of his brow, which explains perhaps why so many men still enjoy working hard on their gardens and making things for themselves that could just as cheaply be obtained from a shop or a specialist. There is no need for people to be bored today even if some have no regular work.

There are leisure facilities galore in the town. With an ageing population, too, more and more voluntary workers will be needed to give the disabled and the elderly assistance, companionship and general support.

I would like to end with one or two observations made by the late Kenneth Clark:[18]

I believe that order is better than chaos, creation better than destruction. I prefer gentleness to violence, forgiveness to vendetta . . . I believe that in spite of recent triumphs of science men haven't changed much in the last two thousand years; and in consequence we must still try to learn from history : . . I believe in courtesy the ritual by which we avoid hurting other people's feelings by satisfying our own egos. And I think we should remember that we are part of a great whole which for convenience we call nature. All living things are our brothers and our sisters. Above all, I believe in the God-given genius of certain individuals, and I value a society that makes their existence possible.

Well, we cannot all be geniuses but we can, each in our small way, make some contribution to the society in which we live, sometimes simply by just 'being there' when our presence is most urgently needed. Lord Clark, who was writing in the late 1960s when many of the old values and standards were being swept away on a tide of cynicism and self-destruction, ended his work on a note of pessimism which today I cannot share. There are now hints of a growing change of attitude in the minds of many of the more creative members of the rising generation. Those of us who reckon we have done our bit through years of war and peace must look to them to safeguard the future of our country, of our way of life and of our (? new) Sussex town.

Chapter Ten

Later Days

by Mark Dudeney

Hugh Matthews' in-depth study of Burgess Hill first appeared in 1989 and ever since has provided general readers and students alike with a comprehensive background to the community in which they work and live. However, more than seventeen years have elapsed since the publication date and, even in such a short space of time, the town has continued to grow beyond the most sanguine expectations of planners and public. The purpose of this additional chapter, therefore, is to describe that progress while at the same time preserving the history of the area affected.

In 1989, the Clayton side of the district was bounded by London Road, Victoria Road and Victoria Avenue, including sections of Royal George Road, West Street, and all of Dunstall Avenue. And while, in a few places, small residential estates were already encroaching onto land beyond, these thoroughfares still formed the outer framework of the town.

All this has now changed. A new road branches off from the A273 opposite the junction to Chanctonbury estate. This western bypass eventually veers to the north, crosses both Malthouse and Gatehouse Lanes, then swings back to the east where it rejoins London Road at the foot of Fairplace Hill. The area enclosed, consisting entirely of farmland and open spaces, was then transformed into houses, a school, a leisure centre, a supermarket, factories and even a burial ground. In short, everything (save a church) that may be found in a modern society.

The effect of this development, the largest building project ever undertaken at Burgess Hill, is still being measured. The town's population has trebled since 1951 and now exceeds 28,803 persons, which is greater than neighbouring Haywards Heath, and the portents are that it is just beginning. More chapters may yet be added to this work!

In the preface to the first edition, Hugh Matthews indicated that the general thrust of his book would be 'Land and Folk'. The theme in this chapter remains the same.

Our tour will commence at the large roundabout situated where the A273 (the London Road) forms the southern approach to the town. A traveller arriving at this junction may proceed in one of four directions: east into Chanctonbury estate, north to the town centre, north/west along Hammond's Ridge, or due west on the bypass known as Jane Murray Way, so named after a popular town clerk.

The Jane Murray Way cuts through former parkland belonging to Clayton Priory, a private occupancy set back from the road and concealed from view by trees. Built in the Georgian style, the Priory is an imposing dwelling, yet apart from the circumstances of construction – which will be alluded to later – the place has no history worth relating, or none that I can discover. One has to rely on fables for any real interest. For instance, from time to time, the nonsense is repeated that once, long ago, it really had been a

168

priory or religious house of some sort and, what is more, was connected to the nearby *Friars Oak* by a secret tunnel! But like the legends clinging to that old hostelry, the tales are entirely without foundation, the facts being that at the conclusion of the Napoleonic Wars (in 1816 or thereabouts) the premises were built and the grounds landscaped as a mansion house for a Captain Higgins. There is no record of property, monastic or otherwise, on the site before that date.

To the north of Jane Murray Way, on land that belonged to Hammonds Place (once known as Atwoods), stands a pleasant residential estate shaded by fine oak trees. The roads that service the area have been well named in that they reflect their association with the 'Big House', a truly venerable dwelling. Partly-timbered and capped with a roof of Horsham stone, Hammonds Place is beyond doubt the oldest building in the district. The porch entrance is Elizabethan, and on the doorway jamb – almost obliterated by age – are the initials E.M. They probably denote Edward Michelborne, the person who is credited with constructing the property, although it is possible that he just extended a premises already existent on the site. Above the porch is a carved shield and, high on the gable, an inscribed date: 1566. The freehold was once much larger, but during the 19th century, in an act of official vandalism, the extraordinary decision was taken to demolish the southern side of the mansion in order to provide the timber and stone with which to build Clayton Priory.

Despite the honour implied by his title, Sir Edward Michelborne (Edward Michelborne's son and heir) was reputed to be a bloodthirsty ruffian with a penchant for piracy. Rumour had it that some of his ill-gotten gains were buried in the grounds of the ancestral home. Should that be the case, it was well done, for none has come to light – or so we are told.

One mystery follows another, for I am reluctant to reveal the precise location of our next port of call. Suffice it to say that a particular meadow to be sacrificed to the housing estate was, back in the 1930s, rented by my uncle, a Burgess Hill fishmonger, who used it as a dumping ground for the waste products of his stock, fish heads, bones, guts and the like. Local children named the area the 'Fish Offal'. 'The stench,' recalled one, 'was awful. You could find your way there blindfold.' The place was at least popular with anglers, because of the quantity of maggots that infested the land.

A few steps along the highway and we come to a spot where past and present blend cheek to jowl, in the form of a footpath severed by the road. Easy to see, especially in the spring, when bluebells flourish in the ancient hedgerows, it is what remains of a tenants' way that, having passed Hammonds Place, skirts the back of Clayton Priory, descends to Hammonds Mill, then forks west to Scotches and south to Clayton Wickham, where it is referred to as Hogs Pudding Lane. Our route lies in a different direction, to the next roundabout and a red-roofed Tesco superstore.

Tesco had operated in the town's Martlets shopping area for many years. Then came the Market Place development comprising 10,300 square metres of floor space and a Waitrose supermarket which began trading in 1991. The continuing implementation of the Burgess Hill Local Plan provided the opportunity for Tesco to expand. Accordingly a planning application was submitted to erect a food superstore alongside the yet-to-be-constructed western distributor road (Jane Murray Way).

Not everyone was in favour of the proposal and, in October 1991, the Action Group for the preservation of Village Life was invited to analyse and comment on the project with specific reference to what was described as 'shopping impact studies'! The report employed phrases such as 'twinge of concern', 'dubious economic benefits' and 'opinion is firmly against this development'. Yet the application succeeded, work went ahead and the new store opened its doors to the public in 1993.

Tesco provided a free bus service to and from the store in recognition of the fact that it was some considerable way out of town. Gradually it has become not only accepted, but has significantly increased shopping opportunities (and employment) in the town. This was borne out by a Mid Sussex survey undertaken in 2002, which showed that, instead of using the facilities in Brighton, Crawley or Haywards Heath, as had previously the case, 92 per cent of Burgess Hill households used local stores for their food shopping and 66 per cent of that number patronised the Tesco store, a figure of course which did not begin to account for out-of-town visitors. Such statistics speak for themselves and it only remains to add that at the present time (2006) thousands of customers from Burgess Hill, Ditchling, Keymer, Hassocks and Hurstpierpoint shop at the premises every day of the week, and the company supplies virtually all of their needs, from cradle to grave! Which neatly introduces us to the next stage of our journey.

With the millennium barely started, the local council was required to face up to the question 'Where will we bury our dead?' It had long been obvious that the graveyard next to St Edward's Church at the foot of Royal George Road, was bursting at the seams, yet a replacement site was extremely difficult to find. That efforts to resolve the matter produced a lot of heat and not much light would be hard to deny, for acres of newsprint packed with conflicting advice and unhelpful comment had been devoted to the subject. They were stressful times for the bureaucrats, but happily the business was eventually settled and a new burial ground may be found along Jane Murray Way opposite the junction with York Road.

Preparation of the area started in January 2003 and was completed 18 months later. It is a non-denominational site and, as such, remains unconsecrated, while the

42. Burgess Hill Burial
Ground.

upkeep is the responsibility of Burgess Hill Town Council. To quote from the official brochure, the place '... has been sympathetically designed to blend with and enhance its rural setting, and will include a commemorative woodland area.' The hope now is that the facility will provide a swiftly growing community with sufficient burial space for at least the next hundred years.

Beyond the Burial Ground, the bypass rolls on – buildings to the right, meadows to the left – and then it crosses Malthouse and Gatehouse Lanes, cutting off the ends of both in the process.

Malthouse lane still leads to Hurst Wickham and Hurstpierpoint, but people travelling there enter only from Jane Murray Way.

Gatehouse Lane, however, goes nowhere at all. Emasculated by the new road, it re-emerges briefly on the other side to link High Hatch Lane with Cuckfield Road, then peters out in the fields. Those seeking refreshment at the *Sportsman Inn* at Goddards Green may either walk from the foot of West Street, or approach by car from another direction. All of which is a far cry from the days when the thoroughfare was the busy western route to Burgess Hill. At one time the London-bound stage coaches rattled by, and in 1915 it was the road that the luckless soldiers of East Lancashire took as they marched to the Western Front by way of Pease Pottage, Crowborough and Dover, a journey from which few would ever return.

St Paul's Catholic College

Our next stop is at the junction of Jane Murray Way with the new A2300 link road to Hickstead, for there, overlooking the roundabout, is St Paul's Catholic College, late of Oathall Road, Haywards Heath where the building was too small and the conditions too cramped to permit any further expansion. Land became available in neighbouring Burgess Hill and the benefits of a move were obvious: they could build a brand new college and at the same time be closer to their junior feeder school, St Wilfrid's, which was situated near Queen Elizabeth Avenue. It was a massive undertaking; from inception to completion the project took seven years and cost £13 million. The result was a clean, spacious, thoroughly modern building, with wide, well-lit corridors, under-floor heating and electronically controlled windows for temperature regulation in the sports hall and passage ways. From the instructional point of view, all the classrooms were equipped with electronic white boards connected to teachers' laptops, while wireless internet connections made it possible for pupils to use their own laptops to access all lessons and private studies, either in the classroom, or at home.

The all-important spiritual aspect of the establishment is identified by the presence of a large illuminated crucifix and a chapel that replicates the shape of a brick kiln, reminding us, should we need such a reminder, of Burgess Hill's industrial history.

St Paul's was scheduled to open on the first day of the autumn term, 2 September 2004. It actually opened a few days later and the delay caused some embarrassing headlines for the Principal. 'Apologise,' demanded disgruntled parents. But the Headmaster had none of it. 'I am not apologising for anything,' he is quoted as saying. 'So they [the pupils] missed out on five days education, but I would reckon that the quality of education they are going to get in this building more than makes up for that. I don't think it's an issue, nor does the education authority or the school governors.'

Triangle Leisure Centre

Connected to St Paul's College by a tunnel that passes beneath the road, the Triangle Leisure Centre is one of the most ambitious projects ever to be undertaken by the local authorities. Prior to its existence, facilities for sport had become somewhat stretched in Mid Sussex, a situation that had arisen because of the dramatic and continuing increase in population, together with an unprecedented public demand to engage in recreational activities. As this edition goes to press, it has been re-branded 'Olympos at the Triangle'.

It is odd to reflect that, back in the 1950s, no one but the most ardent fan would have complained about a lack of amenities. Cricket, football, stoolball, hockey and tennis were played at a variety of grounds, public and private alike. Oakmeeds School, which had recently been built in the meadows of Burgess Hill Farm, benefited from vast playing fields. The Sidney West Centre (which is referred to later) had been opened down Leylands Road, while the open-air pool in St John's Park, probably the most popular venue the town ever possessed, was the headquarters of a thriving swimming club and frequently hosted galas at the premises.

Everything has changed since then. Burgess Hill, accorded as the fastest developing area in the South East, now boasts The Triangle, an all-purpose sports hall that contains a 25-metre indoor swimming pool and an arena with a capacity for tiered and flat floored seating especially designed to accommodate concerts, exhibitions, trade shows and large-scale sporting events, plus an air conditioned arena called the Apex Suite, which caters for conferences, business meetings, training sessions etc, whilst separate facilities are provided for bowling, badminton, table tennis and squash. There is also an open-air swimming pool plus pitches for football and hockey with floodlighting, and courts for tennis and netball.

43.   Olympos at the Triangle.

The entire roof surface spans two acres, over a million bricks were used in the construction, and the scheme cost £13.5 million. On completion in 1998 it was handed over to Mid Sussex District Council, ready for opening the following year.

Friday, 26 March 1999, was the date set aside for the grand occasion. A date of historical significance in that it marked the first time the reigning monarch, Queen Elizabeth II, accompanied by her husband HRH The Duke of Edinburgh would visit Burgess Hill. Around five thousand people lined the streets, some having queued for hours in order to gain a good viewing position. Many had travelled considerable distances to add their greetings to those of the locals, and these included the mayors of Schmallenberg (Germany) and Abbeville (France), towns that have been twinned with Burgess Hill.

With ears ringing from the cheers of the populace and the pealing of bells from St John's Church, the royal entourage slowly made its way via a stop at the Town Council offices to the new Leisure Centre. Crowds lined the route and were gathered in great numbers round the complex itself – which the Queen declared officially open. The party was then conducted round the building, viewing swimming and sporting demonstrations as well as being introduced to sportsmen and sportswomen, members of the staff, schoolchildren, councillors, and those involved in the Centre's design and construction. 'It was,' said a news report '... a very special day for Burgess Hill, and one that will long live in the town's memory.'

There were those who criticised, not because of opposition to the sports centre *per se*, but because of what was perceived to be confused priorities associated with the project, including the importance of the opening ceremony. They had a point, for avoidable mistakes were made; such as an out-of-date reference inscribed on an official plaque at the front of the premises; or tiles improperly affixed that became unstable causing the swimming pool to be closed during school holidays. And what surely should have been foreseen – how lack of space at the poolside, combined with the background noise of the flumes, made it all but impossible for county swimming galas to be held there.

West End Farm

Jane Murray Way ends at the junction with St Paul's College and the Triangle, and

44. *The Woolpack* public house (formerly West End Farmhouse).

from this point the road (until the next roundabout) becomes the A273, passing close to West End Farmhouse, a truly historic building that has suffered the indignity (some say) of being converted to an inn.

In the late 19th century it was the home of Charles Tulley, one of the grand old men of Burgess Hill, who, when congratulated on the condition of his sheep during a particularly dry season, was quoted as saying, 'Yes, nine years out of ten my flock keeps me, and when we get a year like this – I keep my flock.'

The last person to farm West End was the late Victor Marsh, a well known figure in local dairy circles and a stockman whose cattle frequently left evidence of their passing in West Street. Because of this, and other matters, I often visited the premises in my capacity as a local policeman, and the routine was always the same; with business done we would retire to the parlour and broach a bottle of cider. Home brewed and good stuff it was, fruity and mellow and full of sunshine. I viewed the world quite differently after a drink with Victor. What would he think now, I wonder, if he could see his old home, and what would he make of the medical centre, the shops, and the row upon row of houses that have sprung up in the former fields and pastures?

It is interesting to note how, in some cases, the thoroughfares that connect these properties have been linked either directly or indirectly with Burgess Hill and the surrounding district. For instance, we find that Clifton Road (which in times past was sacrificed to make room for Waitrose) has been reborn. A headmaster at the old London Road School is commemorated by Baylis Crescent. Saxby Road does likewise for an inventor from Hassocks and Mocatta Way reminds us of the architect who designed Brighton railway station. But the greatest honour has been accorded to actor Valentine Dyall who lived next to Elmhurst in Station Road. He has been acknowledged twice, by Valentine Drive and Dyall Close.

Neither is local flora forgotten. The Acorns lead into The Oaks, with The Hornbeams and The Rowans close by, while Primrose Close and Foxglove Close are connected by Bluebell Way.

Then there are the cricketers; Tate Crescent – Cornford Close – Cox Grove – Langridge Way, etc. There is even a Wisden Avenue and The Wickets. They are all huddled together, save poor Vallance Close – that particular byway must have incurred the wrath of the naming committee, for it has been posted to 'long stop' and may be found some distance away down Howard Avenue.

As a final comment on the local highway system, throughout the years there was only one street in Burgess Hill. Avenues and drives, courts and crescents, roads, lanes and ways were two a penny, while West Street stood alone. But no longer; a newcomer, Beale Street, celebrating the memory of H. Linford Beale (yet another headmaster), now adjoins Hammonds Ridge.

The Sewage Farm

Having completed the circuitous route – Jane Murray Way, the A273, and finally Sussex Way – we rejoin London Road at the north of the town and slip up winding Fairbridge Way to the sewage farm, an establishment that since 1880, or thereabouts, has served the community well, the first supervisor of which (Mr Edwin Brown) subsidised his income by growing peppermint within the grounds.

But now, it is a scene of abandonment and decay, a wired-off compound containing rusting equipment and derelict buildings engulfed by rank growth and brambles. Nature has taken over and is rapidly transforming the area into a wilderness – and a possibly contaminated wilderness at that. At the time of writing the future of the land is uncertain, but the reason for closure is simple enough. The premises was unable to deal with the demand posed by a rapidly increasing population and so a new gleaming utterly modern treatment plant, serving the needs of Burgess Hill and the surrounding district, was constructed in the fields at Goddards Green. Cleverly concealed from view by coppice and hedgerow, the site's position is betrayed only by the prevailing wind.

Sidney West Hall

A building that played a part in the lives of many Burgess Hillians, and which has since been demolished, was the short-lived Sydney West Hall at Leylands Road. The five-and-a-half-acre site on which it stood was acquired in the early 1950s when a group known as the Mid Sussex Social Welfare and Sports Club was created with a view to providing facilities in the shape of land and buildings for any sport or form of recreation. This included the actual arranging and promoting of tournaments and competitions to benefit both its own members and those of other clubs and affiliations.

As a result, in 1955, a premises comprising a gymnasium and changing rooms was constructed in the grounds and this was later extended to include a kitchen and catering area. In 1978, a rifle range, bar and a lounge were included and then, in 1980, a separate building housing four squash courts was added. All of which meant that, by 1982, as well as the cricketers, who had been there from the outset, 11 clubs were associated with the organisation. Amongst these were:

St Andrew's Cricket Club
Ye Cuckfield Bowmen - a group who used the cricket field for archery and who were involved with Chailey Heritage, St Dunstan's and the Scouts.
Mid Sussex Amateur Boxing Club – the *raison d'être* for the sports centre's existence.
The Westerners Badminton Club
The Butterflies Badminton Club – a group for ladies only.
The Mid Sussex and Burgess Hill Badminton Club
Burgess Hill Rifle Club – formed by members of the Home Guard in 1942, it had several homes in the early years, including Hurstpierpoint College, but finally settled in 1979 at the purpose-built range at Sidney West. The Rifle Club was a particularly well-supported group. Its extensive programme included local leagues, county and national competitions, while, in addition, courses were arranged for scout troops, the Air Training Corps and East Sussex Police.
Burgess Hill Squash Rackets Club

All in all then, it would appear that the Sports Centre had been most successful but, if that were so, where is it now? Admittedly cricket is still played at the ground – but of the boxers, badminton players, squash enthusiasts, riflemen and the rest, there is no sign. Like the building that accommodated them, they have vanished. How can this be?

Before attempting to answer these questions, it is perhaps necessary to write a few words about the man whose name is indelibly linked with the enterprise – the person who gave so much, yet in many ways has become one of the forgotten benefactors of Burgess Hill.

Sidney Herbert West, a former agricultural auctioneer from Steyning who once farmed at Portslade, retired from business in 1925 and moved to Garfield in Park Road, Burgess Hill, where he, his cob and his dogcart soon became a familiar sight.

His interests were twofold: firstly in supporting the Southdown Hunt, both as a committee member and a rider to hounds; secondly in promoting the physical well-being of the younger generation.

He created a private bathing pool on land in the vicinity of Scotches Farm, near Hurstpierpoint. Many boys were taught to swim there and it accorded Mr West much satisfaction to learn that a number of them who later served in the Second World War, either in the Royal Navy or Merchant Marine, and whose ships had been torpedoed, owed their lives to having learnt to swim in 'Westy's' pool. One old-timer, when recalling his childhood said,

> The pool was only for boys and you had to swim naked. The water was usually very cold, and old Westy and his helpers used to chase us round the edge and whack our bottoms with bunches of stinging nettles to make us jump in. It was all good fun and completely innocent, but I doubt if you would get away with it now.

It was at Sidney West's instigation that the Mid Sussex Amateur Boxing Club was formed in 1938, the venue being the *Cricketers' Inn* at Burgess Hill. He became Chairman and his over-riding ambition was to make the Club a permanent institution with its own headquarters. The aim was eventually achieved, but not in his lifetime. He died in 1944 and in his will bequeathed the sum of £16,000 plus a portion of his estate to two friends, with the expressed wish that they use it in some way to benefit the Boxing Club and Scotches Swimming Pool.

For reasons beyond the Trustees' control, the swimming pool was abandoned, but not the Founder's dream of a new HQ and on 25 February 1956 the Sidney West Centre was officially declared open by His Grace, The Duke of Norfolk, Lord Lieutenant of Sussex.

The club became a victim of its own success; the sheer size was such that the Trustees, all of whom worked on a voluntary basis, found it increasingly difficult to devote the amount of time required for full and proper administration. By 1983, the cost of running expenses alone had increased to such an extent that the annual accounts were revealing a regular deficit. On top of this, a structural and maintenance report concluded that the condition of the buildings and drainage required considerable expenditure, probably in excess of £220,000 if it were to be made good. This figure together with the existing burden of loans to the tune of £100,000 was beyond the means of the Trustees, who concluded that the only option left to them was to broker a deal with Mid Sussex District Council in the hope that the Authority would assume ownership, management and operation of the premises, while at the same time ensuring the recreational future of the site.

And so it transpired. Mid Sussex District Council took over the reins, modernised and repaired the facilities to the required standard, but with the understanding that it was a temporary reprieve only, and that in due course the existing set-up was likely to be replaced with buildings deemed more suitable for public requirements.

Quite what 'more suitable' meant is still a subject of debate as nothing yet has been built. What can be said for certain is that Sidney West's pet project, a sports stadium that he never actually saw, was pulled down in 1999 and is now just a memory.

The Swimming Pool and The Providence Chapel
As with Leylands Road, Park Road has also been depleted of some of its institutions, the most notable of which the Swimming Pool, was pulled down in the advent of the

45. The remains of the swimming pool in St John's Park.

Triangle. The powers-that-be obviously believed that it was not commercially viable to operate two such businesses in close proximity.

Many protested, the pool had been part of the local scene since 1935, and they, their parents and in some cases their grandparents had learnt to swim there, on top of which it was such a convenient place to get to; and people were loath to see it go. However, all that is left now to remind us of happy days at the lido is a stretch of wall that once stood between the fountain and the changing cubicles.

The Strict Baptists Providence Chapel has gone as well, insofar that it is no longer a place of public worship, although happily the building, outwardly unaltered (but privately owned), remains a feature of the area. Its closure became inevitable, for the congregation – not large at the best of times – had whittled down to five elderly parishioners and the task of running and maintaining the old structure had become more than could be reasonably managed. So the decision was made to place the property onto the market and for the brethren to practise their faith elsewhere.

46. The former Strict Baptists Chapel.

The *Royal George*

No more does the call 'Time, gentlemen, please' ring out at the crossways. 2001 marked the demise of the *Royal George*, an inn that stood at the corner of Royal George Road and London Road for nearly a century and a half. For the first time in over sixty years, Burgess Hill lost one of its public houses. Flats now stand on the site.

The premises was constructed by George Godly in 1854, on land he had purchased following the Clayton Enclosure. He was also the first landlord (as well as being mine host at the *Friars Oak*) and ran both establishments most successfully. It was under his proprietorship that the *Royal George* gained the reputation for being a businessman's pub, and there is little doubt that many of the proposals to have shaped the district as we know it were first debated within its walls.

It retained its popularity for many years, but, after landlord Jack de Caux pulled his last pint, the heart seemed to go out of the place and it fell into gradual decline. Efforts to revive the flagging fortunes – a lick of paint here, hanging baskets there, even changing the name to *Georgies*, were of no avail. They were too little, too late. Despite a few half-hearted protests, the inn, which took its name from a naval vessel that capsized off Spithead in 1782, has also sunk without trace.

The Pug Mill

Following the demolition of the *Royal George*, a near neighbour, a former pug (clay) mill, which surely must have been the last surviving building in the town to be linked with Burgess Hill's industrial past, was pulled down to make way for a modern warehouse.

The little Mill (which stood on former pottery land to the west of London Road) was hexagonal in shape and had a conical roof, which suggested that the labour required for mixing the pug would have been supplied by a yoked donkey or mule, made to walk endlessly round the perimeter – a method reminiscent of well-wheels once used to draw water on chalk hill farms.

Precisely when the unit was built is a matter of conjecture, but what can be safely said is that following the 1852 Clayton Enclosure Act, and the resultant sale and re-development of the land, the building (which had become redundant) served a variety of uses, mostly as a store place of sorts. Then in 1930 it was transformed into the headquarters of the 1st Burgess Hill Scout Troop, and remained as such for well over twenty years, after which it reverted to storage use.

Although gone, this 19th-century curio is certainly not forgotten. Indeed, the chances are that a day of resurrection, if not immediately at hand, will ultimately dawn and, in anticipation, the premises has been carefully dismantled with every tile, brick and beam numbered and placed in safe custody until a suitable location is found.

Conclusion

It would take a brave man to predict the future of Burgess Hill and I am not about to do so. From wind-swept common to the fastest-growing town in the South East, it has been a story not only of change but continuity; the last exemplified by people whose ancestors were born in the area, and old family firms which can still be found if one looks. Woods the butcher in Church Road is a good example of what I mean; established in the Edwardian era by George Wood, and currently run by his grandson, Richard Wood, the business has been trading in Burgess Hill for more than a hundred years. It is worth adding that Richard Wood, a respected purveyor of poultry, meat and game and excellent sausages, is probably one of the last butchers in the district to understand the request to 'chine', not chop, a delicacy like the best end neck of lamb!

Other companies to have celebrated their centenaries in the town are Burnett's the Printers and Anthony Hole & Son, both of which are located in Cyprus Road.

Envoy

I will gather and carefully make my friends
Of the men of the Sussex Weald
They watch the stars from silent folds
They stiffly plough the field
By them and the God of the South Country
My poor soul shall be heal'd

(*The South Country* – Hilaire Belloc)

Poets, frequently given to flights of fancy, are not always right. This one was: for how many of those who have settled in the town since the second great wave of building began in the 1950s have 'stiffly dug their gardens', and made true and loyal friends of the people of the Sussex Weald? How many 'poor souls' have been healed by the warmth and fellowship of old Burgess Hillians who welcomed them when, strangers and alone, they first came to the town to sink new roots? It is hoped that future 'settlers' will experience the same warmth and the same welcome that has prevailed here for the past century or more.

New housing estates, new commercial and industrial buildings continue to creep inexorably towards the town boundaries. We fervently hope that present and future growth will never, NEVER overwhelm and ultimately destroy the intimate community spirit that exists in the town today.

179

List of Abbreviations

A.V.I.N.   *A Very Improving Neighbourhood – Burgess Hill 1840- 1914* (1984), Ed. by Brian Short

E.S.R.O.   East Sussex Record Office, Lewes

O.E.D.   Oxford English Dictionary

O.S.   Ordnance Survey

S.A.C.   Sussex Archaeological Collections

S.A.S.   Sussex Archaeological Society, Lewes

S.N.Q.   Sussex Notes and Queries

S.R.S.   Sussex Record Society

U.D.C.   Urban District Council – now largely superseded by Mid-Sussex District Council

V.C.H.   Victoria County History

W.S.R.O.   West Sussex Record Office, Chichester

Glossary

Amercement: a fine imposed by the manor court.

Assart: a plot of land cleared of trees and shrubs taken in from the manorial waste for use as farm land.

Beadle: a minor official of the manor court.

Bed: a mattress.

Bedsteddle: a bedstead.

Borough English: inheritance by the youngest son, etc.

Coffer, Cofer: a box, especially for valuables.

Coper: a dealer in horses.

Copyhold: land and premises held of the lord of the manor by tenants paying rents, heriots and fines and transferred from one owner to another through the manor courts.

Cord: a measure of cut wood, usually 128 cu. feet.

Customary freehold: similar to copyhold land and premises except that transfers could be made without using the manor court.

Demesne: manorial land held by the lord of the manor as his home farm.

Enfranchisement: the purchase of the lords' rights to rents, heriots, etc., by tenants to free themselves of manorial dues.

Engrossment: the practice of amalgamating two or more smallholdings to form a larger, composite farm.

Fines: (i) these manorial dues could be fixed (usually 6d.) or 'at the will of the lord' (i.e. variable) payable when a copyholder took possession of his land; (ii) the term is also used in connection with the disentailment of customary freehold premises.

Frankpledge, view of: in the context of this book the court of the Hundred of Buttinghill which was convened from time to time to administer local by-laws.

Furnace: a copper used for brewing beer.

Fustian: a thick, twilled cotton cloth.

Guinea: a unit of currency, but not always a coin, worth £1 1s. 0d.

Headborough: a local constable.

Heriot: a fine, sometimes a man's best beast, sometimes a nominal 6d., payable to the lord of the manor on the death of a tenant.

Homage: the jury of the manor court.

Hundred: an administrative sub-division of a county, having its own court.

Hutch: a cupboard.

Imprimis: firstly, in the first place.

Inholme: land taken in from the manorial waste or the lords' hunting ground.

Inventory: a list of the goods and moveable assets taken when a person died, required for probate purposes.

Keeler: a shallow tub without a top.

Mercy: liable to a fine for infringement of manorial customs.

Messuage: a house, usually with land and buildings.

Moiety, moitie: a half.

Nonsuch: a clover-like plant used for animal feed.

Pain: penalty.

Pound: a small enclosure used to detain straying animals.

Presentment: (i) an appearance of a person at the manor court to answer charges of contravening local customs; (ii) a formal statement to the court by the homage.

Quarter Sessions: a court of law which met every three months to try minor criminal cases and which performed many of the functions later taken over by the County Councils.

Quern: a hand mill for grinding small quantities of grain.

Quit rent: see manorial rent below.

Reeve: an official of the manor court responsible for collecting rents, heriots, fines, etc.

Relief: a small sum (usually one year's rent) payable to the lord of the manor by a customary freeholder when claiming ownership of his land.

Rent, manorial: a fixed sum usually a few shillings or a few pence, payable annually to the lord of the manor by his tenants.

Rod, pole, or perch: a linear measure of $5\frac{1}{2}$ yards or a square measure of $30\frac{1}{4}$ square yards.

Steddle or stettle: a bedstead; a 'bed' in the 18th century was what today we call a mattress.

Steward: the lord's officer who usually conducted the business of the manor court.

Tithing: ten men selected to represent their village at the Hundred Court.

Tow: a coarse and broken part of flax or hemp.

Wain or wayne: a wagon.

Wenyer or weanyer: a newly weaned animal.

Notes and References

Preface
1. Short, Brian (ed.) *A Very Improving Neighbourhood – Burgess Hill, 1840-1914* (1984).

Introduction
1. Blencowe, Robert Willis, 'Roman Remains', S.A.C., Vol. 14, p.177.

Chapter One
1. ABER 1-22.
2. Dyke Hutton Rolls 1121.
3. ADA 1-5.
4. ADA 16-17.
5. Turner, Rev. Edward (ed.) S.A.C. Vol. 25, p.172.
6. Dyke Hutton 1121.
7. Reproduced in S.A.C. Vol.58, p.7.
8. But see p.8.
9. See p.6.
10. See Chapter Eight p.131.
11. Discussed more fully in Chapter Eight.
12. ABER 1 f.21v.
13. Finally stopped up in 1826 (QR/E 789, Oct. 1826).
14. Lady Day, 25 March.
15. Op. cit. p.81.
16. See p.49 *et seq.*

Chapter Two
1. Acc. 968 p.264.
2. ABER I f.135r.
3. In many years no cases were reported.
4. ADA 1 f.47v.
5. Opposite the premises of Meşsrs. Frank Wright Limited.
6. QO/EW2 ff.48v. and 57r.
7. Later called Firtoft.
8. The site lay to the south of the lane leading to the Chapel of Rest.
9. A7.168.
10. Dyke Hutton 1121.
11. Acc. 965 vii (i).
12. ADA 1 f.52r. – see also p.16.
13. A8.128 (1586).
14. I am indebted to Mr. Fred Avery for giving me a copy of this interesting map.
15. QR/E 80.
16. Of Penny's Cottage now part of Dinnage's Garage in Wivelsfield Road, Haywards Heath.
17. Copper, Bob, *A Song for Every Season* (1971), p.130.
18. Bird, Ruth (ed.) SRS 1971 p.75.
19. QO/EW5.
20. I am grateful to Dr. Graham Mayhew for this information.

Chapter Three
1. 1983 Edition (Phillimore).

2. QO/EW 32 & 33.
3. SRS 43, p.56.
4. A4.211 References of individual wills will not normally be given again. They can easily be found by referring to the Index of Susses Wills in E.S.R.O.
5. SRS, Vol.42, p.23.
6. Not 'Keymer [and] Strete' as shown in S.R.S., Vol.43, p.57.
7. ? red-shouldered.
8. What was a chip petticoat?
9. Keeler, a shallow tub without a top.
10. See for example QO/EW 12 October 1706.
11. QO/EW 11, January 1699/1700.
12. I am grateful to Dr. Graham Mayhew for this helpful suggestion.
13. It paid an annual rent of 5d. or 5 broad arrows.
14. QO/EW2 f.64r.
15. Not from our immediate area. We include the case as a typical example of the harsh sentences meted out for minor offences.
16. Beattie, J.M., *Past and Present*, Vol.64 (1974), p.83.

Chapter Four
1. Enfranchisement is discussed more fully in Chapter Eight.
2. S.A.S. Calendars, N.5.
3. Cants and Woodwards were both once part of the lord's hunting ground that extended from Fragbarrow farm in the south to Valebridge common in the north. The early development of this part of the town is discussed in Heather Warne's article 'The Place Names and Early Topography of Burgess Hill' (S.A.C., Vol. 123, pp.127-43).
4. Checkland, S.G., *The Rise of Industrial Society in England, 1815-85* (7th Edition, 1979), p.325.
5. There are gaps in the records at this time and I am grateful to Mr. Christopher Whittick for his help in establishing the outcome of this case.
6. Acc. 968 pp.275-6.
7. QR/E 473 (54).
8. My thanks are due to Heather Warne for helping me to identify this site.
9. Later called the Meeds site.
10. ADA 1 f.111v.
11. See p.48.
12. Inventory no. 2537.
13. Originally enclosed by Henry Marten in 1649 (see p.17).
14. Jenkins, J.G., *Traditional Country Craftsmen* (1978), p.204.
15. QR/E 251 (May 1717).
16. Based on Indices kindly provided by the Bank of England Reference Library.
17. QR/E 516 f.57 and Keymer Parish Registers.
18. Inventory 432.
19. ABER I 121v.
20. HOW 75/2 (E.S.R.O.).
21. A.V.I.N., p.27.
22. Land Tax Returns at W.S.R.O.
23. Historicus, p.19.
24. See p.34.
25. The number of people was not specified.
26. QR/E 313 July 1707.
27. ADA 3, p.232.
28. A detailed description of these holdings, all of which have been identified, is, sadly, outside the scope of this book.

Chapter Five
1. Tate, W.E., *The Parish Chest*, Chapter Eight, p.193.

2. Acc. 968 p.75. Thanks are due to Heather Warne for showing me evidence of this case.
3. The great Act of 1601.
4. See, for example, QR/E 229 m.26.
5. QR/E 455 f.44.
6. See Chapter Four, p.52.
7. A few years earlier we read of grants of small pensions made to men who had fought in the Civil War and who could no longer work.
8. QO/EW 30.
9. See QO/EW 45, April 1822; and QO/EW 46, January 1823.
10. Pronounced, and sometimes spelt, Laffham.
11. See QO/EW 12, April 1703; QO/EW 13, April 1708 *et passim*.
12. QO/EW 13, July 1709.
13. QR/E 396.
14. But see SAC, Vol.123, p.135.
15. Office of Population Censuses and Surveys Monitor (FM185/3).
16. A52.478.
17. Inventory No. 2144.
18. Inventory No. 3004.
19. A58.56.
20. A69.391.
21. This adjoined Mill Road in the Crescent Road/Middle Way area.
22. When they were accurately measured for the tithe survey in 1845 the two holdings (including allocations of Valebridge Common made under the Inclosure Award) totalled nearly 225 acres.
23. See QO/EW 36, April 1804.

Chapter Six
1. Acc.966 p.22.
2. Acc.966 p.36.
3. Op. cit. p.85.
4. In fact he was allocated nearly 17 acres or one-fourteenth of the net area.
5. *The English Village Community and the Enclosure Movements* (1967), pp.103-4.
6. Acc.981.
7. Op. cit. p.24.
8. S.A.S. Misc., Box 25. (E.S.R.O.).
9. His memory was slightly at fault. There were four, see p.90.
10. We had long suspected that such an arrangement had been made. It was gratifying to see this confirmation.
11. About £2m today.
12. Journals of the House of Commons, Vol.83 p.30. Messrs. Curteis and Burrell were Sussex M.P.s.
13. Ibid p.210.
14. Although she died in 1815.
15. Copies at Brighton Reference Library.
16. These two ancient inns can still be visited today.
17. Valebridge mill ponds then about 7-8 acres in extent.
18. In Leylands Road, formerly the Congregational now (1987) the Pentecostal Church.
19. Now the site of the District Council yard and private commercial premises.
20. Book of John Rowe p.33.
21. Near the corner of Dunstall Avenue.
22. Now the site of 73 and 75 London Road.
23. A little to the north of Fairfield Road.
24. A little to the west of the garage and petrol filling station on the corner of Fairfield Road.
25. The present Post Office and stores.
26. Actually in Clayton at that time.
27. Later the site of Fair Lea opposite Leylands Road.
28. Part of Grovelands farm in London Road.

29. See Chapter Two p.19.
30. Acc.968 p.151.
31. Plot 40 on the Enclosure Map: it adjoined Valebridge Road to the west.
32. Issue dated 25 August 1828 p.2 which also contained the notice of extinguishment of common rights not reproduced here.
33. Responsibility for roads rested with Justices of the Peace until the formation of County Councils in 1888.
34. S.N.Q. Vol.15 pp.181-86.
35. Enfranchisement is discussed more fully in Chapter Eight p.129.

Chapter Seven

1. Howard-Turner, J.T. *The London, Brighton and South Coast Railway* (1977), Vol.1, p.21.
2. Course, Edwin, *Railways of Southern England – the Main Lines* (1973), pp.123-4.
3. See also QDP/EW 145 and QDP 130 at E.S.R.O.
4. Course, op. cit. p.151.
5. Census Returns of 1841 and *V.C.H.*, Vol. 2, p.223.
6. See p.121.
7. Tate, W.E., *The English Village Community and the Enclosure Movements* (1967), pp.133-4.
8. Historicus, p.9.
9. House of Commons Journal, Vol. 107.
10. *Sussex Express*, p.1.
11. Ibid., 24 and 31 October 1854.
12. *Sussex Express*, 25 August 1855.
13. Ibid., 18 October 1856.
14. For a brief account of the life of Charles Tulley see A.V.I.N., Chapter Eight, p.85.
15. Historicus, p.10.

Chapter Eight

1. Copies in both County Record Offices, Burgess Hill Library, Hove and Brighton Reference Libraries, etc.
2. Gregory p.171.
3. This is, of course, very much an over simplification of a complex procedure.
4. 4 and 5 VIC.
5. ADA 4 p.421.
6. S.A.S. EG 484 (E.S.R.O.).
7. He also owned West End farm held of the manors of Clayton and Wickham. He died in 1858 worth about £45,000.
8. See Halsbury, *Laws of England*, Vol. 8, para. 465.
9. Ibid., para. 644.
10. S.A.S. Acc.982 (E.S.R.O.).
11. Published by Cecil Palmer, London, 1892 Revised 1922.
12. When 'Hilgay' in Keymer Road was advertised for sale on 19 October 1869 the premises were described as having '. . . a good supply of spring and soft water and gas might be laid on at a small outlay'.
13. Chapter Ten, p.40.
14. Discussed more fully in Tate, *The Parish Chest*, p.140 *et seq.*
15. PAR 294/6/4 and 5 (W.S.R.O.).
16. Historicus, p.12.
17. *Sussex Advertiser*, 3, 10 and 17 September 1861.
18. *Sussex Express*, 9 November 1861 p.4.
19. Historicus, p.16; but *Surrey Standard* of 16 May 1863 (p.2) quotes figure of £5,000.
20. Now divided into two shops.
21. Now the site of houses and bungalows in Brookway.
22. A.V.I.N., p.79. The building was demolished some years ago.
23. Much of the material in the following four paragraphs is based on Chapter Seven of A.V.I.N. which

contains a much more detailed account of the religious activities in Burgess Hill during the 19th and early 20th centuries.

24. Ibid., p.73.
25. Census Returns 1841.
26. The words 'Clayton and Keymer U.D.C. School Board' in a terra cotta panel can still be seen on the front of the building.
27. A.V.I.N., p.73.
28. 16 August 1887, p.5.
29. Avery, op. cit. p.6.

Chapter Nine
 1. Warne, Heather M., S.A.C., Vol.123 (1985).
 2. QR/E 270 and QI/EW7 f.73r.
 3. Historical Notes p.67.
 4. Teg: a sheep in its second year.
 5. Animals of the ox kind: an ox or bullock, a cow or heifer.
 6. See, for example, *Sussex Express* 7 July 1855 and 11 July 1857.
 7. In the *Sussex Advertiser* of 12 July 1870 is an interesting table showing how the numbers penned and prices of animals varied in the decade 1860-70. The lowest number recorded in this 11-year period was 6,020; and the highest 10,260.
 8. Exceptionally, the mid-summer fair in 1986 was held at Haywards Heath.
 9. *Mid-Sussex Times*, 9 July 1912.
10. Other minor adjustments were made in London Road south of Hammonds Place, and near West End farm.
11. Gregory, p.202.
12. See draft Consultation Plan of January 1981 prepared by Mid-Sussex District Council.
13. A.V.I.N., p.38.
14. *Sussex Express*, 22 March 1851.
15. Ibid., 8 September, p.2.
16. Gregory, p.59.
17. *Sussex Express*, 23 August 1851.
18. Clark, Kenneth, *Civilisation*, pp.346-7.

Bibliography

The following is a list of some of the more important primary and published sources consulted in the course of research for this book.

(A) Primary Sources

In East Sussex Record Office:

Court rolls and books of the manors of Clayton, Keymer, Wickham and Ditchling.
Inventories, 18th century.
Parish register for Keymer, 1600-early 19th century.
Quarter Sessions rolls and order books 17th-19th century.
Sussex Archaeological Collections.
Sussex Notes and Queries.
Sussex Record Society Publications.
Land Tax Returns, Ditchling 18th-early 19th century.
Miscellaneous deeds and other documents.
Tithe Awards, Ditchling and Wivelsfield.

In West Sussex Record Office:

Enclosure Awards, Clayton and Keymer.
Land Tax Returns, Clayton and Keymer, 18th-19th century.
Parish Register for Clayton, 1601-early 19th century.
Miscellaneous deeds and other documents.
Tithe Awards, Clayton and Keymer.

In Burgess Hill Library:

Census Returns, 1841-81.

In Sussex University Library:

Journals of the House of Lords and House of Commons, 19th century.

(B) Published Sources

Avery, F.M., *Development of Burgess Hill and its Potteries, 1828-1978* (1979) [this had very limited distribution].
Barley, M. W., *The English Farmhouse and Cottage* (1961)
Bird, Ruth (ed.), *The Journal of Giles Moore, 1656-79.*
Brandon, Peter, *The Sussex Landscape* (1974)
Checkland, S.G., *The Rise of Industrial Society in England, 1815-1865* (7th ed., 1979).
Copper, Bob, *A Song for Every Season* (1971).
Course, Edwin, *Railways of Southern England – The Main Lines* (1973).
Durrant, Peter, *The Parish Church of St Andrew, 1898-1983.*
Evans, George Ewart, *Ask the Fellows who cut the Hay* (1965); *The Farm and Village* (1974); *The Horse in the Furrow* (1967).
Gelling, Margaret, *Signposts to the Past* (1978).

Gooder, Eileen A., *Latin for Local History – An Introduction* (1961).

Gregory, A.H., *The Story of Burgess Hill* (1933); Mid Sussex through the Ages (1938).

Halsbury, *Laws of England*, Vol. 8.

Harper, E.C., *The Brighton Road* (1892, rev. 1922).

Historicus (C.D. Meads), *Historical Notes of Burgess Hill* (1891).

Hoskins, W. G., *The Age of Plunder, King Henry's England 1500-1547* (1976); *Local History in England* (1972); *The Making of the English Landscape* (1977).

Howard-Turner, J.T., *The London, Brighton and South Coast Railway*, Vol. 1 (1977).

Jackson, W. Eric, *Local Government in England and Wales*.

Jenkins, J.G., *Traditional Country Craftsmen* (1978).

Kellys (and Post Office) Directories, 19th and 20th centuries.

Local Newspapers: *Sussex Express, Sussex Advertiser* and *Mid-Sussex Times* (mainly 19th century)

Macfarlane, Alan, *Reconstructing Historical Communities* (1978).

Postan, M. M., *The Medieval Society and Economy* (1978).

Short, Brian (ed.) *A Very Improving Neighbourhood – Burgess Hill, 1840-1914* (1984).

Tate W.E., *The Parish Chest* (1983); *The English Village Community and the Enclosure Movements* (1967).

Wilson, Charles, *England's Apprenticeship – 1603-1760*.

Index of Persons and Places

Index of Subjects